The Little General
and the Rousay Crofters

The Little General

Early in spring the little General came
    Across the sound, bringing the island death,
And suddenly a place without a name,
    And like the pious ritual of a faith,

Hunter and quarry in the boundless trap,
    The white smoke curling from the silver gun,
The feather curling in the hunter's cap,
    And clouds of feathers floating in the sun,

While down the birds came in a deafening shower,
    Wing-hurricane, and the cattle fled in fear.
Up on the hill a remnant of a tower
    Had watched that single scene for many a year,

Weaving a wordless tale where all were gathered
    (Hunter and quarry and watcher and fabulous field),
A sylvan war half human and half feathered,
    Perennial emblem painted on the shield

Held up to cow a never-conquered land
Fast in the little General's fragile hand.

Edwin Muir

Edwin Muir spent his early childhood on Burroughs' 145-acre farm of the Bu on the island of Wyre. It lay a mile across the sound from the laird's mansion at Trumland. In his *Autobiography* he recollected how the General "drove my father out of the farm by his exactions".

The Little General
and the Rousay Crofters

Crisis and Conflict
on an Orkney Crofting Estate

WILLIAM P. L. THOMSON

JOHN DONALD PUBLISHERS LTD

The publishers acknowledge the
financial assistance of the Scottish
Arts Council in the publication of
this volume.

ISBN 0 85796 062 6

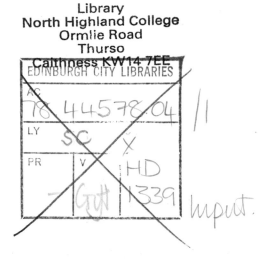
Printed in Great Britain by Bell & Bain Ltd., Glasgow

Acknowledgements

IN Orkney the past is never far below the surface. Reminders take many forms — the windswept bleakness of neolithic Skara Brae, the warm sandstone of the Viking Cathedral of St Magnus or the square green fields of the nineteenth century agricultural improvers. For me, other reminders have been particularly close. This book has been written at Papdale House, Kirkwall, formerly the home of Robert Scarth, factor of General Burroughs' Rousay estate. It seems very probable that he worked on his accounts on the very spot where I have used them for a very different purpose 130 years later. His meticulous records have provided a unique picture of the economy of an Orkney crofting estate during years of change and conflict. Papdale was also the birthplace of Andrew Thomson, the Kirkwall lawyer who was often called on to champion the Rousay crofters in their struggle against their landlord. I have another link through a predecessor at Kirkwall Grammar School, Dr Hugh Marwick. He was Rousay born and appears on these pages as a pupil in the Sourin school. His *Place Names of Rousay* provides a store of local knowledge which I have frequently used. As he once did, I now teach island children who are the descendants of Rousay 'Crofters' and 'Respectables'. While they retain a sturdy independence they are, on the whole, more amenable than their great-grandparents.

To many people in Rousay I am indebted, not only for the information they have been able to give me, but also for their hospitality and the interest they have taken in my work. The help of a number of descendants of the Rousay crofters, now living outside the island, is also gratefully acknowledged. Miss Alison Fraser, Orkney Archivist, the staff of the Regimental Museum of the Argyll and Sutherland Highlanders at Stirling Castle, and the staff of the National Army Museum have all been particularly helpful. Mr. A. J. Skinner, St Albans, made available material from his postal collection including a number of anonymous threatening letters received by General Burroughs. I also thank Mr R. P. Fereday and Mr J. D. Robertson who read preliminary drafts and suggested many improvements.

Plates 1, 7a, 7b, 8a and 8b appear by permission of Orkney Library (all except the first from the T. Kent collection); for Plate 2a I am indebted to the late Major R. Ritchie, formerly of Trumland House; Plate 2b has been provided by Mrs C. McKinlay who has kindly allowed me to use this portrait of her great-grandfather; Plate 3b is from the G. W. Wilson Collection, Aberdeen University Library, while 3a, 4a, 4b, 5a, 5b, 6a and 6b are by Phoenix Photographs, Kirkwall. The drawings of the Sikanderbagh (Fig. 8) appear by permission of the Trustees of the National Library of Scotland. Edwin Muir's poem, *The Little General*, is reprinted by permission of Faber & Faber Ltd from his *Collected Poems*. The quotation from Muir's *Autobiography* which I use in Chapter 18 appears by permission of Hogarth Press.

Contents

Tables

Figures

Plates

1. Frederick William Traill-Burroughs

2a. Shooting party, General Burroughs third from left

2b. James Leonard, implacable opponent of General Burroughs

3a. Trumland House from the air

3b. The *Orcadia* and the *Lizzie Burroughs*

4a. Tafts, the original nucleus of the vanished community of Quandale

4b. Tafts, interior

5a. The Free Church and Manse at Sourin — centre of opposition to the laird

5b. Digro, Sourin, home of James Leonard

6a. Wasbister

6b. Westness and Eynhallow Sound

7a. Oxen

7b. Harrowing by hand

8a. Threshing corn with flails

8b. The hens that paid the rent

1

Homecoming, 1870

'No connection between man and man ought to be more carefully guarded than that betwixt landlord and tenant.' John Gibson, Rousay farmer[1]

GENERAL Frederick William Traill-Burroughs of Rousay and Viera had the reputation of being the worst of the nineteenth century Orkney lairds. To be so regarded was an unenviable reputation since Orkney lairds were a far from popular class and it was not easy to earn the distinction of being the worst. In some parts of Scotland landowners could claim that they commanded the loyalty of their tenantry and that a bond of affection existed between them. Often such a relationship owed more to the landlord's imagination than to reality but sometimes such a bond did indeed exist. In Orkney, however, centuries of hard-fisted exploitation had destroyed any paternal or clan relationship. Orkney lairds had a reputation for being grasping business men, patronising and autocratic in dealings with their inferiors. The attitude of the tenant was, at best, one of wary suspicion but often a sullen subservience concealed smouldering hostility. This was not the hostility arising out of hopeless poverty such as was found in the West Highlands. Orkney is a fertile land and, by the second half of the nineteenth century, it had undergone its own agricultural revolution. Crofters and small farmers were a much more substantial class than their Highland counterparts. Their attitude to their lairds sprang not so much from despair as from the elusive prospect of a more prosperous life always denied them by the profits of improvement being swallowed up by successive rounds of rent increases. In mid-century the lairds had been in the forefront of agricultural progress and had transformed much of Orkney into a landscape of square green fields. But by the last quarter of the century the Age of Improvement was over. Rents exacted from an increasingly depressed farming community were no longer being invested in the land but were going to maintain the lairds in a life style which they were reluctant to modify in keeping with less prosperous times. Yet the tenant's hostility was seldom of a revolutionary kind. It smouldered but only occasionally flared up in the way that it did on Burroughs' Rousay estate. Orkney farmers regarded lairds and their rents as unpleasant facts of life like winter gales, late springs and bad harvests. They did not expect the natural order of things to change.

To be the worst of these lairds is no ordinary reputation but it was one which Burroughs often deserved and which he did nothing to avoid. In no part of Orkney were relations between the proprietor and his tenants so notoriously bad as in Rousay although other estates could match, and sometimes exceed, his record of rack renting, eviction and petty acts of tyranny. The difference between Burroughs and other lairds was that he acted, not from malice, not even from motives of profit, but from principle. Principles can often lead a man to the most unreasonable of actions. He had a strongly developed sense of ownership, and any attack on the rights of property was a matter of principle which he never compromised for the sake of mere popularity or even profit. Inevitably the trouble came to a head with the passing of the Crofters Act which bitterly divided the community. The point was reached where Burroughs hated all crofters. He hated them as a class and would have cleared every one of them from his estate had not the security provided by the Act prevented him. The trouble culminated in acts of violence, numerous legal battles, the sending of a gunboat to Rousay and even a special Act of Parliament rushed through to curtail Burroughs' attacks on his tenants.

Yet his relationship with his tenants did not begin in this way. The casual observer, unaware of undercurrents which already existed on the estate, would have formed a very different impression on that day in July 1870 when Burroughs arrived with his bride to make his home in Rousay. He had already been laird for twenty-three years but he was almost unknown to his tenants since these years had been spent in the army, mostly in India. Before he came of age he had travelled north to his estate each summer, but since then his only visit had been a few weeks' stay in 1859 when convalescing from wounds received in the Indian Mutiny. His tenants knew him as a public figure, for he was something of a minor national hero, but of Burroughs the man and Burroughs the laird they knew almost nothing.

The homecoming of the laird was an important occasion and *The Orkney Herald* reported it in detail.[2] Word reached Rousay that Burroughs had arrived in Kirkwall and that Thursday 28th July was the day he planned to come over to the island. The whole of the previous week was one of active preparation and the imminent arrival of the laird was the one subject of conversation. When the day came, small groups of farmers with their wives and children, all in Sunday best, might have been seen making their way from all parts of the island, while other families crossed in small boats from

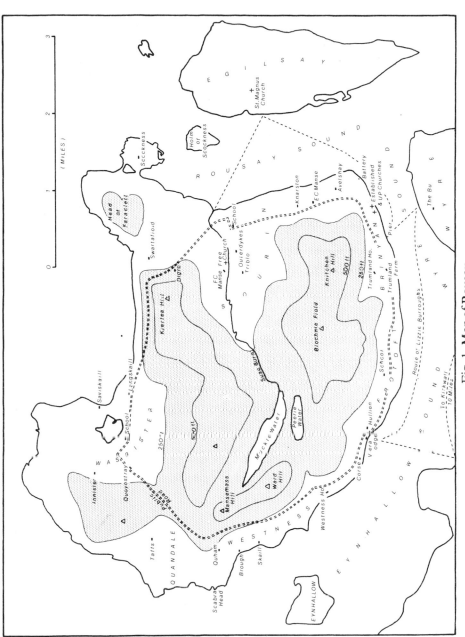

Fig. 1. Map of Rousay

the neighbouring island of Wyre. They gathered on the grassy slopes surrounding Westness House, sitting in the sunshine and awaiting the arrival of the stranger who was their laird. The whole south side of the island had a gala appearance with flags and bunting flying from the flagstaffs at Westness House and the landing place. At Hullion, Corse, and other places along the Frotoft shore, attempts had been made at similar displays.

It is easy to be cynical about such a welcome. It was organised by the factor and was a routine drill for welcoming the laird home. The same procedure had been followed on Burroughs' previous visits and similar mandatory displays of affection subsequently marked his promotion to general, his knighthood and even his return from holidays abroad. The tenants knew what was expected of them and it was the kind of occasion when it was better to be seen to be present. Yet it was more than that. No doubt curiosity played a large part since the tenants were anxious to see this man who wielded so much power over them. It could be a power for good as well as ill. There was much to be gained from a supposedly wealthy laird residing on the island, spending money and providing employment. The calculating tenant might also reflect that it was usually possible to get a better bargain from a laird than from his factor. But mixed with this cynicism, curiosity and profit-seeking was a genuine respect. Their laird was a brave soldier, the hero who had so nearly won the Victoria Cross at Lucknow. It was an age when military prowess won unqualified admiration unclouded by the doubts of a later age which has seen the decline of empire and the barbarity of twentieth century warfare.

At about half past one his boat was seen leaving the Evie shore and, with colours flying, she made good speed across the mile and a half of Eynhallow Sound to Westness where the colonel and his lady were helped ashore to the accompaniment of three hearty cheers from the assembled tenantry. He was a diminutive figure, little over five feet in height, with an erect military bearing and a neatly trimmed military beard. He walked with the merest trace of a limp, the result of a leg badly fractured at Lucknow, but his figure was slim, fit and active. He was thirty-nine years old and planning to retire from the army. On a more private occasion he could be kind and charming but in public he was a less sympathetic figure. He appeared stiff and unbending, with a demeanour which suggested a temper not always under control.

On the road from the landing place a triumphal arch had been erected bearing the single word 'Welcome'. In view of later events, the motto was singularly inappropriate, but the assembled tenants were, as yet, unaware of the irony. The laird and his bride were led through the arch on to the lawn where introductions were made and where John Gibson of Langskaill was waiting to read a speech of welcome. As the tenant of the largest farm, it was a role which he often performed. He began:—

> Colonel and Mrs Burroughs, We representing the whole tenantry of the islands of Rousay and Wyre, have this day the greatest pleasure in welcoming Colonel Frederick William Traill-Burroughs to his island home. This we now do most cordially and, if possible, the more so as he brings with him a lady regarding whom we have already heard good reports as being well fitted to aid and encourage him in every good work.

He went on to speak about the relationship between landlord and tenant:—

> No connection between man and man ought to be more carefully guarded than that betwixt landlord and tenant, and every good man who loves his country should do what within him lies to cement that tie and to continue what in troublous times has formed the strength of the nation — that union and co-obligation of classes which make a brotherhood of all claiming the same country — landlord and tenant standing back to back and facing the enemy at all points.

It was exactly this relationship which was to go so disastrously wrong in Rousay. As yet this lay hidden in the future and the islanders nodded their agreement as Gibson painted a picture of the laird, in happy retirement, going among his tenants, directing them with his advice and encouraging them with his approval.

He next spoke of their 'gracious remembrances' of Burroughs' uncle, George William Traill, from whom Burroughs inherited the estate. It was a sour phrase to many of the audience. Standing there in the sunshine and looking out at the twelve great squared fields of Westness Farm lying one beyond the other along the shore, green with corn and divided by the hard straight lines of the new dykes, there were many islanders who had no 'gracious remembrances' of George William Traill. Among those listening were descendants of the udallers who had owned the vanished farm of Brough. There were ploughmen and farm hands who had once worked their own land, cottars and casual labourers who had tenanted their own crofts and others who had been brought up over the hill in Quandale where a whole community had been cleared to make way for sheep.

Burroughs was probably unaware of any such undercurrents of feeling, and important farmers like John Gibson took a different view of the changes:—

> You will see (he continued) that we have not been idle since you last visited Rousay and that, while you have been fighting your country's enemies on the hills of the Crimea and in the unhealthy jungles of India, we too have been fighting against a rugged soil and an uncertain climate, endeavouring to make two blades of grass grow on your islands where one, or rather none, grew before.

And that was true. His audience consisted of farmers practising essentially the type of farming found in present day Orkney, but any man over the age of thirty would well remember a time when agriculture had been medieval. No generation before or since had to adapt to greater changes.

Burroughs replied briefly to this speech of welcome. He thanked the tenants for the honour done to Mrs Burroughs and himself and expressed the hope that he would soon be able to visit them all on their own farms. He concluded by requesting their presence inside the house where refreshments had been prepared for them. Shortly afterwards the tenants began to leave for home, apparently well satisfied with what they had seen of their laird.

A fortnight later there was a dinner for laird and tenants. Again this was standard procedure and similar festivities had marked his earlier visits. In 1852 the main ingredient, according to the estate accounts, had been an almost unbelievable 2 cwts of cheese, but in 1859 the expenses were mainly for the purchase of whisky, payment to the fiddler and breakages of crockery. It had been altogether a livelier affair! This time the dinner took place in the large barn at Westness which had been cleared and decorated with flowers and branches of evergreens.[3] As well as Colonel and Mrs Burroughs, the party from Westness included the laird's younger brother, Charly, who had recently passed out from Sandhurst. Robert Scarth, the factor, was also present. He was now nearing the end of his career and, more than any other man, he was the architect of agricultural improvement in Orkney, for he factored other estates besides Rousay. He had a reputation for being a hard, competent, knowledgeable man who always knew just how much rent a tenant could afford to pay. He never took less, but he never took more, for one does not kill the goose that lays the golden eggs. Mr Gardner, the aged minister of the Established Church, was there with his colleagues, Mr Rose of the Free Church and Mr McLellan of the United Presbyterians. Impartiality demanded toasts from all three on an occasion like this and, for good measure, further toasts from the three schoolmasters. Yet for all the number of toasts, the dinner was a sober affair. By 1870 Rousay was strongly in the grip of the temperance movement and drunkenness was extremely rare.

At last Burroughs rose to reply to these expressions of the community's affection and he spoke at some length. He enjoyed speaking in public and, given the opportunity, he would willingly discourse on farming matters. His social status and his sense of superiority permitted him to do so with perfect confidence although his knowledge of farming was very limited.

He began by endorsing the comments which by now had been frequently made about the need to maintain good relations between landlord and tenant. Despite what 'popular agitators' might say to the contrary, it was in their mutual interest to keep on the friendliest terms. When he had last spoken to the tenants eleven years earlier he had expressed the hope that some day a good road round the island might be built. Now that task had been completed. He had also spoken of the need for farms and fields to be squared according to the latest scientific principles and now he saw that work largely accomplished. Enclosing, draining and dyke building had gone ahead in his absence. He also noticed that the standard of housing was immeasurably improved. The peat fire in the middle of the floor was now consigned to the past and had been replaced by proper fireplaces and even patent stoves. This had greatly improved the standard of cleanliness — a subject in which Burroughs had an almost morbid interest — and consequently even the humblest cottages now had plastered walls and wallpaper.

He concluded by assuring his audience that during his recent travels through France, Belgium, Prussia, Austria, South Germany, England and Scotland, he had seen examples of farming a good deal worse than anything which might be found in Rousay. It was a curiously negative compliment.

Apart from his reference to 'popular agitators', who had certainly not penetrated to Rousay by 1870 and who always existed mainly in his imagination, there were certain other ominous features of his speech which the applauding audience failed to notice. The very scale of the improvements which had taken place since his last visit gave him a false sense of the prosperity of his tenants. By 1870 the rate of improvement was slowing down and a decade later it was to stop entirely. Burroughs never really understood this and, long after the days of prosperity were ended, he continued to believe that his tenants had substantial sums of money hidden in their bank accounts. His praise of the factor's improving leases also sounded a note of warning for the future. 'The rent increase after each seven years,' he said, 'separated those tenants who wanted to advance from those who were content to stand still.' But those tenants who wanted to advance can have seen little benefit in a system where the profits of their improvements were largely creamed off in increased rent. There was a limit to the rack renting which the estate could bear and rent increases, perhaps tolerable in good times, became impossible to meet with the onset of agricultural depression.

The initial festivities over, Burroughs prepared to settle into his estate and to make a new life for himself in Rousay. As long as the laird and his tenants were speaking in generalities it had been easy to agree on the need for a good relationship between them. The time had now come for these generalities to be put into practice.

2

The Family in India

Sheriff Nicolson. — Mr M'Callum said the people are fond of remaining at home?
General Burroughs. — I suppose it is so, but I don't know any family in Great Britain who are all at home. I know my brother is on the northermost frontier of China; I have sisters in England and one in China. *Napier Commission*[1]

ONE reason why so little was known about the new proprietor was that his connections with Orkney were most tenuous. He had no Orcadian forebears and none of his direct ancestors had ever lived in Orkney or, as far as is known, even visited it. His surname, Traill-Burroughs, had an Orcadian component, for Traill was a familiar landed name. Traills had owned Westness for over two hundred and fifty years, but this part of his surname was adopted at the wish of George William Traill from whom he inherited the estate. Burroughs always referred to Traill as his uncle, but the relationship was actually more remote. After the early death of Burroughs' great grandfather, his great grandmother had married again and Traill was the son of this second marriage. This was the sum total of Burroughs' connection with his estate.

The founder of the family fortunes had been Sir George Colebrooke, the head of an old and wealthy firm of merchant bankers in the middle of the eighteenth century. By his marriage to Mary Gaynor, the rich heiress to a West Indian sugar fortune, Sir George became very rich indeed. He entered Parliament as M.P. for Arundel and made himself useful to the East India Company by defending its privileges. He was rewarded by being invited to join the Court of Directors and rose to become chairman in 1769. It was an appointment sufficient to secure profitable careers in India for most of his descendants over the next five generations. George William Traill, laird of Rousay from 1840 to 1847, and Frederick Burroughs, laird from 1847 to 1905, belonged to this network of Indian-based descendants.

Sir George Colebrooke's eldest daughter, Mary, was married first to the Chevalier Charles Adrian de Peyron, a member of a recently ennobled French family in the service of the King of Sweden. On a visit to Paris in 1784 he was involved in a duel with the Comte de la Marck.[2] Peyron was killed and Mary Colebrooke was left a widow with an infant son. She married again and her second husband was William Traill, a member of a cadet branch of the Traills of Westness. It was a fortunate marriage for Traill. As Burroughs put it bluntly, he had 'married a lady, with whom he got a lot of money'.[3] Even more important than money, he had gained the influence of the Colebrookes and the likelihood of profitable careers in India for his son and stepson. For Traill it was a dazzlingly successful marriage. Possibly he owed his acquaintance with the Colebrookes to the kelp trade. Orkney was at that time the leading kelp-producing area in the British Isles, and among Colebrooke's many business interests was a chemical works on the Forth whose kelp purchases caused a minor boom in Orkney in the 1760s.

Traill's stepson, Charles Adolphe Maria de Peyron, went out to India in 1797 at the age of sixteen and served for ten hectic years in the 3rd Native Cavalry Regiment. In 1807 he was invalided home and died in England later the same year at the age of twenty-six. Indian careers could be glamorous and profitable but sometimes they were very brief. He died unmarried but left an illegitimate daughter in Calcutta, a daughter who never saw her father, for she was born five months after he left India. She was Caroline de Peyron and was Burroughs' mother.

Although left fatherless, she had powerful friends, the chief of whom was Mary Colebrooke's brother. Henry Thomas Colebrooke was the most distinguished member of the family.[4] Through his father's influence he had gone to Bengal in the Company's service and rose quickly to become a judge. The heavy drinking and excessive gambling of the Warren Hastings era held little attraction for him and, as an opponent of the Company's trading monopoly, he was shunned by many of his fellow Company employees. He fell into habits of unremitting private study and, despite a heavy workload, found time for an immense volume of scholarship. His writings covered a wide range of subjects including trade, commerce, Hindu civil law and studies of Indian literature. He was also the first European systematically to study Sanskrit. The advent of Wellesley as Governor-general brought him recognition and rapid advancement. In 1801 he was appointed to the bench of the new Court of Appeal in Calcutta; from 1805 he also held the position of Professor of Hindu Law and Sanskrit and in 1807, the same year as his illegitimate grand-niece was born, he was appointed to a seat on the Council of the East India Company.

Later Caroline lived under the protection of her uncle, George William Traill, at Simla.[5] It was there that she met Frederick Burroughs, a young lieutenant in the 17th Native Infantry, son of Sir William Burroughs of Castle Bagshawe, County Cavan. Sir William had been a judge in Calcutta in Henry Colebrooke's time and, by the sale of the Castle Bagshawe

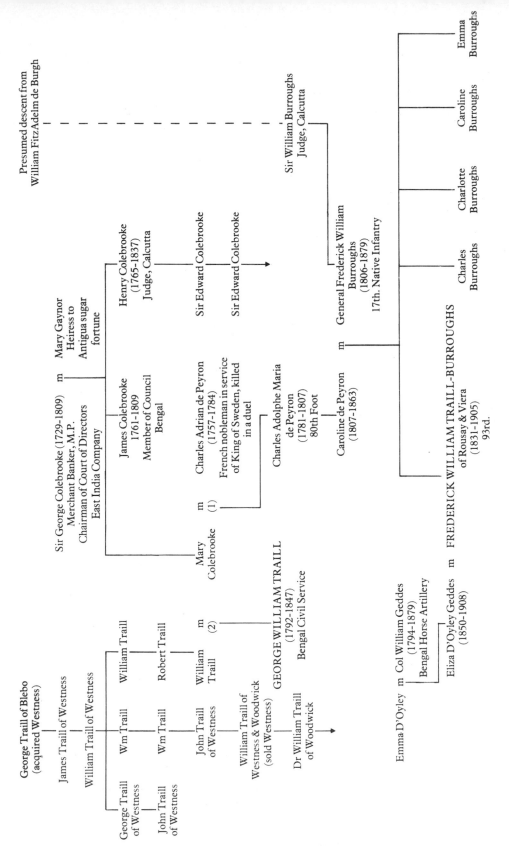

Fig. 2. The Traill and Burroughs Families

property, he had left his son a comfortable income to supplement his army pay.[6] Frederick and Caroline were married in 1830 at Fatehgarh, a military post on the banks of the Ganges not far from Cawnpore, and their first child was born the following year. He bore exactly the same name as his father, Frederick William Burroughs, and he was the future laird of Rousay. For three happy years his home was a typical army bungalow lying between the parade ground and the river. The more senior officers lived on the actual bank of the Ganges but Burroughs' father, only fairly recently promoted to lieutenant in the 17th Native Cavalry, had to be content with a house in the second row and separated from the parade ground only by the engineers' yard. Yet for a junior officer it was a sizeable establishment. During the Indian Mutiny Burroughs visited the burnt-out shell of his birthplace and drew a quick plan of the building in his pocket diary.[7] The house had deep verandahs on all sides and consisted of a large central room surrounded by no fewer than sixteen smaller rooms and compartments with curtain-covered interconnecting doorways. The household of even a junior officer could not function without its retinue of specialist servants — cooks, water carriers, laundry boys and gardeners. In the cool season Fatehgarh was a delightful station — it reminded Burroughs of Oxfordshire — but in the hot season dust, heat and the intensity of light made life unbearable outside the dark interior of the bungalow. Burroughs' earliest memories must have been of this bungalow beside the Ganges and his father's native soldiers drilling on the sunbaked parade ground.

Much earlier, the year after his half-brother came home to die, George William Traill entered the service of the East India Company. Peyron was a soldier but Traill made his career in the Bengal Civil Service.[8] He was one of the first of the new men, a product of Haileybury, the East India Company's newly founded 'university'. Territorial expansion and the corruption of the Warren Hastings era had created the need for a new type of administrator in India. George William Traill was a good example of the type of man it was intended Haileybury should produce — confident, immensely hard working, cultured and reasonably honest.

Before the Haileybury buildings were completed, the East India Company's college was temporarily housed in Hertford Castle. Traill's year at the college (1808-9) began at Hertford and ended in the new premises. In future, entry to the Company's administrative service was to be restricted to Haileybury graduates and nomination to places in the college was one of the most prized pieces of patronage in the control of the Directors. In Traill's case nomination was easily obtained through Colebrooke influence. Haileybury was run on university lines and aimed to turn out a man of broad culture through studies of law, mathematics, economics, botany and oriental languages. Its most distinguished professor, Malthus, imparted to Traill an enthusiasm for the collection of statistics and for the study of the economy and population of the regions in which he was to serve.

Traill arrived in India in 1810 when his uncle, Henry Colebrooke, was at the height of his power. His first important appointment came five years later when he was attached as assistant to the Hon. E. Gardner, political officer in the Nepalese Campaign. Despite a good deal of military incompetence, the campaign was eventually successful and Nepal was forced to cede the Himalayan province of Kumaon. Gardner was appointed the first British Commissioner in Kumaon and Traill remained as his assistant. The following year a general settlement was made with Nepal and Gardner departed to become first Resident in Kathmandu. Traill succeeded him in Kumaon and so, at the early age of twenty-four, found himself governing 11,000 square miles of newly conquered mountain country. It was rapid advancement which he owed not only to family influence and to the rapid expansion of British India stretching the resources of the Civil Service, but also to his undoubted energy and ability.

For the next thirty years Traill exercised what was described as a 'benevolent and active despotism' in Kumaon.[9] It was said that, although the Governor-general might rule in Calcutta, Traill was 'King of Kumaon'. He was firmly of the opinion that a frontier administrator knew what was best for his territory and was much better placed to make decisions than desk-bound officials hundreds of miles away. Successive Governor-generals let him have his own way. It was not only that his Himalayan kingdom was very different from the rest of India and difficult of access, but also that Traill had been there since the beginning of British rule. It was as if he had succeeded to his 'kingdom' by right of conquest.

The province of Kumaon consists of some of the most difficult mountain country in the world. Few parts, even of the Himalayas, have such a vertical range of height, from a mere 2,000 to 3,000 feet in the deeply incised valleys of the Ganges, Jumna and Sutlej to 25,645 feet in the culminating spire of Nanda Devi. The low valleys are hot and humid. In these jungles, Traill in one year expended 1,400 rupees in destroying 45 tigers, 124 leopards and 240 bears. There is seldom much flat land and any arable ground is found perched high on the steeply sloping valley sides or in remote tributaries. Higher ridges are covered in oak and rhododendron forest above which rise the alpine pastures and the snows.

The province which young Traill took over presented problems other than its obvious physical difficulties. His task was to create order where for seventy years there had been chaos and misrule. Since it had been overrun by Nepalese gurkhas, Kumaon had been oppressed and over-taxed. There was little effective control from Kathmandu. The province had been divided into military districts, each under an officer responsible for raising a fixed sum, but in practice free to collect as much more for himself as he was able to exact. The rule of the gurkhas had resulted in a quarter of the villages being deserted and perhaps half of the arable land going out of cultivation.

Traill's main task was fiscal. It was his responsibility to assess and collect taxes. His first move was to halve the gurkha assessment on the province, and this reduction soon resulted in a revitalisation of the economy and eventually restored the former tax-paying capacity. Initially taxation was on an *ad hoc* basis, but Traill embarked on a major survey of the province to put the levy on a permanent footing. This involved him in sorting out a tangle of outdated taxes, for the pre-1790 taxation system was half forgotten and gurkha taxes had been superimposed on the original system. He had to investigate the intricacies of taxes on goods in transit, on cultivation, mining, lawsuits, weaving, grazing and on the manufacture of clarified butter, as well as 'gifts' on such occasions as births and marriages. The system was further complicated by the fact that not all villages were revenue-paying. Some owed military service in lieu of revenue, others were assigned to temples or were free villages. Anyone who could master Kumaon taxation might even hope to understand the *skat* payments on an Orkney estate.

With a handful of assistants, Traill undertook the task of surveying some 8,000 villages. It was a project which involved enormous difficulties of travel — fording mountain torrents, crossing precarious bridges and scaling mountain passes. Estimates were made of livestock numbers and the extent of arable land. Systematic enquiries were made into population, history, language and social institutions. Malthus would have been proud of his ex-pupil — Traill even made a classification of the different kinds of Kumaon ghosts! It was all gathered together under the title *Report on Kumaon for 1822-23,*[10] much of which was incorporated verbatim in all nineteenth century official publications on the province.

One of his many journeys included a high crossing of the main axis of the Himalaya. In 1830 he made the first crossing of the 17,700 ft. pass immediately east of Nanda Devi,[11] thereafter known as Traill's Pass. Even by modern mountaineering standards it is by no means easy and it was a notable achievement for that time.

As well as possessing personal energy, Traill had the ability to get the best out of his young assistants and to stamp his personality and methods on them. One of these men, Brian Hodgson, later British Resident at Kathmandu, assisted Traill in the survey of Kumaon and left a brief portrait of him at that time:—

I was much struck by the simple yet efficient method of administrating the province, a new acquisition tenanted by very primitive and poor tribes. The Commissioner (i.e. Traill) who spoke and wrote the local language, dispensed with all formalities, settled cases in court like the father of a family, and encouraged everyone who had a complaint to put it in writing and drop it into a slit in the court door, of which he kept the key. Answered viva voce, in court or out. He was of active habits, and went everywhere throughout the province, hearing and seeing all for himself. His cheerful, simple manner and liking for the people made him justly popular.[12]

In his youth Traill was an attractive figure but it was the misfortune of all of this family that they were more likeable in India than they ever were at home. Traill retired from the service in 1836 and used his wealth to buy property in Rousay as it came on the market. It was not to be expected that the efficient frontier administrator would allow his new estate to continue undisturbed in its old-fashioned ways. He was to be remembered, not as the enlightened and vigorous 'King of Kumaon', but as the tyrannical laird of Rousay who effected the most thoroughgoing clearance to take place on any Orkney estate. His ultimate achievement was the purchase of the lands of Westness in 1845 (but not Westness House). For a member of a junior branch of the family, the acquisition of the ancestral lands was a final mark of success, but it was a success which he did not long enjoy. In November 1847, aged only fifty-four, he died as a result of a heart attack. He had dined quietly in the Oriental Club in the company of his cousin, Sir Edward Colebrooke, and was last seen in the drawing room where, according to his usual routine, he was served with a cup of hot milk and water. The following morning a housemaid reported that one of the water closets was locked. A policemen was summoned to break down the door and Traill's body was discovered. An autopsy revealed a heart condition of long standing.[13]

Much of this family background was known to those tenants who turned out to welcome Burroughs to his home in July 1870, but there were certain ominous features which they could not have fully appreciated yet. The Burroughs were originally a family of Irish landowners, and in no part of the world were landlord-tenant relations so notoriously bad as in nineteenth century Ireland. Burroughs liked to believe that his family were descended from the original William FitzAdelm de Burgh who was sent by Henry II to receive the surrender of the King of Connaught but, although he took an interest in Irish affairs, he owned no property in Ireland nor did he maintain contact with any relatives he may have had there. The great Irish issues — home rule, the land question and the disestablishment of the church — dominated the politics of his time and on all of these he was an implacable opponent of Gladstonian Liberals. Crofting legislation in Scotland was modelled on Irish land reform. Burroughs' Irishness meant

1. Frederick William Traill–Burroughs of Rousay and Viera.

2a. Shooting party, General Burroughs third from left. Very conscious of his small stature, he seldom consented to appear in group photographs.

2b. James Leonard (1835–1913). Stonemason, weaver, Free Church precentor, Temperance lecturer, evicted crofter and General Burroughs' implacable opponent.

3a. Trumland House from the air, 'a very compact, complete and nice looking house' built 1873–6 to the design of David Bryce.

3b. The *Orcadia* (left) and the *Lizzie Burroughs* (right). The coming of steamships revolutionised farming in the North Isles of Orkney. Most islands were served by the *Orcadia* but from 1879 until 1892 Rousay, Egilsay and Wyre relied on the erratic service provided by Burroughs' little steamer.

4a. Tafts, the original nucleus of the vanished community of Quandale, cleared by George William Traill in 1846. The corn kiln on the right was built only four years previously.

4b. Tafts, interior. Tafts was a superior dwelling, a mansionhouse in miniature. The main room, although very small, had two stone window seats and a chimney.

5a. The Free Church and Manse at Sourin—centre of opposition to the laird.

5b. Digro, Sourin, home of James Leonard. The two houses, high on the margins of cultivation, look out over the sound towards Egilsay. In 1883 there were fifteen people living on the croft.

6a. Wasbister. The farm of Langskaill is in line with the left end of the Loch of Wasbister. Saviskaill stands near the shore in line with the other end of the loch.

6b. Westness and Eynhallow Sound. Westness House, built in 1792, was originally the principal mansionhouse on Rousay. Along the shore lies the arable part of Westness Farm, squared and improved by George William Traill c.1846.

7a. Oxen. Crofters often co-operated with a neighbour, each providing one beast in the pair. When asked by the Napier Commission about the relative merits of horses and oxen, George Leonard replied, 'I could not keep a horse for a week.' In this case, a flagstone is being used to break clods.

7b. Harrowing by hand.

8a. The threshing of corn with flails was part of the routine of barn work. Usually this was done indoors in the draught between two doors (seen on left). The building is a typical nineteenth century farm with dwelling, barn, stable and byre in a single low building. Note the remains of a turf cover on the flagstone roof.

8b. The hens that paid the rent. As grain prices slumped, crofters increasingly fed corn to hens and Orkney egg production expanded. The Crofters Commission, however, did not take this secret income into account when fixing fair rent, much to the annoyance of General Burroughs.

that he met the Crofters Act with preconceived ideas and a predetermined opposition.

It is tempting to believe that Burroughs inherited his bravery from the aristocratic and mercenary Peyrons and with it his hastiness and easily ruffled sense of honour. One may even imagine that he had the same temperament as his great grandfather who was killed in a duel. A century later such affairs were out of fashion and one did not fight duels with crofters, yet his battle with them was akin to an affair of honour. Away from the battlefield even bravery may turn out to be rashness and pigheadedness. The qualities which so nearly won him the Victoria Cross were not obvious qualifications for managing a crofting estate.

Nor were thirteen years in India a good preparation for such a task. David Balfour, laird of the neighbouring island of Shapinsay, had first-hand experience of the dangers. Like the Burroughs estate which owed its existence to George William Traill's career in the Bengal Civil Service, the Balfour estate owed its prosperity to an Indian fortune. David Balfour's great uncle, John Balfour, had been a writer with the East India Company in Madras. David's early years had been spent under the shadow of this rich but parsimonious and long-lived relative. It was from personal experience and with his great-uncle in mind that he wrote to Burroughs in 1866 warning him of the danger of an over-long stay in India:—

> I still look forward to the hope that we shall welcome yourself before long. I do not at all believe that your Estate and Tenantry are suffering under such excellent management as Scarth's — everything is done that can be done without the sunshine of the laird's own eyes — What I fear most is that if you delay long your tastes and habits of thought will be so Indianized, that you will not be happy among us when you do come — that the changes to our climate, scenery, customs and character may be so violent as to disgust you with a life in Orkney and you will not be able to judge fairly between conditions so contrasted.[14]

Although Burroughs, unlike John Balfour, was able to settle happily in Orkney on his return from India, David Balfour's other fears were fully justified. The long years in India had inculcated habits of command but had impaired his judgment. They were years devoid of any experience which fitted him to guide the destiny of a community of Orkney farmers.

Rootlessness was perhaps the most fundamentally ominous feature of the new laird's background. Both he and his wife sprang from generations of empire builders, from families accustomed to ruling 'natives' with a perfect confidence that they knew what was best for other people. They had little sense of 'home', that close identification with a place and that immediate understanding of the aspirations of the people and the subtleties of their culture which only a long and intimate connection can provide. In a place like Orkney even one generation may not be enough.

Burroughs came from a family the members of which were scattered throughout the outposts of empire. It was not easy for him to understand the close-knit society of Rousay or to sympathise with the crofter's attachment to the few infertile acres he had reclaimed from the stubbornly resisting heather.

3

Early Development of the Estate

'Since they were severed, more than three centuries ago, from the kindred rule of Norway, their history has been a continuous tale of wrong and oppression, of unscrupulous rapacity and unheeded complaint.' David Balfour, *Odal Rights and Feudal Wrongs*[1]

WHEN Traill bought land in Rousay and when Burroughs inherited it, they did not represent some new type of exploiter coming to disrupt a stable and idyllic island community which previously had existed immune from any such pressures. Usually there had been a dominating family in Rousay, often incomers, and since Traill and Burroughs enjoyed incomes which were independent of their estate, they were less systematically ruthless than most of their predecessors.

Something of the early development of the estate can be reconstructed from the evidence of sixteenth century rentals. The earliest of these, *Lord Sinclair's Rental Book of Orkney*,[2] does not include bishopric land, so the whole district of Sourin is missing. These lands, however, were enumerated in a tack of 1563[3] and both earldom land and bishopric were included in *The Rental of King and Bischoppis Lands of Orkney, 1595*.[4] Besides giving detailed information on the sixteenth century, the rentals throw light on an even earlier period and are the basis for understanding the later development of the estate.

Land was measured in *pennylands* and *farthings*, the farthingland being a quarter of a pennyland. Eighteen pennylands composed an *uresland*, a division which formed a basic district for fiscal and ecclesiastical purposes. Rousay consisted of 6½ ureslands with individual districts varying in extent from half ureslands to 1½ ureslands. Along the south shore of the island, the half uresland district was the normal unit. Here a narrow ribbon of coastal settlement, often on steeply rising ground and overlooking the tidal streams of Eynhallow Sound, was divided into the districts of Inner Westness, Frotoft and Brinyan. The east side of Rousay looking across the quieter waters of the sound to the island of Egilsay with the ruined tower of St Magnus Church on the skyline, comprised the half uresland district of Knarston, the 1½ ureslands of Sourin, and the peninsula of Scockness, a further half uresland. The main settled area in the east was the wide, semi-circular bowl formed by the lower part of the Sourin Burn which drains the greater part of the uninhabited hilly interior of the island and serves as an outlet for the two lochs, Muckle Water and Peerie Water. Leaving Sourin, the track to Wasbister climbed steeply over the shoulder of Kierfea Hill then slanted down the Leean, the precipitous north coast of Rousay. The beautiful district of Wasbister lies in the north-west of the island. It centres on the Loch of Wasbister with cultivated land sloping down to the loch on three sides. The rentals divide Wasbister into two parts, the half uresland unit of Langskaill on the east side of the loch and the remainder, Wasbister proper, forming a whole uresland. The western parts of Rousay formed the remaining and rather artificial uresland which contained two quite distinct districts, the exposed and windswept township of Quandale facing out to the open sea and, over the shoulder of Scabra Head, the district of Outer Westness.

It seems fanciful to try, as Dr Marwick has done, to relate the ureslands to original Norse land takes, the whole uresland the property of important leaders and half ureslands of lesser.[5] While ureslands may sometimes reflect the boundaries of properties at a remote period, it is not necessary to think of them as anything more than convenient units for church purposes fitted as nearly as possible to the natural districts of the island. The uresland division is an ancient one, pre-dating the parishes. Each district had its chapel and, although it is a unit which has now entirely faded from memory, last century the tradition was still remembered that neighbours had an obligation to attend any funeral which took place in the uresland. In Rousay, several little graveyards served uresland districts, and interments in these local graveyards took place well into the present century.

Marwick also seems to be surprised to have to conclude that the uresland was not the 'toon' (a term unknown in Rousay), the basic working unit of run-rig agriculture, the unit within which rigs were shared among farmers. This unit, of course, must have generally been much smaller and corresponded with the component parts of the uresland as enumerated in the rental (Table 1). These places did not necessarily form a single holding but might comprise a farm with satellite holdings or else a community of small farmers. The fact that most farms outside the bishopric consisted of a mixture of udal property and rented land indicates a complicated structure.

The extent of the pennyland in earlier times cannot now be determined. By the eighteenth century, when it is possible to convert pennylands to acres, the pennyland was a decayed and corrupt measurement. Cases can be found in Orkney where the pennyland consisted of as little as 4 acres and other instances where it contained nearly 60 acres.[6] Perhaps it had never

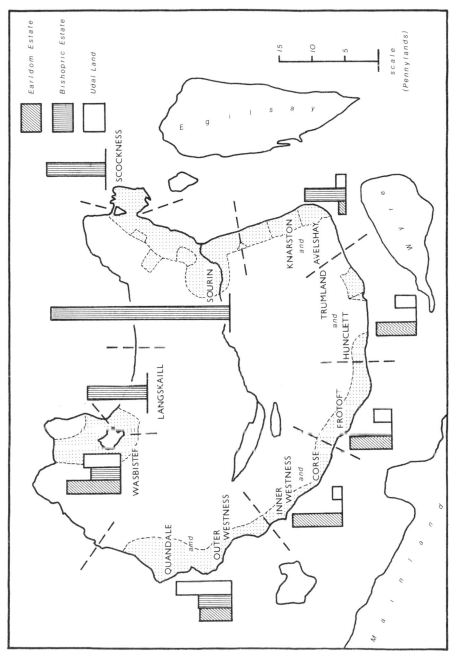

Fig. 3. Sixteenth Century Rousay. The map shows the uresland divisions and the ownership of land within each. There were extensive bishopric lands in the east of the island and elsewhere a complicated mixture of rented earldom land, church property and land held by udal tenure. The township dykes are drawn from a map of later date (O.C.L. E29, c.1780).

been a unit of area but rather a measurement of worth relating to fertility and taking into account such factors as the availability of seaweed for manure. An eighteenth century suggestion was that the pennyland was a measure of the area of land which could be sown by a certain quantity of seed, traditionally sown thick on well manured land near the coast and more thinly on less fertile inland ground.[7] If this was the case, George William Traill would have understood the Orkney pennylands, for it was exactly this method of valuation which was traditionally used in the mountains of Kumaon.

But there were other reasons for the variability of the pennyland. Whatever it may have been originally, the pennyland came to be a measurement of the run-rig land excluding the *tumails*, that part of the land which was not subject to run-rig sharing but was permanently attached to one particular house.[8] There was a natural tendency for farmers to extend their tumails at the expense of run-rig 'townland' whenever they were able to do so. Reclamation might also affect the size of the pennyland which was a fixed value and did not increase to take account of additional arable ground. Expansion of cultivated land could take place even without the 'flitting out' of the original hill dykes, for interspersed with scattered arable rigs there were grass sections which were often easily reclaimable. Thus Orkney, which had to cope with a corrupt system of weights, had also to contend with an even more decayed method of measuring land. But the system was not quite so bad as at first appears, for the main use of pennylands was internal, to indicate a share in the farm rather than to compare farms. Thus if a tenant rented a pennyland on a three pennyland farm, he was entitled to every third rig, and his *coogild* or right to keep stock was similarly related to his pennyland holding.[9]

Shortly after Sir Laurence Dundas acquired the Earldom Estate in 1766, he commissioned a survey from which it is possible to calculate the extent of 39 of Rousay's 119½ pennylands inclusive of tumails:[10]

	Pennylands	Scots Acres	Acres/Pennyland
Wasbister	22	499	22.7
Swandale	3	67	22.3
Houseby	6	69	11.5
Knarston	6	83	13.9
Trumland	2	34	17.0
Total	39	752	19.3

Pennylands in the North Isles were usually much smaller than on the Orkney Mainland and it was a common rule of thumb that a North Isles pennyland was equivalent to a Mainland farthingland.[11] Rousay occupied an intermediate position. The average Mainland pennyland (22.3 acres) was only slightly bigger, while pennylands, for example, in Sanday and Westray were much smaller than in Rousay.

Turning next to a consideration of the various Rousay properties, it is appropriate to begin with Westness, the heartland of the Burroughs estate. Westness House stands in Inner Westness but the original centre was Brough and Skaill in Outer Westness. Here three brochs, including the Broch of Midhowe and a much earlier Neolithic stalled burial chamber, point to the continuing presence in Westness of an authority able to command the obedience and the labour of the district. It was here too beneath the ward (or beacon) hill that the island's main estate was centred in the Norse period.

The Orkneyinga Saga provides a vivid glimpse of Westness in the twelfth century when it was the home of Sigurd of Westness, an important landowner and one of the foremost supporters of Earl Paul. It was while on a visit to Westness that the earl was abducted by Sweyn Asleifson in one of the most daring and dramatic saga incidents. After a night spent feasting at Westness, Earl Paul was out early the following morning otter-hunting in the rocks under Scabra Head when he was surprised from the sea by what he had taken to be an innocent merchant vessel and carried off to captivity in Scotland and eventual death.[12]

From the 1503 rental it is possible to reconstruct the outline of Sigurd's twelfth century estate. From information contained in the saga, it is clear that Earl Paul visited Westness as a *veizla*, the technical term for a superior who guested with a vassal, consuming the produce of his estate. Thus it appears that Sigurd, in addition to holding udal land of his own, was also a tenant of earldom land, which is hardly surprising since he was the earl's friend and supporter and was married to his cousin. One must therefore look to the 1503 rental to discover earldom lands in that part of Rousay, and there one finds the seven pennylands of *Auld Earldom* land of Inner Westness which surely must have been the land in question. To this can very probably be added the four pennylands of *Auld Earldom* land in Wasbister and either all or part of Quandale. It is equally certain that Sigurd's own property must have included the seven pennylands of udal land at Brough. Whether he owned Skaill is less certain. At a later date it was in the hands of the church but originally it had been udal. If it was not already church property in Sigurd's time, it was most probably part of his estate. The estate of Sigurd of Westness therefore comprised the western part of Rousay and had boundaries similar to the estate George William Traill was to control seven hundred years later.

Another large unit which can be identified from the same period is Sourin. The entire district, along with Scockness, was bishopric property, one of four large blocks of land with which the bishopric was originally endowed. Again the date of the gift is uncertain but the saga makes frequent reference to the bishop residing in Egilsay in the twelfth century and, since Sourin formed a single unit with Egilsay, it is reasonable to assume that Sourin became church property at this time. The link between Sourin and Egilsay continued for a long time. In 1678, when James Traill was trying to compel the Sourin people to contribute to the repair of the parish church seven miles away at Skaill, a church which was 'unthecked' and in danger of becoming ruinous, he complained that Sourin was 'annexed to Egilsha without any law'. Official enquiries were made and it was found that the inhabitants of Sourin had attended service at Egilsay 'past memory of man', and the arrangement was confirmed.[13]

This link is a good example of two communities joined by the sea. When Rousay was roadless, travel by land was difficult and Sourin was rather isolated from the rest of the island. Three miles of steep hillside lay between Sourin and Wasbister and, in the other direction, the then sparsely inhabited district of Brinyan separated Sourin from Frotoft. In these circumstances it was natural that the two sides of the sound should form a single unit. The union of the districts in the bishopric simply recognised the natural unity which the sea provided.

There can be little doubt that the original grant of Sourin was made by the Earl himself. No one else was likely to have been in possession of such an extensive block of land undivided by udal inheritance. This is confirmed by the evidence of the 1503 rental. The rental was concerned with investigating cases where revenues had been misappropriated, but it makes no comment on the fact that Sourin paid no *skat*. Whereas an individual might dispose of his land to the church if he chose to do so, *skat*, the original land tax, was still payable to the Earl. As Sourin paid no *skat*, nor does the rental claim that it ought to be paid, Sourin must have been gifted by the Earl since no lesser person had the right to give away the *skat*. Sourin therefore represents a large block of *Auld Earldom* land gifted to the church as part of the original endowment. Possibly this was an atonement for the murder of St Magnus in Egilsay, a murder which was certainly quickly forgiven.

Outside the main block of Sourin and Scockness, there were three other properties belonging to the bishopric — the nine pennylands of Langskaill, five pennylands of Skaill and four and a half pennylands of Hammer in Wasbister. None of these places paid *skat* in 1503 although the rental claimed that payment was due. The implication is that they were originally udal properties and not the gift of the Earl. They were later acquisitions by the church possibly as pious endowments, business transactions or expiation for misdeeds and, by astute management, the church had

	Total Pennylands	Kingsland and Auld Earldom	Conquest Land	Bishop	Vicar	Udal Land	More Recent Enclosures
Knerstane	9	•	1¼	4	2⅓	1⁵/₁₂	•
(½ uresland)	9						
Trumland	2	•	1½	•	•	½	•
Nether Howclett	4	•	3½	•	•	½	•
Ovir Howclett	3	•	1	•	•	2	•
(½ uresland)	9						
Frowtoft	9	•	6½	•	•	2½	•
(½ uresland)	9						
Corse	2	•	⅝	•	•	1⅜	•
Inner Westness	7	7	•	•	•	•	•
(½ uresland)	9						
Skaill	5	•	•	5	•	•	•
Brugh	7	1	•	•	•	6	•
Quham	3	•	¾	•	•	2¼	•
Quendalc	3	•	3	•	•	•	•
(1 uresland)	18						
Wasbister	18	4	4³/₂₀	4½	•	5⁷/₂₀	•
(1 uresland)	18						
Langskale	9	•	•	9	•	•	•
(½ uresland)	9						
Bankis	3	•	•	3	•	•	•
Ove	3	•	•	3	•	•	•
Ovirdaill	3	•	•	3	•	•	•
Brindaill	3	•	•	3	•	•	•
Ossaque	½	•	•	½	•	•	•
Brewland	1	•	•	1	•	•	•
Suandaill	3	•	•	3	•	•	•
Bigland	3	•	•	3	•	•	•
Pow	½	•	•	½	•	•	•
Hertiso	½	•	•	½	•	•	•
Ferraclott	3	•	•	3	•	•	•
Mydfra	1½	•	•	1½	•	•	•
Eistafra	2	•	•	2	•	•	•
(1½ ureslands)	27						
Scockness	9	•	•	9	•	•	•
(½ uresland)	9						
Quoyskow	1¼	•	•	•	•	•	1¼
Quoyeister	¼	•	•	•	•	•	¼
Lequy	No Pennyland Value			•	•	•	•
Quyis	1	•			1	•	•	•
Quynenea	No Pennyland Value			•	•	•	•
	119½	12	c.22¼	59½	2⅓	c.22	1½

Table 1. The Lands of Rousay from Sixteenth Century Rentals (in pennylands). By this date comparatively little udal land remained and this consisted of scattered portions. Rousay was dominated by the two big estates, the Bishopric and the Earldom.

engrossed not only the rents as was their right, but also the *skat* which still should have been paid to the Earl. In the case of Langskaill, the rental is quite explicit and notes that 'bishop William quhen he had our Soverane Lordis landis in tak wes the first that evir began to tak ony of the Kingis scattis contenit in this buik'.[14] The bishop referred to is William Tulloch, Bishop of Orkney from 1368 to 1382, who held the skats in tack from 1374 to 1378.

The final piece of church property consisted of part of the lands of Avelshay. Avelshay contained $2\frac{1}{3}$ pennylands which made up the vicar's glebe, but there were a further four pennylands which had been granted by Earl William (Earl from 1434 to 1471) to Sir Hew of Randale for undertaking a mission to Norway on the Earl's behalf. The 'sir' was a clerical courtesy title and, although the grant had been for his lifetime only, his successors had succeeded in retaining the property and annexing it to the income of the Prebendar of Wyre, an official of St Magnus Cathedral in Kirkwall.[15]

Earl William's time also saw the acquisition by the Earldom of what were known as the *Conquest Lands*. These were properties acquired by purchase or other means and this *Conquest Land* amounted to a total of $22\frac{1}{4}$ pennylands. This implies that Earl William acquired almost exactly half the udal land which existed in the island at that time. Storer Clouston has suggested that these sales were related to the transfer of Orkney from the Danish to the Scottish crown, and were the result of uncertainty about the future. It is more likely that the cause was economic. The fourteenth and fifteenth centuries experienced a shrinking population popularly associated with the Black Death (1347-51) but comprising both earlier and later periods of high mortality. Economic conditions were depressed from about 1300 onwards, reaching a low point in the first half of the fifteenth century. It is significant that the *Conquest Lands* of Rousay were in small scattered units through most townships although never, except in the case of Quandale, forming the whole of a township, and even in Quandale the *Conquest Land* was acquired through at least two separate transactions. One would expect the larger landowners to be more responsive to political threats but smaller udallers to be more likely to succumb to economic depression. It might well be that small and marginal farms had difficulty in meeting *skat* payments and that the Earl bought or confiscated the property of the bankrupt udaller as a means of clearing the debt. It is difficult to imagine that the Earl was pursuing a vigorous policy of buying up property at the same time as he was allowing the church to make inroads on his *skats*. Economic depression can account for his accumulation of small properties and his simultaneous neglect of his estate.

The 1503 rental provides other evidence to support this view. It reveals a fall in the *landmails* (the rent). Some examples are quite explicit — Over Howclett and Quham were rented at 'a third part fall' (a one-third reduction in rent) and seven places in Wasbister at a one-fifth reduction. When rents in kind are converted into money terms, it becomes clear that the decline in the level of the rents was widespread. There was also a tendency to collect rent in produce reflecting a more pastoral type of economy. Marginal at the best of times, grain growing in Orkney's northern climate must have provided a precarious livelihood in the fifteenth century.

The archetypal Orcadian society is often thought of as a community of sturdy udallers recognising no superior and holding their land with an absolute ownership provided they paid their skats — a primitive peasant democracy of equals. Reality was somewhat different. Even by the sixteenth century quite a small proportion of Rousay was udal, less than 22 out of a total of $119\frac{1}{2}$ pennylands. These udal properties varied from the substantial estate of Brough to numerous small plots of land. The church with 62 pennylands held rather more than half the island, and $35\frac{3}{4}$ pennylands were earldom property. Church and earldom land was rented to tenants who varied greatly in economic status and who in turn rented land to a numerous sub-tenantry.

The two blocks which we have identified in the twelfth century — Westness-Brough-Skaill in the west of the island and Sourin-Scockness in the east — continued to exist as units right up to the nineteenth century but with very different histories. In the fifteenth and early sixteenth centuries the Craigies were the udal owners of Brough and were the dominant resident family in the island, various members successively holding the offices of *lawrikman, lawman* and *roithman*. The fact that a family with a Scottish surname were udallers indicates that the property had passed into their hands through marriage. The founder of the family may well have been James Cragy, 'dominus' of Huip in Stronsay and liegeman of the King of Norway who married a granddaughter of Malise Sperra (killed 1389).[16] Malise Sperra owned $2\frac{1}{4}$ pennylands in Quham and $1\frac{1}{2}$ pennylands in Quandale and may also have owned the larger adjacent property of Brough. However they achieved it, the Craigies, a family of Scottish incomers, had established themselves as the leading family in an island with a basically Norse population well in advance of the transfer of sovereignty to the Scottish crown.

The Reformation provides a good example of how an immoral and profiteering clergyman could turn events to his advantage and become a landed proprietor. The clergyman was Magnus Halcro, Cathedral chantor in St Magnus Cathedral in Kirkwall and the illegitimate son of Malcolm Halcro, Archdeacon of Shetland. Magnus Halcro's first move was to purchase Brough from the Craigies in 1556. The property he acquired was a substantial one and included the 'fortalice', head house and mill besides carrying the right of patronage to the chapel of St Christopher in the Cathedral. The fortalice referred to was a small, thick-walled tower standing adjacent to the old parish church near Brough. The Reformation provided Halcro with opportunities to consolidate and add to his estate. He immediately took advantage of the new order to marry Margaret Sinclair, heiress to Sir James Sinclair. The fact that the bride was married to some one else and the groom already had a family of three illegitimate children seems to have carried small weight against the political advantages of the match. Such difficulties could be overcome by an influential churchman. Influence also obtained for him a tack of the bishopric lands in Rousay and his position in the island was supreme.

Halcro was able to live out his life in peaceful enjoyment of his ill-gotten estate, but his widow fell foul of Earl Robert Stewart, half-brother of Mary Queen of Scots and the equal of Magnus Halcro as an unscrupulous collector of property. In 1584 the Earl claimed arrears of skat amounting to £1,009 and, in default of payment, he proceeded to confiscate the estate with unseemly haste and by dubious means. An assize was convened packed with the Earl's henchmen and they heard how a search had been made for moveable goods but 'none found'. The estate was accordingly offered for sale but there were 'no buyers' — it was not politic to bid when Earl Robert was interested — and the property was therefore declared forfeit.[17] Two years later it was granted to George Stewart, Earl Robert's illegitimate son, but by 1593 it was again in the hands of the Halcros and remained their property until it was sold to the Traills a generation later.

Before his confiscation of Brough, Earl Robert had already acquired Sourin by other means. He was Commendator of the Abbey of Holyrood and in 1568 he exchanged this for the bishopric lands in Orkney. It was an astute move by which he not only added the bishopric to his Earldom property, but also removed the influence of his only possible rival in Orkney. It gave Earl Robert and his son, Earl Patrick, a dangerous monopoly of power, and their rule is usually regarded as the most notorious period of oppression and exploitation. After the removal of Earl Patrick, a thorough reorganisation of the bishopric and earldom estates was undertaken in 1614. Sourin was unusual in that it consisted of a large block of bishopric land which elsewhere mostly lay in small scattered lots throughout every parish of Orkney and Shetland, often run-rig with the lands of other proprietors. By excambion the bishopric property was now consolidated in a limited number of parishes and Rousay was not one of them. Thus all the bishopric lands in Rousay were transferred to the earldom. For the people of Sourin it was a fortunate move for, over the next two centuries, the bishopric estate was the most consistently mismanaged of all Orkney properties. The earldom passed first to the Mortons and then to the Dundas family. The Dundases, after some initial enthusiasm for agricultural improvement, were content to manage their estate in the traditional way and were regarded as easy-going landlords. When Traill began to develop his estate at the other end of the island and to evict many of his tenants in the process, a number of them found a haven of refuge in Sourin. The aristocratic and absentee Dundases put no barrier in the way of evicted crofters who squatted on the common and were sometimes allowed to reclaim and occupy crofts rent-free. Others settled on existing crofts as sub-tenants. These policies resulted in small, fragmented holdings, many of them on marginal land and often supporting more than one household. It led to the development of a crofting community in marked contrast to the capitalised high farming on the Traill estate. When Burroughs bought Sourin from the Dundases, there was a natural apprehension that the same vigorous policies would now be pursued in Sourin.

In the early seventeenth century the Traills had established themselves in Westness. They were a Fife family, originally the Traills of Blebo descended from an Archbishop of St Andrews, and they first came to Orkney as followers of Earl Patrick. The date when they acquired Westness is not known but George Traill appeared as a member of assize in 1615 and was described as 'of Westnes'.[18] The dominant figure for much of the eighteenth century was John Traill. As a young man he had, like other Orkney lairds, flirted with Jacobitism, and in later years his 6 ft 6 ins frame was bent with rheumatism which he attributed to the time he spent hiding in the Gentlemen's Cave in Westray. In the aftermath of the rebellion Westness was one of those houses plundered by Benjamin Moodie of Melsetter who harried the Jacobites in the North Isles in a rampage of Hanoverian zeal. Moodie's marines burned down both house and outbuildings[19] and the present Westness House, built in 1792,[20] is its replacement. John Traill lived for fifty years after the rebellion, and when he died in 1795 he had long outlived his Jacobite past.

George William Traill's first purchase was the small estate owned by the Traills of Frotoft. Thomas Traill and his son William were only remotely related either to George William Traill or to the Traills of Westness. Their land consisted of the 6½ pennylands of Banks, Frotoft, a little property which had existed intact at least from the fifteenth century. These Traills were good examples of landowners in the merchant-laird tradition, the older style of Orcadian proprietor which people like Traill and Burroughs were superseding, thanks to their Empire careers and independent income. The fate of these Traills of Frotoft also illustrates the ruin and bankruptcy caused by the collapse of kelp prices.

Originally Thomas Traill was involved with his son-in-law, William Watt of Skaill (in the parish of Sandwick, not Rousay) in business ventures on a more or less equal footing.[21] Their enterprises included shipping joint cargoes of kelp to Newcastle, Dumbarton and other kelp ports aboard Traill's ships, the *Robina Miller* and the *Madora*. Return shipments of glass, slates, grain and general cargoes were disposed of through Watt's extensive retail business. Although the Traills styled themselves *of Frotoft*, their Rousay property was quite small. They usually resided at Wideford near Kirkwall and they also owned land in the west Mainland. As well as their shipping interests, they owned a brewing and distilling business in Kirkwall.

Like most Orkney shipowners in the eighteenth century, Watt and Traill supplemented their legitimate trade with some smuggling. Traill had 20 ankers of Rotterdam gin (about 160 gallons) on Watt's sloop, the *Peggy*, which was captured off Montrose in 1770 when returning to Orkney.[22] Apart from accidents like this, smuggling by the nature of the activity left few explicit records, but a fragmentary and unsigned note, preserved among the correspondence between Watt and Traill, refers to two further cargoes brought to Kirkwall from Rousay.[23] Stories of their narrow escapes passed into folklore.[24] Traill's circumstances were ideal for smuggling and it seems likely that this was a regular and important part of his business. He was a shipowner; he owned an island property where a cargo might be brought ashore without attracting attention; he owned a distillery which was a convenient cover for having large quantities of spirits in his possession and Watt, his partner, could handle distribution through the most extensive retail business in Orkney.

His son, William Traill, ran into serious financial difficulties when kelp failed although Watt, with a more diversified business, continued to prosper. The relationship between the brothers-in-law, once one of equality, became increasingly strained. A bone of contention was an annuity of £50 per annum which Thomas Traill had left to his daughter, William Watt's wife, and which her brother found difficulty in paying. His letters to Watt, a voluminous correspondence, became increasingly vague and subservient. He found endless excuses for failing to reply to Watt's letters about the annuity — his eyesight was too poor to allow him to write, the weather had been too bad to send a messenger, he had been ill, he had been away from home. In exasperation Watt advised him to sell his ships and his brewery and to cut his losses while something might yet be salvaged. But it was already too late. His ships had run him heavily into debt and, in December 1832, his estate was put into the hands of trustees.

From then on Traill's position became progressively worse. He had secured the post of Surveyor of Taxes in Orkney, but this too was lost. By 1839 he was in desperate straits and was reduced to writing a begging letter to his rich but tight-fisted Watt relatives, attempting to borrow £1 to buy a cow. The trustees sold the bulk of the property in 1835 but kept Banks for a further five years when it was sold to George William Traill. In 1850 William Traill's debts were finally paid off at 9d in the £1 but by that time a new kind of laird was firmly established in Rousay.

In 1601 there were almost 40 landowners in Rousay[25] but by 1653 the number had decreased sharply to 18, a decline which reflects the difficulty which udallers had in maintaining the unwritten right to their land against the Stewart earls and their Scots followers. After 1653 the decline continued, but at a slower rate, reducing the number to 13 by 1820.[26] This number decreased still further in the 1830s and 1840s when the collapse of kelp brought about a fall in the value of landed property. Not only was George William Traill able to buy up bankrupt kelp-making properties but the price he could offer was attractive to a number of small owner-occupiers. The final stage came in 1853 when Burroughs bought the Earl of Zetland's Sourin and Wasbister lands to become the proprietor of virtually the whole island. Whereas some earlier landowners had been more deliberately rapacious, they had never had that monopoly of power which was now concentrated in the hands of Frederick William Traill-Burroughs.

4

The Age of Improvement

'Altogether the Orkneys have passed out of the picturesque stage of history, and are at the present time, probably as thriving as any portion of Her Majesty's dominions.' John R. Tudor, *The Orkneys and Shetland*[1]

THE term 'Agricultural Revolution' is a familiar one, a useful phrase to bring together the great number of individual changes which were taking place in farming through most of the eighteenth and part of the nineteenth century and useful, too, as a means of emphasising that the changes were not haphazard individual improvements but were interrelated, the constituent parts of new farming systems. While it was a time of fundamental change, it does seem that 'revolution' is hardly the correct term for developments which were spread over such a long period of time. One expects a revolution to bring fundamental change, but one also expects the change to be rapid.

But 'revolution' is a good description of what happened in Orkney. The old methods of farming survived much longer than in other parts of Britain and were still to be found little modified as the middle of the nineteenth century approached. When change came, it was not a gradual process but an abrupt break with the past. Large-scale improvements began quite suddenly about 1848, by 1870 the main changes were largely completed, and the Age of Improvement came to an end about 1883. It was a revolution which was entirely accomplished within the span of a man's working life and it transformed not only the landscape and farming methods, but also the way of life and the values and expectations of the agricultural population. The trouble in Rousay has to be seen against the background of these changes. The Rousay crofters were the casualties of the Age of Improvement, struggling even when farming prospered and bearing the brunt of the subsequent agricultural depression. The causes of the tension in Rousay therefore lie deeper than the mere personality of General Burroughs. It is no coincidence that relations between the laird and his tenants were superficially good as long as prosperity lasted but were ruptured in 1883 when this prosperity came to an end.

An examination of exports from the islands reveals that there was little growth in the Orkney economy between 1800 and 1848, and indeed in the period 1833-1848 there was a small decline.[2] Although the total value of Orkney's trade remained fairly constant, this figure disguises important changes which were taking place in its composition. At the beginning of the century, the economy was totally dominated by kelp-making to the neglect of everything else, and when the kelp market collapsed in spectacular fashion in the early 1830s it was fishing rather than agriculture which enabled Orcadians to survive hard times. Yet, although of limited importance as a money earner, agriculture was the subsistence basis of the whole community. The small farm provided the family with the greater part of its food and it was the home from which its members went out to earn a money income as kelp-makers, fishermen, whalers, seamen on English fishing smacks and servants of the Hudson's Bay Company. For centuries grain had been an important export, but live cattle, the future basis of Orkney's prosperity, were exported only in very small numbers in 1800. Caithness dealers were the main buyers and the cattle they purchased were ferried across the Pentland Firth in flat-bottomed open boats each capable of holding about a dozen animals. At the end of the summer they were herded south to the market at Bonar Bridge where they entered the droving trade supplying markets in central Scotland or even England.[3] Orkney, however, was too remote and the crossing of the Pentland Firth too difficult for the demands of the droving trade to have much impact. It was only the advent of steamship communications which made the export of cattle a regular business for Orkney farmers.

The thirteen years from 1848 to 1861 saw Orkney's exports expanding at the phenomenal rate of 20% per annum under the stimulus, not only of the new steamers, but also of Government loans for drainage which made capital available for agricultural improvement. They were confident years when a prosperous future seemed assured. Estates were eager and able to invest large sums of money in programmes of draining and dyking, run-rig was abolished and commons divided. On large farms model steadings were built at estate expense and on smaller farms new byres and barns were erected by the tenants. Lairds, farmers, crofters and cottars all set about the task of reclaiming land from the hill, adding about 75% to Orkney's arable acreage.[4] Land capable of reclamation seemed to offer hope for the future even to the poorest cottars.

Although this new prosperity was based on beef, the arable crops remained of surprising importance throughout the Age of Improvement. Grain exports were larger than they had ever been before and potatoes were also an important cash crop. After 1870 there was less concentration on the arable crops as the building of American railroads and the

Government's cheap food policy brought about a fall in grain prices. Orkney, although now more thoroughly committed to beef cattle, remained prosperous for another decade, but in the early 1880s the price of store cattle slumped disastrously. Prices, perhaps down about one third on average, fluctuated considerably from year to year and in bad years cattle were barely saleable. In the 1890s stores from Canada were selling in the Aberdeen market below the price at which they could be produced in Orkney. Prices of wool and dairy produce also fell by nearly as much.

Writing in 1883, perhaps the high point of nineteenth century farming when the Age of Improvement was coming to an end but before the agricultural depression had made itself felt, Tudor vividly described what had been achieved:—

> Now rotation of crops on the five-shift course is the usual thing, the fields are squared off with almost painful regularity, and well dyked in, and the voice of the steam threshing machine is heard in the land . . . Altogether the Orkneys have passed out of the picturesque stage of history, and are at the present time, probably as thriving as any part of Her Majesty's dominions . . . Bankruptcy among the small farmers has, it is said, never been known, and over a million was, in 1880, stated to be lying on deposit in the banks at Kirkwall, Stromness and St. Margaret's Hope, to the credit of the farmers and 'peerie lairds'.[5]

Even when Tudor wrote this description, men still in the prime of life remembered a very different time. They could remember when many of the trim, square fields they now cultivated had been hill land beyond the boundaries of the township, land which was devastated by the widespread removal of the top soil for turf-manuring and by the uncontrolled grazing of cattle, horses, sheep, pigs and geese, a hungry horde banished beyond the flimsy protection of the township's turf ring-dyke during the summer when crops were growing. Traditional controls of grazing rights had largely broken down with the disappearance of Baillie Courts, and hill land was grossly mismanaged. Such land was usually *commonty*, common not only in the sense that it was used in common, but also in the sense that boundaries between neighbouring properties were not established, hence it was owned in common. In practice this joint ownership gave squatters freedom to build houses on the common and to carve out new holdings for themselves. Many of the smaller farms had grown from such humble beginnings.

The commons were of great importance to the poorer people. They provided almost unrestricted grazing for animals, building material for houses, peat for fuel, turf to manure the land and, above all, a supply of reclaimable land from which the enterprising cottar might hope to build up a small farm. The legal division of the commons resulted in large-scale reclamation by lairds and farmers. It brought about rapid expansion and improvement. But for the poorer people, deprived of these traditional resources, the future was suddenly uncertain.

Even as the middle of the nineteenth century approached, the greater part of the arable land consisted of unenclosed run-rig. The *New Statistical Account* presents a uniform picture of parishes where the experiments of a progressive laird or an enterprising minister stood out as oases of progress in a bare and open landscape of steep-crested rigs separated by ill-drained and weed-choked channels. The rigs were an attempt to overcome difficulties resulting from a total lack of artificial drainage. A contemporary writer described how 'instead of taking the water off the land, they have laboured to raise the land above the water, by piling high, broad serpentine ridges between which boats may sail in wet weather'.[6] In Orkney's damp climate the soil lay waterlogged for much of the year and in winter it became a sea of mud. The animals, back from the hill, grazed the township lands in common, ranging at will over the recently harvested arable land which became incredibly poached as a result. The old breed of Orkney pig was particularly destructive. They were kept in vast numbers 'to the regret of all good farmers'[7] and rooted around to such effect that farmers on light land were sometimes able to dispense with ploughing and sow a crop of oats without further cultivation.[8] Their depredations even invaded the kirk yard and, in South Ronaldsay, Governor William Tomison, who had retired to his native parish from the Hudson's Bay Company, preferred to make arrangement for his burial in a private mausoleum in his garden rather than in the kirk yard where, it was believed, pigs had disinterred several corpses.

There was no possibility of growing either turnips or improved pasture on land exposed to such ravages. Traditionally the arable land was alternately cropped with oats and bere (a type of barley) without any period of fallow, a monoculture made possible only by very heavy manuring with ware (seaweed) where this was available and elsewhere by turf-manuring. The harvest was a meagre one. The old *black oats* had a low seed/yield ratio, on average about 1:3, and the yield from the bere crop was only marginally better at about 1:4½.[9] Not all of the harvest was available for consumption. One third of the oat crop had to be held back for next year's seed, and a further third went to pay the rent and the heavy superior duties, leaving the farmer with the remaining third for his own use.[10] One implication of the low seed/yield ratio was the great variability of the surplus available to the farmer. A good year which increased the yield from 1:3 to 1:4 would double his surplus whereas a poor year which brought the yield down to 1:2 would leave him with nothing. Thus he could only survive bad times by falling behind with rents or encroaching on the precious seed which he needed for the following year. As yields actually varied from about 1:2 to 1:5, the lot of the farmer varied from a comfortable surplus in good years to deprivation and famine in years of poor harvests. A single bad harvest caused hardship, but a run of bad harvests such as might be expected twice a century resulted in total disaster and, in earlier times, in considerable loss of life. Such were the periods 1623-36, 1695-1700, 1739-42 and 1782-85.

A further implication of the low yield was the variability of the surplus which could enter trade. In good years there was a large surplus of bere (oats seldom entered trade and exports of meal tended to be balanced by imports) and Orkney conducted a lively trade with Shetland and Norway. After a poor harvest the grain trade dried up entirely. While one may admire the tenacity of the old Orkney farmers who were able to sustain remarkable exports of grain despite their cool northerly climate and low yields, a modern farming economy could never be built on a cash crop which produced, on average, no surplus for sale in one year out of five.

It is easy to be patronising about the old methods of farming. The things which needed to be changed now seem so obvious, and in most parts of Scotland the old ways had disappeared long before the middle of the nineteenth century. Many people in Orkney saw what had to be done and the parish ministers in their descriptions for the *Old Statistical Account* in the 1790s were full of ideas about the abolition of run-rig, the division of commonty, reclamation, enclosing, and introducing new crops like sown grasses and turnips. Yet progress was painfully slow. Turnips were grown as a garden crop in Orkney as early as 1688[11] but were still quite uncommon as a field crop in the early nineteenth century, being first grown in Rousay, for example, in 1821. Improved English ploughs and a turnip-drill plough appear in a Burray inventory of 1747[12] at a time when such implements could seldom be found elsewhere in Scotland, yet in the nineteenth century most Orkney farmers were still using the ancient single-stilted plough. The ambitious South Ronaldsay enclosure, the stone-dyked Park of Cara, also dates from the first half of the eighteenth century, but a hundred years later the work of enclosing had advanced little. Experiments were made with sensible crop rotations as the eighteenth century drew to a close, yet when the *New Statistical Account* was written around 1840, continuous grain cultivation was still the almost universal practice. Good example was never enough and progressive ideas were consistently ignored.

There was more to the slow rate of progress than merely the farmers' innate conservatism. One must see the old and the new as two entirely distinct farming systems, the traditional farming directed to grain production and the new system geared to beef cattle. One of the main

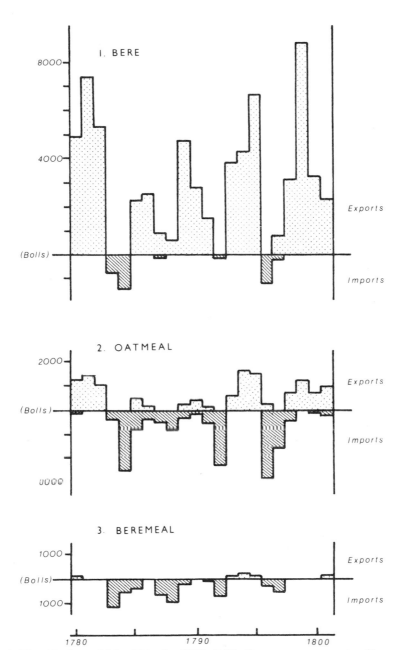

Fig. 4. The Grain and Meal Trade, 1780-1801. Due to an uncertain climate and low yielding varieties, harvest failures were frequent. Successive bad harvests caused subsistence crises. The amount of grain and meal entering trade was consequently highly variable and provided no basis on which to build a cash crop farming economy. (Based on John Shirreff's *General View of the Agriculture of the Orkney Islands*).

reasons for abolishing run-rig and creating a landscape of square fields surrounded by expensive stone dykes was to give protection to crops of turnips and improved pasture, but there was little incentive to make this investment until the export of cattle became a viable proposition. Even progressive farms tended to prefer herding to the expense of dyke-building while they followed the traditional pattern of grain monoculture. Nor was there need to worry about the management of the commons as long as grain rather than cattle or sheep was the priority. In the expert opinion of Shirreff, the author of the *General View of the Agriculture of the Orkney Islands*, the commons contributed so little that if they were to be 'totally annihilated or destroyed' the real value of the islands would not be materially lessened.[13]

Kelp-making was a further cause of the delay in agricultural improvement. During the boom years when some three thousand people were employed in the summer months, there was little labour to spare for agriculture. Kelp-making fitted easily into the old pattern of farming with its summer slack season after the bere crop was sown in May and before hay-making in late August, but the new farming made heavy demands at that time, particularly for the hoeing of turnips. Kelp also encouraged attitudes where scant thought was given to investment. It was an industry where for a small outlay — little more than the purchase of rakes and spades — enormous fortunes could be made in the boom years. Easy profits were looked on as money to be spent rather than reinvested.[14]

During the kelp years there was a good deal of talk about agricultural improvement but little was done. There were a number of obstacles in the way of progress which, although by no means insuperable, had to be cleared away before the work of improvement could begin. One such difficulty was the traditional payment of rents and superior duties in grain rather than money, a tradition which tended to perpetuate the old grain-growing system. Another problem was the existence of large areas of crown lands in many Orkney parishes, originally the bishopric property. Crown lands were specifically excluded from the 1695 Act concerning the Dividing of Commonties. Under the terms of this Act commons had almost entirely disappeared from Scotland during the course of the eighteenth century, but no division could legally take place in any Orkney parish where there was former bishopric property. Since the former bishopric was leased to the Dundas family from 1775 to 1825 and the Dundases owned the even more extensive earldom estate, the legal restrictions on one estate created an attitude where no improvement to either estate was contemplated. It was not until 1828, when the end of the kelp boom was already in sight, that a further Act of Parliament[15] permitted the division of commons in which the crown had an interest.

This Act resulted in the disappearance of all major Orkney commons within the following thirty years.

Although the failure of kelp forced the lairds to turn their attention to the agricultural potential of their estates, the Age of Improvement had not yet come. On the contrary, the kelp collapse resulted in bankruptcies, a fall in the value of landed property and a general lack of confidence in the future. It was not until the 1840s that two new factors restored confidence and brought about change.

The first of these was the coming of the steamships. A regular service was inaugurated in 1833 and, in the years that followed, it began to bring Aberdeenshire cattle dealers with ready cash to pay for their purchases. This new market reinforced a trend which had been apparent for more than a hundred years. In the eighteenth century both grain and cattle prices had been rising in Orkney, but cattle prices rose at a rate about twice as fast as those of cereals. In the nineteenth century grain prices remained fairly static or actually declined as the impact of the Corn Laws and American imports were reflected in market prices, but at the same time the price of cattle rose to levels beyond the dreams of earlier generations of farmers. The relative value of grain and cattle, as summarised in Fig. 5, was a powerful incentive to change.

The other cause of change was the government loans for drainage which were available from 1846 onwards. The effect was not only to provide money at attractive rates of interest — and this was, of course, important — but it was as if the drainage loans had introduced the very idea that capital might be profitably invested in agriculture rather than trade. As Robert Scarth, the great improver and factor on the Rousay estate wrote, 'small lairds ... who formerly kept their savings in a bank at $2\frac{1}{2}\%$ ... would as soon have thought of throwing it in the sea as of laying it out on drainage or lime or any attempt to improve the waste lands'.[16] The few previous attempts at drainage had been primitive, and lack of drainage more than anything else perpetuated the run-rig landscape. The Balfour estate in Shapinsay was the biggest borrower and was a model of what might be achieved through drainage loans. Deep stone drains were driven across the island without regard to the boundaries of existing farms or fields and a grid landscape of ten-acre squares was created. Drainage served not only the existing arable which extended to only 800 acres, but it provided a framework within which a further 1300 acres were reclaimed in the next few years.[17]

The ruthless improvements typified by the Balfour estate could not be achieved without cost to the crofter-cottar class. It is a mistake to think of the normal farming community before the Agricultural Revolution in Orkney as a society of equals practising a primitive communism in a run-

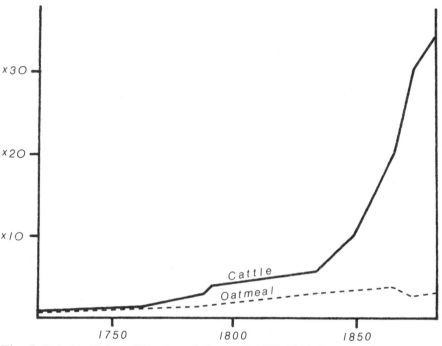

Fig. 5. Relative Value of Cattle and Oatmeal, 1720-1883. Improved cattle prices,
   particularly after the advent of steamships, provided a powerful stimulus to
   change from an old-fashioned grain-growing farming economy to an up-to-
   date beef-rearing system.

rig township. Most districts were dominated by one big farm or several
farms. The great majority of the agricultural population were of a status
somewhere between the extremes of independent farmer and landless
labourer. An enormous amount of labour was employed, particularly
before carts became common. In the late eighteenth century, for example,
Patrick Fea of Stove in Sanday employed twenty men carrying seaweed to
manure the land. On another occasion thirty-four men with horses were
engaged in carrying grain to Stove while on the same day a further five men
were working in the barn.[18] On big farms as many as seventy people might
be employed during the harvest.[19]

In a society where money was scarce it was easier to pay labour in kind
and with land rather than with cash. Land was plentiful and the holdings of
the sub-tenant cottars were not distinct units but consisted of rigs scattered
over the entire area of the big farm and intermingled with the rigs
cultivated by the farmer. Such a farm was described as being in 'a state of
cottarage'.[20] On the biggest farms the cottar was occasionally a full-time
agricultural labourer, a *bu-man* (Old Norse *bú*, a farm), but a much more
common arrangement was for the cottar to be obliged to provide his
services when required. This was aptly known as *on ca' work*. The number

of days' services were seldom defined and besides the normal agricultural routine of winter barn work, ploughing and sowing in the spring and harvesting in the autumn, the cottar's duties might include kelp-making, undertaking errands and transporting goods by land and sea — the obligation of *flitting and furing*.

In the nineteenth century there was a growing hostility to any kind of system which bound one man to another by 'feudal' obligations. Liberalism saw in a money relationship a means of bringing freedom to the servant and profit to the master. A comment by the Rousay factor, Robert Scarth, typifies this attitude:—

> The cottar system . . . is perhaps the most degrading to the labouring class, the most discouraging to industry and exertion, and consequently the most injurious to morals, which can be conceived. A youngster, when he has hardly attained manhood, and before he can have saved as much as will purchase a bed and blankets, makes an improvident marriage, and only then thinks of looking for a hut to shelter him and his fast increasing family. Having got the hut and a small piece of land, he has to go in debt for the purchase of a wretched cow and a still more wretched pony, and, paying his rent in small but never ending and ill-defined personal services, or, as it is expressively called in the country 'on-ca-work', he becomes the slave of the principal tenant, who is so blind to his own interests, as to prefer the slovenly, half-executed work of this hopeless, ill-fed and inert being to the willing and active services of a well-paid and well-fed farm servant.[21]

Changes were pioneered by the brothers Malcolm and Samuel Laing on their farm of Stove on Sanday, changes which were widely imitated throughout the county and created a class of *crofters* as opposed to the old *cottars*. Crofters' holdings were adjacent to the main farm but entirely distinct from it. They held their land directly from the proprietor, not as sub-tenants of the farmer, and they paid a money rent. All obligations of service were abolished but crofts were deliberately of a small size and designed to provide a pool of labour which the farmer could employ for a money wage.

Thus the Rousay crofters in their struggle with General Burroughs were not members of an ancient class fighting for survival in an age of change. Their crofts were the products of the new system. They were also the fortunate members of the former cottar class, for not all cottars became crofters. Others had become perforce full-time agricultural labourers, and the least fortunate, deprived of their land, were dependent on whatever work they could find. The successive decline of linen, kelp-making, whaling, straw plaiting and fishing meant that they were increasingly dependent on casual farm work and likely to be under-employed except during the harvest.

D

Hard though the crofter's life might be, he had made considerable progress and he knew it. To describe his condition in his younger days as 'medieval' or approaching a 'state of serfdom' is no flight of literary exaggeration but sober fact, as can be seen from the comparison in Table 2 between Bodo, a *villein* of the Abbey of St. Germain-des-Prés near Paris about the year 820 and James Linklater, a small tenant farmer in the Parish of Sandwick, Orkney, in 1834, over a thousand years later. The payments in kind and the obligations of service show a quite remarkable similarity. The difference between them was one of legal status only, for whereas Bodo was 'unfree' and was tied to the estate, James Linklater could abandon irksome on-ca' work for the freedom of the frozen seas of Greenland or the snow-covered wastes of Northern Canada.

	The Villein Bodo [22] A villein of the Abbey of St. Germain-des-Pres, c.820	*James Linklater* [23] Tenant farmer in the Parish of Sandwick, Orkney, 1834
Farm Size	30 acres, not all arable	30 acres, not all arable
Money Payments	2 silver solidii for commutation of military service	£2 rent
Payments in Kind	28 gallons of wine 100 planks every third year	14 lbs of butter 2 bolls of bere
Poultry Payments	3 hens 15 eggs	3 hens 36 eggs 2 geese
Payments in Services	Maintain 10 metres of fencing	Maintain section of hill dyke
	Winter and spring ploughing and 2 days' corvée per week	On-ca' work — ploughing, barn work, harvesting
	Carrying services as required	Carrying services as required
Handicrafts	1 day per week	Required to spin 6 hanks of linen
Mill	Payment of 2 silver solidii for use of the mill	Multure
Legal Status	Unfree; tied to estate	"Free"

Table 2. *Orkney Crofter and Medieval Villein: a Comparison.* To a greater extent than crofters in other areas, those in Orkney were burdened by obligations of labour service (on ca' work). These two examples, divided by a thousand years, show a remarkable degree of similarity between the nineteenth century Orkney crofter and the ninth century villein.

The crofters who turned out to welcome General Burroughs on his return to Rousay had known this way of life in their younger days. The agricultural boom years had converted the more fortunate of them into small farmers contemplating their bank accounts with some degree of satisfaction. But they felt that they had prospered despite the laird rather than with his assistance. They saw him as a threat to the progress they had made and standing in the way of further advancement.

5

The Quandale and Westness Clearances[1]

'The Earth is the Lord's and the fullness thereof.'   Rev George Ritchie's rebuke to George William Traill

QUANDALE was the one community in Rousay which was a crofting township of the type commonly found in the Highlands. Here alone small tenants lived on terms of approximate equality and were not overshadowed by the presence of big farms. High ground to the north concealed the Wasbister farms while the shoulder of Scabra Head separated them from Westness to the south. Quandale lies in the extreme west of Rousay, a broad and bare semi-circular depression facing the open sea. In westerly gales the full force of the Atlantic breaks along a line of low cliffs and sheets of salt spray are carried hundreds of yards inland. The crofters complained that their corn suffered badly from 'sea gust'.[2]

While many Orkney crofts were engulfed by neighbouring farms, 'clearance' is seldom the appropriate description of what happened. The usual process was for farms to be enlarged by spasmodic evictions and amalgamations over a period of time, a steady and unspectacular erosion rather than a traumatic change. But the Quandale episode was different. It was a clearance of the kind often found in the Highlands — a whole community removed to make way for sheep — for, like the Highlands, Rousay had extensive hill grazings which made it more vulnerable than other more arable islands. The Quandale clearance left a searing impression on the community but, although it was Burroughs who is remembered as the 'wicked laird', the evictions were the work of his predecessor, George William Traill, the efficient and enlightened 'King of Kumaon'.

On his return from India, Traill used his considerable fortune to buy up property in Rousay as it came on the market. In 1840 his estate was confined to Frotoft and the island of Wyre, but in 1841 he made three further purchases which gave him possession of the whole of Quandale and parts of Wasbister. Quandale had been a detached portion of an estate owned by yet another Traill, Thomas Traill of Westove, the main part of whose property lay twenty miles away in the island of Sanday. His estate in Sanday was perhaps more thoroughly geared to kelp-making than any other in Orkney and so, when kelp prices slumped, Westove found itself in serious trouble. With a large population and few other opportunities, the estate continued to make kelp in the hope that, although profits might be marginal, the tenants could at least earn sufficient to pay their rents. Other landlords, cutting back on their own production, saw that it would be 'very difficult to keep poor Tom Traill above water', and so it proved.[3] The bankrupt estate passed under the control of a trust which decided to sell out, but with a crisis of confidence in the economy it was not easy to find a buyer for a kelp estate.

Unlike the Sanday part of the estate, Quandale's shores were too exposed for kelp-making, but since it was part of a larger property organised for kelp, Quandale was subjected to the same kind of management — policies favourable to an increasing crofter-cottar population and with little thought for agricultural improvement. The trust had hoped to interest John Balfour with his Indian fortune but his nephew dissuaded him, reporting that:—

> The lands of Quandale, in Rousay, which pay about £70 of the (total Westove rental of) £650, have no kelp worth naming; and no advantage to compensate for their great exposure, but the extensive range of Common Hill pasture belonging to the island. The tenants of this part of the estate are proverbially poor.[4]

Indian money was indeed to buy Quandale but the purchaser was George William Traill, not John Balfour. The new owner did not clear the land immediately but a further purchase which Traill made in 1845 opened up new possibilities. It was the purchase of Westness which changed the fate of Quandale.

The acquisition of the land of Westness gave Traill possession of the three elements which were brought together to create the 2,800-acre Westness Farm. The first of these elements was Inner Westness where a large farm had existed at least since the Reformation. The second was the district of Outer Westness where there had been large farms in the days of Sigurd of Westness and later when the Craigies of Brough had dominated Rousay, but by 1845 Outer Westness comprised eight small farms and a number of cottar holdings. Although the farms were small, three of them were held on nineteen-year leases which prevented their immediate incorporation. The third element, Quandale, consisted of a large number of very small crofts, all of them held on a year-to-year basis with no leases to protect them.

The House of Tafts stood at the centre of Quandale. Although small, it was a building of distinction and originally a place of some importance.[5]

The name *Tafts*, or a variation of it, is a common house name deriving from the Old Norse *thopt* (house site). Such names are usually to be found at the centre of a township, marking the original nucleus of the community, and this was the position which Tafts occupied in Quandale, with the other crofts arranged in a semi-circle of satellites. Its pre-eminence is confirmed by a 1668 sasine by which William Douglas of Egilsay disposed of Tafts to his son 'with the priviledge of the *uppa* thereof as the samen has been in use in all times bygane past memorie of man'.[6] The *uppa*, the first rig in each field or block of rigs distributed among run-rig sharers, was a privilege reserved for the most important house in the community.

Tafts was one of the earliest two-storied houses in Orkney. It consisted of two downstairs rooms, each 12 ft. 6 ins. by 12 feet and separated by a passageway running straight through the house connecting a front and back door. Stone window seats of good construction were a feature of the design and one downstairs room had a fireplace. The upper storey was reached by a stairway from within one of the downstairs rooms and consisted of two further apartments with low sloping ceilings. Arguing that the two doors, the narrow passage, the deep-set windows and the stair leading from the downstairs room rather than the passage are all features designed for defence, Storer Clouston consequently dated the building from before 1471 when persistent raids by Lewismen ceased. Such a dating seems highly conjectural, but there is no doubt that Tafts was old and had once been a place of importance. Unlike the traditional Orkney farm, Tafts had quite separate outbuildings. These consisted of a barn with its threshing floor between two doors, a corn kiln attached to the barn, and a separate byre.

Despite its original importance, by quite an early date Tafts had very little land. In 1601 it consisted of only a half pennyland of udal land and, although it was occupied by a single tenant, John a Toftis, it did not belong to a single owner but was shared by Craigies and Yorstons. It would appear that Tafts was a victim of the sub-division which udal inheritance often caused. Deprived of much of its land, Tafts became the dower house and in 1705 it was occupied by Jean Traill, the widow of Magnus Craigie of Skaill.

Had Tafts retained its importance, it might have become a large farm gradually absorbing its smaller neighbours in the traditional Orkney way, but the very nucleus of the community had decayed. By 1841 Tafts was tenanted by Magnus Murray and, with 13 acres of arable land, he was of the same economic status as the other crofters although his holding still remained marginally the biggest and he paid rather more rent than anybody else.

When Traill bought Quandale it was already a declining community. Fifty years later, when the Deer Forest Commission took evidence in

Orkney, it was something of a mystery how a sizeable community could ever have existed in such a bleak and windswept place. Burroughs' lawyer suggested that they had depended on kelp-making and said that he had himself seen the old kelp kilns. But he had to admit that the exposed coastline did not look particularly suitable.[7] From the size of the crofts, it is clear that agriculture could not have been the only or even the main means of support. As the lawyer suggested, crofters' income from the land was supplemented by kelp-making, but probably at other places rather than at Quandale itself. Fishing and casual labour on the land were other sources of employment. After the collapse of 1831 very little kelp was made in Rousay and fishing too was an industry in decline. Hence Quandale's troubles stemmed not only from the laird's plans for improvement, but also from a lack of employment in the subsidiary occupations on which the crofters had depended for a living.

Earlier in the nineteenth century there would appear to have been about 28 households in Quandale. By 1841, when Traill acquired the property, this number had already been reduced to 22 through a series of amalgamations (see Table 3). This process was continued by the new laird and a further six crofts disappeared before Quandale was cleared. These amalgamations must have given hope that viable farms were being created from over-small crofts since the average holding had been increased from $3\frac{1}{2}$ acres of arable with 13 acres of run-rig grassland to $6\frac{1}{2}$ acres of arable with 24 acres of grassland. By Orkney standards these units were no longer unusually small and they were veritable farms in comparison to the fragmented holdings to be found in other crofting counties.

Writing less than a dozen years after the clearance, Alexander Marwick remembered how 'in summer the hills swarmed with horses, cattle, sheep, pigs and geese'. The 40 families between the Dyke of Grind (the southern boundary of Westness) and the Lobust (the northern limit of Quandale) owned 70 horses, 220 cattle and between 600 and 700 sheep. 'There was more beef and mutton used in Rousay in one year,' he wrote, 'than is now used in ten years.'[8] Perhaps time had already lent a degree of enchantment to Marwick's memories. Westness and Quandale were districts which knew poverty although he was right to emphasise that they were by no means reduced to absolute destitution. In human terms the communities were very vital ones. The 1841 census reveals that the area to be affected by the clearances supported a population of 215 persons — a greater population than the whole island contains at the present day. It was a youthful community with 38% under the age of 15 and a mere 4% over the age of 65. There were young children in nearly every house.

Traill's other actions also seemed to promise a future for Quandale. In 1842 the estate undertook repairs to the ancient farm steading at Tafts. A

		Arable (acres)	Pasture (acres)	Inhabitants 1841
Nether Quandale	Amalgamated with Mid-Quandale before 1841	*	*	0
Upper Croolea	Amalgamated with Claypows before 1841	*	*	0
Lower Croolea	Amalgamated with Claypows before 1841	*	*	0
Hasley	Amalgamated with Breck before 1841	*	*	0
Cairn	Amalgamated, probably with Breck, before 1841	1	*	0
Smook	Amalgamated before 1841	*	*	0
Cut Claws	Farmed by tenant of Windbreck in 1841; amalgamated with Knapknowes in 1843	8	20	0
Hestival	Amalgamated with North House in 1842	4	0	2
Braehead	Amalgamated with Breck in 1843	1	1	2
Nether Mouncey	Amalgamated with Upper Mouncey in 1842	*	*	5
Upper Mouncey I	Amalgamated with Mouncey in 1843	0	1	5
Upper Mouncey II	Sub-tenant of Upper Mouncey I	0	0	2
Stirling	Amalgamated with Deall before 1841; thereafter house occupied as sub-tenancy until cleared in 1846	0	0	3
Upper Quandale	Cleared in 1845	12	38	5
Mid Quandale I	Cleared in 1845	13	67	5
Mid Quandale II	Sub-tenant of Mid Quandale I; cleared in 1845	0	0	8
Claypows	Cleared in 1845	3	26	3
Breck	Cleared in 1845	11	25	5
Tafts	Cleared in 1845	13	94	7
Deall	Cleared in 1845	4	10	4
Knapknowes	Farmed with Tafts in 1841; thereafter a separate farm until cleared in 1845	8	30	0
North House	Cleared in 1845	½	0	5
Breck	Cleared in 1845	11	25	3
Mouncey	Cleared in 1855	3	9	2
Flintersquoy I	Cleared in 1855	4	7	7
Flintersquoy II	Sub-tenant of Flintersquoy I; cleared in 1855	0	0	1
Stouramira	Cleared in 1855	½	7	3
Old Parochial School	After 1846 the school became the shepherd's house, the only occupied house in the district	0	0	1
		97	360	78

Table 3. The Quandale Crofts

* Where no figure for arable and pasture has been given the land has been included in the holding with which the croft was amalgamated.

new corn kiln was built and the barn was extensively repaired. As late as 1843 other repairs were being carried out by the estate at Flintersquoy and Knapknowes. Nor was Traill unusually severe in his rents. When he bought Quandale, it was rented at a total of £74 per year. Following the amalgamations and improvements, he undertook a general revision which brought the rental to £77, a very modest increase. Nevertheless rents were high for such exposed land and the Quandale community were generally 10% to 30% in arrears, a greater degree of indebtedness than in any other part of Rousay. A few tenants, like William McInlay who farmed Upper Quandale, were inveterate debtors. His farm was substantial enough to have been the first in Rousay to possess a cart, yet he was always behind with the rent.[9] Some tenants were offered crofts elsewhere in Rousay after the evictions but the only place McInlay could find was temporary accommodation in the wash-house at Westness until he was able to leave the island. Yet not all tenants were in arrears. Magnus Murray of Tafts paid regularly until the last year of his life when a debt accumulated which his widow had some difficulty in clearing. Indeed some of the smallest crofters were never in arrears but continued to find sufficient subsidiary employment to meet the rent.

The purchase of Westness in 1845 altered Traill's plans for Quandale's future. It opened up the possibility of creating an improved farm incorporating the crofters' land rather than trying to make something of the existing holdings. The suddenness of this change of plan, and the evictions coming just when crofters hoped for better times, contributed to the bitterness of the clearance. Traill in his brief summer visits to Orkney entered into the improvements with enthusiasm but the architect of the Quandale clearance was Robert Scarth. The factor's acute business mind had grasped the possibilities which low-interest government loans for drainage presented. He acted as factor for other estates besides Rousay and had already been involved in agricultural reorganisation of the most drastic kind. The kelp collapse of 1831 had left North Ronaldsay in a desperate position, over-populated, deprived of its livelihood and practising a debased form of run-rig agriculture. The following year Scarth abolished run-rig over most of the island and squared the land into small farms, a reorganisation accompanied by rent increases which the population had difficulty in paying in their reduced circumstances. Four years later Scarth had to assist with the emigration of thirty-two families from the island.[10] He was now to preside over equally thorough-going changes in Rousay.

The Quandale crofters were given notice to quit after the harvest of 1845. Some were found crofts elsewhere in Rousay, some became landless labourers, while others left the island. They were reluctant to go. In 1846 several obtained leave to cultivate potato ground in Quandale or to graze a cow, but at prices calculated to discourage such uses. As late as 1848 summonses for removal were served on 'squatters', former tenants who still had nowhere to go.

It had been Traill's original intention to let the new farm of Westness and Quandale and it was advertised in the *John o'Groat Journal* in February 1846.[11] Although he received offers from within the county, Traill failed to find a tenant. He had hoped to attract a farmer from a more advanced district who was not only able to pay the high rent but was possessed of sufficient capital to stock the farm properly and undertake the work of improvement. The farm remained in the proprietor's own hands for the next twenty-nine years. Traill therefore set about the business of improving the Quandale pastures in 1847. The land was thoroughly drained by means of almost 45 miles of open ditches and was enclosed by six miles of dry stone dykes. Some of the former crofters found employment in these improvements, which included the demolition of their former homes. Purchases of rib grass, cocksfoot and fescue indicate that the former arable was reseeded as pasture, and applications of guano and bone dust indicate farming practices well in advance of what was commonly found in Orkney at that time.

Although the heartland of Quandale was cleared, three small crofts were allowed to remain for a further ten years. These were Stouramira, Mouncey and Flintersquoy, all high up on the margin of the township reclaimed from common land beyond the original hill dyke. The very names of the crofts — Flintersquoy (the enclosure of the sharp stones), Stouramira (the great mire) — indicate the poor quality of the land. Deprived of hill grazing, meadowland and the grassland interspersed with former run-rig, these places had little future. Until the 1845 clearance, William Corsie of Mouncey had always managed to pay the rent but now he slipped ever deeper into arrears. In 1851 the factor's accounts noted that he 'has nothing' and arrears of £5:10s:6d were written off. New arrears accumulated and had to be written off a second time in 1855, 'he having been removed and no effects'. Life was hard too for George Leonard of Stouramira. Many years later he was brought forward to tell the story of the Quandale clearances to Lord Napier and his Royal Commission.[12] As a young man he had settled in Stouramira in 1842, rebuilt the house and set about reclaiming land. Although the croft was very small, originally with only one acre arable, he had been able to keep a cow and had grazed a number of sheep on the common grazing. Even after the 1845 evictions he still managed to pay his rent, supplementing his income with fishing, shoemaking and any other work he could find. Despite paying his rent, he too was removed in 1855 and had to make his way through the hills with his few belongings and an infant in arms to a bare and uncultivated hillside in

Sourin where he had permission to settle.[13] The land occupied by these crofts was not immediately improved, but in 1872 expensive works were undertaken at Flintersquoy involving trenching, dyke-building and removing the very stones which had given the croft its name.

Westness was a different kind of community. Whereas Quandale was an egalitarian society where the crofters were all of comparable economic status and all were tenants-at-will, Westness was a stratified community with holdings of five different kinds:

1. In a class by itself there was the dominating presence of the big Westness farm.
2. There were three small farms in Outer Westness, Brough, Skaill and Upper Eastaquoy which, although little different from crofts in either size or rent, had the additional status and security of nineteen-year leases.
3. Also in Outer Westness five crofts were held on a year-to-year basis.
4. There were eight cottar holdings which, since their occupiers cultivated land and owned stock, were not very different from crofts apart from the fact that they were sub-tenancies either of Westness itself or of other farms or crofts.
5. In Inner Westness there was a cluster of eleven houses, mainly of nineteenth century construction, occupied by farm servants and landless labourers.

The number had once been greater. Even before Traill purchased Westness there had been the same contraction in the number of holdings as has been described in Quandale, and this at a time when the population of Rousay was increasing steadily. It was a process continued by the new laird who began by abolishing some of the smaller cottar holdings. Then, two years after the Quandale evictions, the remaining crofters and cottars were served notice to quit. This time, warned by the delay in the final removing of some Quandale tenants, the factor obtained a signature or mark to a 'submissive letter' by which the tenants obliged themselves to flit and remove at Martinmas 1848, acknowledging their liability to pay damages if they remained in their homes after that date.[14] Only one croft, the little holding of Magnus Mass Hill, was allowed to exist for a further nine years. The laird may have felt a special responsibility for the tenant, James Kent, a navy pensioner and veteran of the Napoleonic Wars. In any case his croft was beyond the hill dyke where it interfered little with the operation of the new farm.

It was no doubt their leases which prevented Brough, Skaill and Upper Eastaquoy being immediately added to Westness. The leases of Skaill and

Upper Eastaquoy expired in 1855 and were not renewed. Last to go was Brough which was incorporated in 1859. Curiously, its last tenant was a Magnus Craigie who bore the same name as the Magnus Craigie who had sold Brough to the Halcros complete with its 'fortalice, head house, mill and right of patronage to the Chapel of St Christopher'. The nineteenth century Magnus Craigie had no such property to dispose of. He found irregular employment as a ploughman on Westness and was moved into the cottar house of Quoycare.

For cottars the changes were more subtle. On the traditional big Orkney farm, cottar houses were scattered throughout its area. Cottars cultivated rigs intermingled with those of the farmer and they also owned stock. They were sub-tenants, holding their land from the farmer rather than directly from the laird, and bound to the farmer by the ill-defined ties of *on ca'* work. When the cottar's methods of cultivation and the quality of his stock were little different from those of the farmer, cottarage was an acceptable system, but there was no place for it on an improved farm. The farmer had no desire to see half-starved and possibly diseased cattle mingle with his well-bred herd or to have slovenly rigs disfigure his carefully cultivated square fields. After Traill bought Westness, traces of the old system lingered for a decade. The evicted widow Murray of Tafts was given leave to graze a cow in Quandale, and a number of cottars were able to rent potato ground, in each case for a charge of £1:10s. In 1855 this high rate and the advent of a new and more efficient farm manager finally brought an end to cottars farming on their own account.

The effect of these changes was to abolish every kind of independent holding, leased farms, crofts and cottar pendicles. The crofters in their prepared statement to the 1883 Napier Commission claimed that 'almost exactly forty families' were ejected from Quandale and Westness.[15] Their estimate was no exaggeration. Tables 3 and 4 list 62 households of which 13 still remained in 1883, leaving 49 as the number which had disappeared. The crofters were telescoping events by suggesting that this number was removed in a single clearance, since some of these holdings were gone before 1840 and the process was completed only in 1859. The 62 had been reduced to 51 by the time Traill bought the property and, through further amalgamations, to 42 at the time when the evictions began. The clearances comprised two main phases. In the first, 1845-8, most of the tenants-at-will and cottars were removed from Quandale and Westness, a total of 20 in all. In the second phase, 1855-9, the leased farms and the crofts on the hill margins were taken over, 9 in all, and at this time cottars finally lost residual rights to keep animals and cultivate land.

Eviction did not necessarily mean leaving the district, since the clearances were accompanied by the erection of new houses in the

		No. of Inhabitants 1841	Still inhabited 1879
Hammer	Disappeared at an early date	0	No
Oldman	Disappeared in early 19th century	0	No
Cringlaquoy	Disappeared at an early date	0	No
Eastaquoy	Disappeared shortly before 1841	0	No
Scabra	Disappeared shortly before 1841	0	No
Giorhouse	Sub-tenant; disappeared shortly after 1841	3	No
Garson I	Sub-tenant; disappeared shortly after 1841	5	No
Garson II	Sub-tenant of Garson I; disappeared shortly after 1841	2	No
Quham I	Croft on year-to-year basis; cleared 1848	5	No
Quham II	Sub-tenant of Quham I; cleared 1848	2	No
Quoycare	Croft on year-to-year basis; cleared 1848	6	Yes
Clyver	Croft on year-to-year basis; cleared 1848	6	No
Windbreck	Croft on year-to-year basis; cleared 1848	8	No
Pow	Cottar sub-tenant; deprived of land c.1848	8	No
Quoygreenie	Cottar sub-tenant; deprived of land c.1848	3	Yes
Cott	Cottar sub-tenant; deprived of land c.1848	4	Yes
Skaill I	Leased farm; cleared in 1855 on termination of lease	7	Vacant but habitable
Skaill II	Sub-tenant of Skaill I; cleared 1855	10	No
Upper Eastaquoy	Leased farm; cleared in 1855 on termination of lease	6	No
Brough	Leased farm; cleared in 1859 on termination of lease	5	Yes
Magnus Mass Hill	Croft on year-to-year basis; cleared 1855	3	No
Haagate	Cottar sub-tenant; deprived of land c.1848	4	No
Blow High	Built mid-19th century; cottar house with no land	0	Used as isolation 'hospital'
Mounthooly	Cottar house with no land	2	No
Helziecliff	Gardener's house built by G. W. Traill	0	Vacant but habitable
Bridge End	Grieve's house built by F. W. T. Burroughs	0	Yes
Gue I	Farm Servant's cottage	4	Yes
Gue II	Farm Servant's cottage	5	Yes
Gue III	Farm Servant's cottage	2*	Vacant but habitable
Scar I	Farm Servant's cottage	7*	Yes
Scar II	Farm Servant's cottage	2*	Yes
Hynd's House	Farm Servant's cottage	8*	Yes
Hynd's House	Farm Servant's cottage	0	Yes
Westness House		18	Let to shooting tenants
		135	

Table 4. Westness Farms, Crofts, Cottar Holdings and Houses

* For the Westness farm servants' cottages marked thus the 1841 census gives insufficient information to make it certain that the correct family has been attributed to each cottage.

Westness area. The regular farm servants were accommodated in a group of houses on the steeply sloping south side of the Westness Burn while on the opposite side stood Bridge End, the farm manager's house, and Helziecliff, the gardener's cottage. High on the slopes above stood two small cottages, Mounthooly and the aptly named Blow High, both occupied by less regular farm workers. Some of those accommodated in these Westness houses were families evicted from their former homes. For them the clearance had meant only a resettlement and a reduction in their status from tenants farming their own land to agricultural labourers. It was a change which was not always resented. While some of the former tenants had the bitterest of memories of the clearances, memories which now have been handed down to the third and fourth generation, there were others who were not unhappy to escape from the precarious livelihood and under-employment of a small croft to the security of a regular job on the Westness Farm. They were the lucky ones; for many more people the only source of income in the future was casual agricultural work. They contined to be under-employed as before but they had lost their base on the land.

These were the people who, in later years, would remember how their minister, the formidable Rev George Ritchie, who had led nearly all of his congregation out of the Church of Scotland at the time of the Disruption, had descended on George William Traill like an Old Testament prophet. When Traill had protested that the land was his and he had a right to do with it as he pleased, Ritchie had answered him with the text, 'The Earth is the Lord's and the fullness thereof'. Traill was undeterred by the minister's warning, and to the superstitious the text seemed like a curse for, in little over a year he was dead, struck down by a heart attack in the lavatory of his London club.

The farm he had created extended to about 2,800 acres of which about 220 acres were arable and a further 1,000 acres consisted of low ground pasture. While it was in the proprietor's own hands, it generally provided full-time employment for nine to eleven people and casual work for a great many more. The most important of the full-time employees was the farm manager or 'overseer' as he was commonly called. His duties were more extensive than merely the management of the farm. Since the factor lived in Kirkwall, the overseer was the estate's resident agent, undertaking such duties as supervising the construction of the island roads and inspecting improvement on tenant farms on which a rent reduction was claimed. The first overseer was George Lyall who was engaged when Traill purchased Westness. He was paid a salary of £25 per half-year, later reduced to £20, and occupied Viera Lodge rent-free with additional benefits such as free coal. The trustees who administered the estate in Burroughs' minority

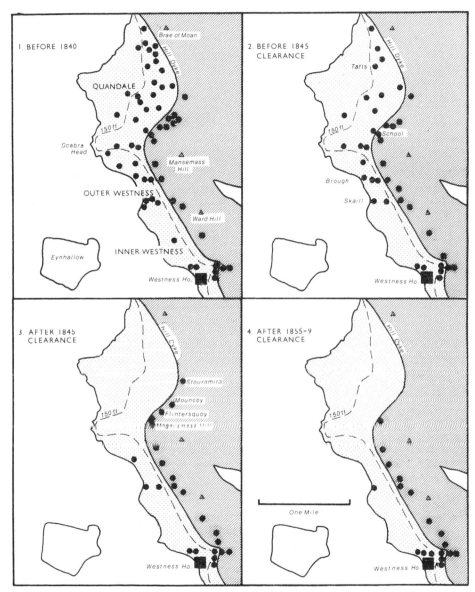

Fig. 6. The Westness and Quandale Clearances. The maps show the contraction of the Quandale and Westness communities even before the 1845 clearance. Thereafter a number of farms remained until their leases expired (1855-9), at which time a number of crofts high on the hill margin were also cleared. In the final phase the remaining houses were occupied by farm servants and landless cottars.

were not entirely satisfied with his management and, on their advice, he was replaced soon after Burroughs took control of his own affairs.

Some care was taken with the selection of a successor. On the recommendation of Donald Horne who had acted as judicial factor to the trust, Robert Scarth journeyed south to Dollar where he engaged George Learmonth as the new overseer. Horne had previous dealings with the Learmonth family since he and a brother of George Learmonth were members of a syndicate which leased and improved the farm of Houseby in Stronsay, a farm comparable to Westness in size but with even more arable ground.[16] George Learmonth was to remain as overseer in Westness for the next twenty years and he then took the farm on a nineteen-year lease when it was let in 1875. Meanwhile his brother was the active member of the Houseby syndicate and he took the tenancy of that farm when the lease expired and the syndicate was dissolved. Thus both brothers rose from being farm managers to become tenants of two of the biggest farms in Orkney.

Next in the hierarchy of farm servants came the grieve and the shepherd, and both, like the overseer, were invariably incomers in the early years. The shepherd lived in the old Parochial School on the edge of Quandale, the only inhabited house left in the whole district and where he was well situated for the new sheep run. He was assisted by an under-shepherd, always a local person, and sometimes had extra help from a boy who acted as herd. The grieve was in charge of arable operations and had charge of the ploughmen of whom there were usually four. Several of the ploughmen had been tenants of their own places including James Gibson, ex-crofter of Flintersquoy, and Magnus Craigie who at one time had a nineteen-year lease on the now vanished farm of Brough. The sons of the overseers, first Lyall and then Learmonth, were also employed as ploughmen, and one of Learmonth's sons eventually rose to become grieve. Other ploughmen drifted in and out of employment, in some terms being engaged on a regular basis and in others forming part of the pool of casual labour. There was, however, much less mobility than, for example, among the farm workers of north-east Scotland — the result of few alternative places of employment. Some, like Robert Logie, spent a lifetime on the farm, rising from herd to under-shepherd to ploughman and eventually becoming the first native-born shepherd. A cattleman and cattlewoman completed the full-time complement. Cattlewomen or dairy maids seldom stayed long, a year or two at the most but more often only a single term. The cattleman, on the other hand, was one of the longest-serving farm workers but was paid less than half the wages of a ploughman and, as he grew older, his wages gradually diminished.

		Nov-May	May-Nov	Meal (bolls)
George Lyall	Overseer	£20	£20	—
James Burns	Grieve	£5:5s	£7:5s	8
George MacLeod	Ploughman	£4:10s	£6	6
James Logie	Ploughman	£4	—	3 (half year)
George Lyall jnr.	Ploughman	—	£4:10s	3 (half year)
William Couper	Ploughman	£3:10s	—	3½ (half year)
Samuel Harrold	Ploughman	—	£4:10s	3 (half year)
Donald Sutherland	Shepherd	£6	£6	8
Robert Logie	Under-shepherd	£4	£4:10s	7
James Mainland	Herd	£1:10s	£2:5s	6
Alex Johnstone	Cattleman	£2:5s	£2:5s	6
Cecilia Craigie	Cattlewoman	£2	£2	4½
Jean Reid	?	No money payment		4½

Table 5. Westness Farm Servants, November 1853 to November 1854

All farm servants, with the exception of the overseer, were paid partly in money and partly in meal and, despite the fact that oatmeal was more valuable than beremeal, they were allowed to take their payment in either. Table 5 shows the meal and money payments which the farm servants received in 1854. Wages throughout the 1850s were tending to rise but thereafter remained steady. On the whole, the farm servants failed to benefit much from the increased profitability of the farm.

In addition to the regular farm workers, Westness depended on a host of casual workers. This was the traditional Orkney practice, although the distinction between regular workers and casual employees was now more clear-cut than the old division between *bu-men* and those *on ca'*. Casual labour could now be divided into three groups: first, cottar sub-tenants who were now entirely landless and for whom casual work was the main source of income; second, crofters with their own land, often at a considerable distance from Westness, relying to a greater or lesser extent on outside employment to supplement a low income from their crofts; and, third, the wives and families of the regular farm servants.

An interesting feature is that those crofters who, in the early 1850s, were living on crofts soon to be incorporated in Westness Farm, were hardly ever employed as casual workers. There were seven of these crofts, Stouramira, Mouncey, Flintersquoy, Magnus Mass Hill, Brough, Skaill and Eastaquoy. Two of them were tenanted by men who eventually became ploughmen on Westness and another, George Leonard of Stouramira, was willing, according to the evidence which he later gave to the Napier Commission, to take 'any work that offered', yet, in 1853 for example, these seven tenants between them contributed only a total of one half day's casual work. The whole point of the crofting system as it had developed in the early nineteenth century was that small crofts adjacent to big farms would provide a source of ready labour. Their failure to do so,

E

whether as a result of estate policy or the tenants' choice, may have been the cause of the decision to abolish them in the late 1850s.

Although a large number of people were employed, casual work was irregular. The demand for labour was greatest in the harvest when workers engaged for its duration and, like regular farm servants, received payments in meal and money. At other times of the year, casual workers did not receive a meal allowance nor did they receive their food except on special occasions such as sheep shearing. They were normally paid a money wage only. Summer provided opportunities for working with peats, hoeing turnips and gathering stones off newly reclaimed fields, but in winter fewer workers were required for tasks such as barn work, spreading dung or carting seaweed for manure. The most regular work was obtained by men skilled in dry stone dyke-building or in draining.

In 1853 there were no fewer than 39 people employed on a casual basis at one time or another during the year. Of these only one was employed for as much as a third of the available time and 20 were engaged for less than 5% of the total working time. In the aftermath of the Quandale and Westness clearances, under-employment was endemic. As time went on, the demand for casual labour grew, increasing from about 1,000 days in 1853 to about 1,500 days in 1873. At the same time, the total number of people employed in the course of the year dropped from 39 to 25 and thus casual workers were obtaining more regular employment. The difference, however, was merely one of degree, since no casual worker was even then employed for as many as half the possible working days.

Employed Percent. of Total Working Days	1853		1873	
	No. of Workers		No. of Workers	
	Male	Female	Male	Female
0 - 5%	11	9	5	1
5 -10%	4	3	2	5
10-20%	3	5	1	—
20-30%	—	3	4	1
30-40%	1	—	1	1
40-50%	—	—	1	3
Total Casual Workers	19	20	14	11

Table 6. *Casual Workers on Westness Farm, 1853 and 1873*

The tenants were bound by their leases to the *Hard Six Rotation* and this rotation was also originally followed on the farm which was in the laird's own hands. It was a rotation which obliged the tenant to grow a crop of turnips or potatoes the first year, to follow this in the second year with bere or oats undersown with ryegrass and clover for hay and pasture in the third and fourth years respectively, in the fifth year to grow oats and in the final year either oats or bere. By 1874, however, the *Conditions of Leases* had been amended to prescribe the *Five Shift Rotation*, the rotation almost invariably used in Orkney in the final years of the nineteenth century. This followed the same pattern of cropping as the *Hard Six* without the final year's grain crop. Nineteenth century grass mixtures did not allow grass to be laid down for long periods and, indeed, in both of these rotations the second year of grass was often a failure.[17] Consequently what would now be considered unusually large acreages of turnips were grown. The *Hard Six* with three years of grain implied that half of the land under rotation was growing grain, but later, as cereals became less profitable, the *Five Shift Rotation* cut the proportion of land under oats and bere to 40%. Many Orkney farms found that the large acreage of turnips which the *Five Shift* demanded was an embarrassment, but on a farm like Westness with numerous sheep the turnip acreage was a positive advantage. An examination of the agricultural returns shows that the acreage of turnips grown in Rousay actually exceeded the proportion which even the five shift required. The acreage of rotation grassland, however, was always rather less than ought to have been obtained by strict adherence to the rotation.

With half of the arable under cereals, Westness had originally a good deal of grain to sell, yet not perhaps as much as one might have expected. Both the traditional black oats and the higher-yielding white oats were grown, but a seed/yield ratio of 1:7 suggests that a significant proportion of the older variety were still being grown in 1853. About a third of the crop was sold off the farm, a further third was fed to animals and the remaining third went to produce the *bolls* for the regular farm servants and the *harvest fees* for the casual workers.

The large extent of arable land required ten horses to work it and much heavy manuring was also necessary. In addition to farmyard manure, there were regular purchases of guano and bonemeal from 1846 onwards, and cottar labour was extensively used for collecting and spreading seaweed. In the early years cattle numbers were surprisingly small — in 1853 a shorthorn bull, 8 cows and 14 younger animals — but as time passed the numbers grew until there were usually 60 to 70 animals. Westness regularly bought cattle from other farms in Rousay and sold through dealers. A bull bought in Leith in 1848 was an almost unique example of an animal brought in from outside Orkney.

Considerable care, however, was taken in assembling the original Cheviot flock for the Quandale pastures. In 1848 Lyall travelled to Wick, Helmsdale, Berriedale and back to Dunnett driving his purchases, and then hired three boats to transport them across the Pentland Firth. In the early years the animals to be marketed were usually ferried to Caithness and sold at Georgemas, an important occasion when both Lyall and Scarth would supervise the selling, but sheep were later disposed of through dealers or sent south by sea to be sold in Edinburgh. After the sales, the flock numbered about 690. In addition to Cheviots and Cheviot-Leicester crosses, there was also a small number of native sheep (despite prohibitions on tenants keeping any 'wild or Orkney sheep'), and until 1854 there was also an experimental flock of Dinmonts. In 1882 the Cheviot flock was dispersed and replaced by Blackfaces.

Under Lyall's management, it is not possible to separate the profits of Westness and Trumland, both farms being in the proprietor's own hands, but the combined profits were not large and were also rather variable. When George Learmonth took over Westness (but not Trumland), his costs were more than twice as great as Lyall's had been. He employed much more labour and spent much more on cattle purchases. But, if his costs increased, the sales from the farm increased by even more and, after 1858, the profit from Westness never dropped below £500 a year and, in the best year, 1865, reached £863. When a farm servant might be engaged for £12 a year and when the overseer himself received only £50, the profit to the proprietor can only be described as princely. Learmonth's methods were typical of mid-century high farming — he spent freely and expected to reap large rewards. In addition to the money spent on dyking, draining and reseeding the Quandale pastures, Learmonth undertook the work of building a completely new steading (1859-66) and built new houses for farm workers.

After remaining under the profitable management of George Learmonth for over twenty years, Westness was eventually let in 1875. Once again it proved difficult to find a tenant. The farm was advertised without success in the *Glasgow News* in August, in November in *The Northern Ensign, The Field, The Edinburgh Courant, Land and Water* and *The Scotsman* and finally, perhaps in desperation, in *The Orcadian* and *The Orkney Herald* in December. Burroughs found his tenant close at hand and George Learmonth signed a nineteen-year lease. The difficulty in finding a tenant was due to the rent which was expected. Learmonth was taking a risk when he accepted the tenancy at a rent of £600 a year since in only ten of his twenty-one years as manager had the farm yielded as much as that. It was only by increasing profitability still further that he could do better than break even. It was not an easy situation. He was aged seventy-one; the son to whom he hoped to pass on the tenancy was soon to be stricken by paralysis, and the years of agricultural prosperity were drawing to a close.

	Sales					Costs						Profit
	Grain	Cattle	Sheep and Wool	Sundries	Total Sales	Farm Servants	Casual Labour	Cattle Purchases	Sheep Purchases	Seed, Fertilisers etc.	Total Costs	
Westness and Trumland Combined 1848-1852												
1848	99	280	260	129	768	172	61	33	132	102	501	267
1849	42	102	147	69	361	64	55	3	13	106	241	120
1850	46	117	280	53	496	104	31	0	20	81	236	260
1851	48	101	428	31	657	103	35	0	0	143	286	371
1852	117	149	720	16	1001	101	19	0	0	150	293	708
Westness only, 1853-1871												
1853	110	105	536	71	822	166	69	1	102	152	528	294
1854	162	268	621	11	1061	107	73	203	72	149	603	458
1855	71	250	604	77	1002	123	100	108	39	185	604	398
1856	53	314	677	95	1139	121	82	148	59	177	587	552
1857	62	247	535	70	915	130	101	123	35	135	490	425
1858	110	217	543	124	995	129	95	134	27	128	516	479
1859	129	328	732	75	1281	148	82	98	54	132	516	765
1860	22	392	684	84	1187	128	95	134	27	131	555	632
1861	11	442	622	148	1222	154	98	195	39	149	636	576
1862	67	414	701	59	1241	162	105	154	37	168	629	612
1863	80	413	762	87	1342	158	91	189	40	132	611	731
1864	83	333	802	92	1310	149	93	139	44	144	570	740
1865	120	353	911	76	1461	159	75	100	65	123	598	863
1866	116	280	602	90	1087	160	70	89	29	152	499	588
1867	109	251	470	101	931	157	59	80	33	128	457	574
1868	154	210	654	104	1121	155	73	75	38	131	471	650
1869	59	269	543	69	941	156	99	34	53	134	441	500
1870	137	281	742	99	1258	156	74	50	22	136	437	821
1871	121	250	850	86	1308	156	103	57	48	163	772	636

Table 7. Westness Farm: Sales, Costs and Profit, 1848-1871 (£'s). Under the competent management of George Learmonth (overseer from 1855 to 1875) the improved Westness Farm regularly yielded a handsome profit to the laird. Note that rounding of figures to the nearest £1 results in apparent discrepancies in the totals.

When George William Traill acquired Westness, it was the land only which he bought. Westness House remained the property of William Traill (1797-1858) and later his widow. In 1863, when Mrs Traill died, Burroughs was able to buy the house, although financially embarrassed at the time, and he set about the work of renovation. The house was repaired and redecorated, the grounds were set to rights, greenhouses built and garden walls reconstructed. In 1872 the house was reroofed and an extension was added. Being himself in India, Burroughs let the house with shooting and fishing rights over the whole of the estate. His tenant was yet another Traill, James C. Traill, a London lawyer who, although not closely related, was a friend from Burroughs' schooldays at Blackheath. Thereafter Westness was occupied rent-free by military acquaintances. While he himself was absent, Burroughs considered it more important to have a tenant he could trust rather than to maximise the profit from sporting rights. When he returned from India, he occupied Westness from 1870 to 1875 but, on the completion of his new mansion at Trumland, Westness was again let as a sporting property. The letting was now on a more business-like basis. The Westness tenant had shooting rights over only half the island, the other half being reserved for the laird, and he was allowed to fish on alternate days on Muckle Water, Peerie Water and the Loch of Wasbister. For these reduced rights, the shooting tenant paid a rent increased to £200 from the £50 it had been when James Traill was tenant. Burroughs felt it was worth much more. He reckoned that it cost him £50 a month to let the house and provide a gamekeeper, gardener, dogs, ponies, boats and boatmen. A rent of £1,360 for a six months' lease would, he considered, be a more realistic figure.[18] It was, however, much more than he was likely to be able to obtain.

Nearly every year Westness House was let to a different shooting tenant. One year it was taken by Thomas E. Buckley, joint author of *A Vertebrate Fauna of the Orkney Islands* who, after his summer in Rousay, read a paper on the mammals and birds of Rousay to the Natural History Society of Glasgow.[19] Another occupant, a military gentleman, quarrelled violently with Burroughs, who noted in his account book that the tenant had been 'expelled' — one would like to know more. Perhaps the most colourful was Lady Florence Dixie, a relative of the Duke of Queensberry, who stayed at Westness with her father in 1885. Lady Florence wore her hair short, commonly dressed in a sailor's suit and was a regular speaker on Scottish nationalism and women's rights. As an ardent champion of the underdog, her presence in Rousay at the height of the trouble between the laird and his crofters was potentially explosive. Lady Florence, however, was a keen sportswoman and a good shot. She appears to have been more intent on killing grouse than involving herself in local crofting politics.[20]

6

Lucknow

'For individual gallantry in the Secunderbagh and being the first who entered one of the breaches. . .' Recommendation for the award of the Victoria Cross to Capt. F. W. Traill Burroughs[1]

'You must be under an hallucination in imagining you entered by the breach . . .' Sir Colin Campbell[2]

FREDERICK Burroughs was only sixteen when he inherited the Rousay estate on the death of his uncle. Born to an Irish father and an Anglo-French mother, he had spent the first nine years of his life in India before being sent home for the sake of his education. Although his father and mother returned to England on leave at about the same time, the boy travelled with George William Traill who was retiring from the Bengal Civil Service and was henceforth to be his guardian. It was Traill, not his parents, who made arrangements for his schooling, first at Blackheath and then at Hofwyl in Switzerland. Traill visited Berne to inspect the school, a select establishment managed by a German count and accommodating thirty boys. Its curriculum combined language teaching with an active outdoor life. Traill approved of this system of education and he hoped that his rather puny nephew might benefit from mountain air and exercise. Burroughs was an apt pupil and quickly acquired a working knowledge of French, German and Italian, with a smattering of Latin. He enjoyed the expeditions into the mountains and proved himself to be fit and hardy but, to his uncle's regret, he remained quite noticeably undersized. It was while he was still a pupil at Hofwyl that Burroughs received the news of George William Traill's death.[3]

The following year, 1848, Burroughs joined the 93rd, the Sutherland Highlanders, as an ensign, the regiment being shortly due to return after ten years' service in Quebec. It was a regiment noted for its good order, discipline and bravery but also for the intensity of its religious beliefs. The 93rd was the Free Church regiment. The controversies which split the Church of Scotland and which led to the Disruption had reached the regiment in Canada, and the men of the 93rd had taken a resolute stand on behalf of the Free Kirk, defying the efforts of their officers to compel attendance at the 'Moderate' Church.[4] They were imbued with a fierce, narrow, bloodthirsty variety of religion and have been compared to a 'military Highland parish'.[5] The regiment contained its own Free Church congregation with six elders drawn from among the private soldiers and non-commissioned officers.[6]

Underlying this adherence to the Free Church was the land question in the Highlands and memories of the Sutherland clearances. The 93rd at this time still retained strong territorial links with the north of Scotland where the Established Church was attended by the laird, his servants and his sheep farmers, while the Free Church was the church of the crofters. Since the immediate occasion of the split between Evangelicals and Moderates was the question of the proprietor's right of patronage, the Free Church was the party of anti-landlordism. The Rev George Ritchie's denunciation of George William Traill's clearance policy was typical of the attitude of the new church, and years later Burroughs was to find that his opponents were drawn from that congregation. His long connection with the 93rd ought to have made him familiar with the attitudes he was to encounter among his tenants.

In a regiment noted for its height, Burroughs must have appeared an odd little figure as a seventeen-year-old ensign. He had always been acutely aware of his lack of inches. While at school, the letters he received from his uncle frequently referred to the matter with a heavy-handed humour which disguised the fact that Traill was worried about his nephew's slow growth. 'I beg that you will without further delay begin growing,' he would write with a bachelor's lack of understanding of how painful a subject this was for the boy. He should not, Traill wrote, allow himself to be overtaken by his young cousin, Rosa Sutherland, since she would then look down on him for the rest of his life! Fred dutifully measured himself both in inches and centimetres and reported progress to his uncle. Later, when Traill was negotiating with the Duke of Wellington regarding a commission for his nephew, he was still urging him to grow and reminding him 'that there is . . no precedent for a field marshall under five feet in height'.[7] Comments of this kind had their effect on Burroughs. He always felt a need to assert his authority and he was quick to resent insults, both real and imagined. The men of the 93rd nicknamed him 'Wee Frenchie' and believed he owed his formal manners and punctilious drill methods to a military training in the prestigious Ecole Polytechnique in Paris.[8] This was not in fact the case but, in addition to his French ancestry, he had a habit of using French words and phrases in his conversation and writing. He was a devout Episcopalian but this, while it separated him from the men, did not make him particularly conspicuous since officers were hardly ever Free Church members. The regiment reflected the social order of the Highlands — Free Church crofters in the ranks while the officers belonged to the Episcopalian or to the Established Church and were drawn from the landowning classes.

His first duty was a memorable one. While awaiting the return of the regiment from Quebec, he was assigned to a detachment of three officers and fifty men who formed the guard of honour on the occasion of Queen Victoria's first visit to Balmoral.[9] The guard travelled by train to Aberdeen, then marched to upper Deeside where they were accommodated in Mar Castle. The two-month stay was a pleasant introduction to army life. There was good shooting and the officers had permission to fish on Loch Muick but, with a reverential respect for royal privacy, they would hide themselves in the woods whenever the Queen and Prince Albert were on the loch. The highlight of the officers' stay was the Braemar Gathering where they struck up a friendship with 'clan' Forbes from Donside and, after the gathering, the guard and the pseudo-clan assembled on the lawn at Balmoral where the Queen appeared in person to welcome them. Queen Victoria enjoyed her first visit to Balmoral. It set a pattern for the fashionable, upper class Highland holiday where shooting and fishing were the main occupations and a loyal tenantry, like the scenery, was part of the picturesque background. It was a way of life which others were to emulate, the way of life which Burroughs was to try to create in Rousay.

Burroughs' easy introduction to army life was followed by more demanding service. After six years in Scotland and England, the 93rd saw action in the Crimean War. Throughout the war, although the regiment was decimated by cholera, dysentery and fever, Burroughs was unaffected and was never absent from duty for a single day. He fought at the Battle of the Alma and commanded a company at Balaclava where the 93rd formed 'the thin red line tipped with steel' which faced a large body of Russian cavalry. In later years a faded print of this single line of red-coated soldiers adorned the walls of Rousay farm houses, and an officer of unusually small stature was widely believed to represent their laird. To oppose massed cavalry with infantry in extended line was a manoeuvre born of desperation which might easily have ended in disaster, but its success made the reputation both of the regiment and the little Glasgow general, Sir Colin Campbell, forging a special relationship which was to be renewed in the Indian Mutiny. The morale of the 93rd was incredibly high and, with Sir Colin Campbell, they felt that there was no limit to what they might accomplish.

The end of the war saw the 93rd in the forward trenches at Sebastopol in readiness for a final assault on the Redan. It is said that Burroughs had volunteered to lead the first assault when the Highland Brigade attacked in the morning but, during the night, it was discovered that the Russians had withdrawn from the defences and abandoned the town.[10] The sudden retreat denied him the chance to distinguish himself but when, two years later, he stood opposite a black and smoking breach in the walls of the Sikanderbagh at Lucknow, he was determined not to miss his opportunity a second time.

On their return to England from the Crimea, the 93rd spent an uncomfortable winter at Dover. There was no proper accommodation and the regiment remained under canvas in wet and stormy weather, experiencing hardships as difficult to bear as any they had met during the war. They were preparing for service overseas. Their destination was to have been India but the worsening political situation in China caused their posting to be altered. In early June, before they embarked for China, the Queen inspected the regiment at Portsmouth. By this time the Indian Mutiny had broken out but, in the absence of a telegraph link, the news had not yet reached Britain. Transport was provided in H.M.S. *Belleisle*, an 84-gun sailing two-decker, and a steamer, the *Mauritius*. Burroughs was fortunate enough to be aboard the *Mauritius*, which provided much more comfortable accommodation.

The voyage out via Madeira to the Cape was marred by a mutinous crew. The captain had forbidden the usual celebrations on the crossing of the line on the grounds that they were only an excuse for drunkenness and scrounging on the part of the crew. Despite this order, several sailors burst into the dining saloon and the captain finally had to call on the assistance of the regiment to restore order. The disaffected attitude spread to some of the men in the 93rd and two of Burroughs' own company received fifty lashes for their part in the trouble.

But news of a mutiny of a more serious kind awaited them at the Cape. Like all of Victorian Britain, the officers of the 93rd saw the Indian Mutiny in simple terms of right and wrong. The conduct of the mutinous sepoys was pure treachery which threatened the very existence of the British Empire. The 93rd were particularly affected by the horrifying story of the massacre of the women and children whose mutilated bodies had been found in the well at Cawnpore. Major Ewart who had been Burroughs' Commanding Officer at Balmoral had lost relatives at Cawnpore and there were rumours that Burroughs' father was among those murdered when his regiment, the 17th Bengal Native Infantry, had mutinied.[11] It was not until he reached Calcutta that Burroughs learned that his father was safe, although his sister Charlotte and his brother Charly had had a narrow escape. Many years later Charlotte was to recall how, as a girl of nine, her hands sticky with bread and jam and clutching a little Indian basket containing a china cat with a blue ribbon, she had been bundled up a ladder to take refuge behind a low parapet of sand bags on the flat roof of a neighbouring bungalow. As she and her brother lay on their stomachs behind this flimsy protection there had been a good deal of rather wild firing. A lieutenant who tried to climb down to fetch help was shot before he could reach the ground. Eventually the sepoys had moved away, attracted by hopes of easy looting, and under cover of darkness the women and children were able to escape from the roof top and eventually made their way safely to Calcutta.[12]

The Governor of the Cape, Sir George Grey, although strictly he had no authority over troops in transit, took the responsibility of diverting the 93rd to Calcutta. The crew of the *Mauritius* continued to be disaffected, much to the disgust of the soldiers who were anxious to reach Calcutta as soon as possible, and the men of the 93rd had to do much of the coaling. They arrived in the Hooghly on 20th September and found Calcutta itself in a very tense state. However, they were reunited with Sir Colin Campbell who had travelled out via Egypt when news of the Mutiny had been received in Britain. Preparations for moving his force up the Ganges were now well advanced.

At that time India had seen few Highland regiments and the kilts of the *gogra wallahs* (skirted men) caused a sensation. Throughout the Mutiny the 93rd wore regimental Highland dress including their distinctive feather bonnets of ostrich plumes mounted on a stout wire framework, a dress not only imposing but cool and providing a certain amount of protection against blows to the head. This wire framework was to save Burroughs' life at Lucknow. The regiment had been issued with brown alpaca coats with red linings for the cold winters of northern China and these were useful for their capacious pockets. When in action and separated from his servants, an officer might go into battle with a spare shirt, towel and toothbrush in addition to the issue of three days' provisions. Officers wore a broad silk sash across the shoulder and were armed with sword and dirk.

Only two days after their arrival the journey up country began. The first forty miles were on the river aboard a barge towed by a tug, and the regiment then disembarked at Chinsurah. There the Free Kirk susceptibilities of the 93rd were shocked by the sight of a naked fakir bedecked with shells, teeth and soda water bottles, strolling down the Mall in the cool of the evening when there were ladies present. Their reaction — to pitch him into the Ganges — was typical of the attitudes which led to the Mutiny.[13]

After a delay of a few days while other troops moved up to Chinsurah, the journey was continued by rail for a further 125 miles to the railhead. Thereafter they travelled by bullock cart and were divided into detachments of ninety men with four officers travelling at intervals of a day. To escape the heat, they rested in bungalows during the day and travelled at night. Considering the urgency which all felt, progress was painfully slow. The bullock carts jolted and bumped throughout the night, stopping every eight or nine miles for a change of animals and barely maintaining an average of two miles an hour. Myriads of fireflies illuminated the night, but even along the Trunk Road there was danger from bands of mutineers who indeed nearly captured Sir Colin Campbell himself. Beyond Allahabad there was another short section of railway and then the detachments marched the final forty-six miles into Cawnpore. No.6 Company, with Burroughs in command, was the first to arrive at Cawnpore, which was already in British hands once again. Traces of fighting were everywhere and batches of mutinous sepoys were being hanged during the four days Burroughs was there, a grisly performance beginning each day at dawn and continuing to sunset or even later. Leave was granted to all officers and men to visit the house where the two hundred women and children had been massacred. The relics of the killing still remained, scraps of clothing in the bushes, bloodstains and gashes of hatchets on the trunks of the trees. It was an emotional occasion, the soldiers removing their hats on entry to the courtyard, many of them in tears and pausing with uplifted hands to swear vengeance on the murderers.

The immediate concern was to prevent a repetition of these events at Lucknow, where a small British force, with many women and children, was holding out in the improvised fortifications of the Residency and was in imminent danger of being overrun by vastly superior numbers. Sir Colin Campbell's purpose was to bring them out safely since for the moment the army he had at his disposal was far too small for him to attempt to capture and hold Lucknow. Even a rescue attempt would be a difficult matter.

Soon after leaving Cawnpore, the 93rd were driven back in full retreat by an unexpected enemy. The regiment had retired to their tents in the heat of the day after stationing a picket in a grove of trees some distance ahead. This picket were soon seen running for their lives although there was no sign of the enemy. The bugle sounded to muster the regiment. Officers and men scrambled out in various states of undress. As the retreating picket came closer it could be seen that they were surrounded by a cloud of fierce Indian hornets which one of the picket had aroused by idly poking at their nest with his sword. The bugle sounded the 'disperse' and in double quick time they sought refuge in their tents. This incident gave rise to the usual crop of jokes about the unsuitability of the kilt, arguments which the 93rd answered in all seriousness and with a total lack of humour.[14]

A week after leaving Cawnpore the relief column reached the Alumbagh, a fortress which had been held with some difficulty by a small British contingent and which lay on the outskirts of Lucknow, only two miles from the Residency. The following day (14th November) the advance into Lucknow began in earnest. Instead of taking the main road into the town as the mutineers had expected him to do, Sir Colin Campbell swung to the right, catching the enemy by surprise and advancing as far as the Dilkusha Park, the summer residence of the kings of Oudh. About midday the 93rd piled arms and fell out in the park since a canal blocked further advance and a way across had to be found.

In the early afternoon Burroughs' company was advanced on outpost duty to the corner of the park nearest the canal. Although the wall of the park had been breached in several places, many of the deer were still grazing. Taking up their position, No.6 Company were surprised to find the enemy within fifty yards of them. They were dressed in pre-Crimea scarlet coatees and huge old-fashioned shakoes and wore white cross belts with ammunition pouches, but they had discarded uniform trousers in favour of native clothing and they wore 'Turkish slippers'. Like so many tourists, the men in Burroughs' company were allowed to mount the rampart in small groups, laughing uproariously at the old-fashioned uniform. Meanwhile the mutineers were doing exactly the same, equally amused by the kilts of the 'gogra wallahs'. Burroughs sent his lieutenant forward to reconnoitre, but before anything could be done the Punjab regiment came skirmishing up and put the rebels to flight.

With only a brief respite, Burroughs' picket remained in position at the corner of Dilkusha Park all that day and the next. Their section of the front was quiet and they had little to do. Elsewhere the British force had to beat off a determined attempt to cut off their line of communication with the Alumbagh. Other companies of the 93rd seized a section of the canal which barred their advance, only to find it was too deep to ford. But although they saw little action, Burroughs' picket discovered congenial company. They found themselves on duty with a troop of Bengal Artillery commanded by George Balfour Traill, who was a remote relative and a close friend from Burroughs' school days at Blackheath. They settled down to enjoy the spiced beef, white bread and hard boiled eggs which the artillery had been able to bring up on their tumbrils. Burroughs and his fellow infantry officers normally fared much less well since they were dependent on native servants who tended to disappear as soon as the action began.

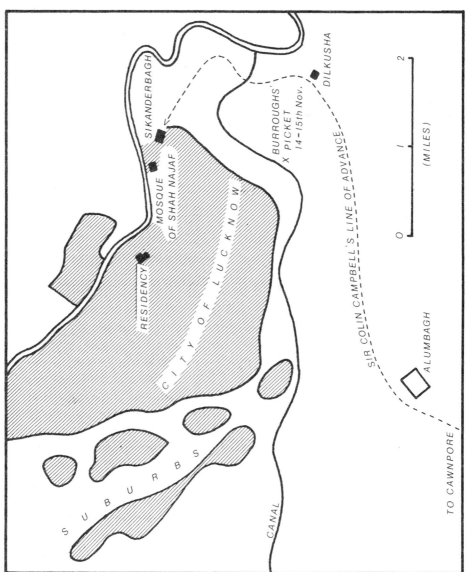

Fig. 7 The Relief of Lucknow

The only excitement on the second day was provided by a contest between a big Irish gunner and a fanatical *ghazi* in single combat. The gunner had wandered down from the picket position towards the edge of a wood, unaware of the scantily clad *ghazi* armed with a *tulwar* (native sword) creeping through the long grass. The picket shouted a warning to the Irishman who fortunately had his sword with him, and ten minutes of fencing ensued with the Irishman parrying the *ghazi's* furious rushes. Meanwhile the picket formed an audience shouting 'Fair play!' when anyone threatened to intervene. At last the Irishman saw his chance and left his opponent for dead but, ten hours later when Traill and Burroughs walked down, they found him virtually disembowelled but still fully conscious. They were able to converse with him in Hindustani and to discover that he had come out to kill a *Feringi* and so win a place in Paradise. On their return Traill sent the Irish gunner down to finish him off with a bullet.

Under cover of darkness Burroughs' company was withdrawn to Dilkusha which in the meantime had been fortified as an advance base from which they were to push on to the Residency itself. Sir Colin Campbell was drawing attention to the extreme left of his position where they had already discovered that the canal was too deep to cross, but the actual advance was planned to take place from the other end of the line where an easy crossing had been found. Burroughs' men, slipping in through the darkness, were enjoined to converse in whispers and to muffle the scabbards of their swords lest any sound betray the plan for the morrow.

The whole force was under arms before daybreak. Companies were inspected and each man issued with sixty rounds of ammunition. The men breakfasted on boiled beef, commissariat biscuit and tea, all of which had been prepared during the course of the night, but for Burroughs there was no breakfast — the native servants had once again failed to appear. The sergeant-major, however, fetched 'tots' of the black stewed tea which was served to the men. Sir Colin then called the officers forward and in low tones directed them to ensure that their men made as little use as possible of their rifles and that they relied on their bayonets. In crowded conditions they might shoot both friend and foe. When the officers had passed on these instructions, the force moved off. It consisted of three thousand infantry of whom about a third were from the 93rd and the remainder consisted of two numerically weak Punjabi regiments, the 23rd (Royal Welsh Fusiliers), the 82nd and two further battalions composed of the remnants of various regiments. Because of the rapidity of the advance, it had not been possible to bring up much in the way of artillery and a naval detachment provided the main firepower.

For the second time the direction of advance took the enemy by surprise. They were able to cross the canal without difficulty and to advance along the bank of the Gumpti, skirting the village of Jia Mau, into the narrow twisting lanes which led to the Sikanderbagh. Hitherto they had met no opposition but the last part of the road lay between high banks and rows of thatched huts and here they met fierce resistance. In this enclosed situation there were, for a time, scenes of confusion but at last the enemy retreated into the Sikanderbagh and Sir Colin Campbell was able to bring both infantry and naval guns to bear on the first major obstacle.

The Sikanderbagh (the Garden of Alexander) was a formidable position. This royal pleasure garden was a square, each side of which measured about 150 yards. It was surrounded by a twenty-foot wall unbroken by windows or doors. At each corner stood a pentagonal bastion and the only entrance was protected by three ornate towers. Efforts had been made to further fortify the garden by loopholing the parapets and throwing up an earthwork before the entrance. In more peaceful times the walls had enclosed lawns and flowerbeds with broad walks lined with shrubs leading to a pavilion in the centre of the garden. The enclosure now contained some two thousand armed men whose cooking fires had blackened the lawn and consumed everything that would burn.

The part which Burroughs played in the events which were to follow was a matter of controversy, not just at that time but for the remainder of the century. Even as late as 1897, forty years after these events, there was a correspondence in *The Standard* about who could rightly claim the honour of being first through the breach in the walls of the Sikanderbagh.[15]

To understand the controversy it is necessary to appreciate the high drama of the occasion, one of the most romantic feats of arms of Victorian times. This small force had been rushed hundreds of miles up country to the relief of men, women and children long besieged in the Residency who might be expected to share the fate of those at Cawnpore should the relief fail. Against overwhelming odds the main hope rested with the Highlanders, fresh from their achievements in the Crimea and reunited with their old commander. For younger officers, such as Burroughs, there was the additional glamour of the newly created Victoria Cross. War at that time still presented opportunities for individual gallantry and the V.C. was awarded much more frequently than was later to be the case. Yet Victoria's reign had hitherto been mainly peaceful and chances of glory came infrequently. Young officers had to seize their opportunities. The old general, however, strongly disapproved of the V.C., which he considered encouraged foolhardy conduct and feats of individual gallantry by officers who ought to have been giving their full attention to their men. He was himself careful not to expose his troops to unnecessary danger and he felt uneasy about the risks which young officers were prepared to take. In Burroughs' mind there may also have been the memory of the Redan, the only other siege at which he had been present, when the surprise withdrawal of the Russians had robbed him of his moment of glory. He may also have been smarting at the recollection of his own rather amateurish first contact with the rebels only two days earlier. But, above all, he suddenly found himself by chance in a position where he ought to be able to distinguish himself.

Whether or not he was first through the breach in the walls of the Sikanderbagh remains uncertain, but it is an uncertainty which does not stem from a lack of evidence. Discounting the many memoirs of those present at Lucknow and later histories of the Mutiny which record the events at second hand, there is a wealth of conflicting evidence from officers and men who were closely connected with Burroughs and who were eye-witnesses of the events they described. Burroughs' immediate superior was Colonel Ewart (of the Balmoral guard), and he wrote his memoirs in 1881.[16] W. G. Alexander, a lieutenant in Burroughs' company, later rose to the rank of lieutenant-colonel and published his recollections of the Mutiny in 1898.[17] The surgeon in the regiment produced two sets of bulky and prosaic memoirs [18] and William Forbes-Mitchell, a sergeant, also published his version of the events at Lucknow.[19]

These eyewitnesses tell differing versions of the story of the storming of the Sikanderbagh, differences understandable after the lapse of years and perhaps inevitable considering the confusion and the excitement of the occasion. Alexander gives the fullest account and he had a particularly good opportunity to examine the Sikanderbagh, having been stationed there for three days after the siege. Although his version was written long after the event, it was based on a diary he wrote at the time. He was openly biased in favour of his old company commander and, indeed, had been prompted to write his memoirs by the correspondence in *The Standard* which cast doubt on the part Burroughs played. Yet he had little reason to be an uncritical admirer of Burroughs. Not infrequently he had to bear the brunt of Burroughs' brusque manner and bad temper, and on one occasion he was placed on a charge by Burroughs for going to the assistance of one of the naval guns without a direct order to do so.

Ewart, like Burroughs and Alexander, entered the Sikanderbagh by the breach and was in a good position to see what happened. His account is unbiased but inconclusive. To Alexander the question of who was first through the breach is a central issue but to Ewart it is only an interesting incidental question. Munro, the regimental surgeon, was not in such a good position to observe at first hand. Forbes-Mitchell's account is biased in favour of the non-commissioned ranks and it tends to be anecdotal in style, sometimes preferring a good story to the facts. Burroughs, a prolific correspondent, was in a position to influence several of these stories. Alexander and Munro both acknowledge the assistance they received from Burroughs as does Burgoyne, the official historian of the regiment.[20]

The bare facts of the storming of the Sikanderbagh were told in a dispatch from Sir Colin Campbell:—

F

The attack (by the artillery) on the Sikanderbagh had now been proceeding for about an hour and a half, when it was determined to take the place by storm through a small opening which had been made. This was done in the most brilliant manner by the remainder of the Highlanders and the 53rd, and 4th Punjab Infantry, supported by a battalion of detachments under Major Barnston. There never was a bolder feat of arms, and the loss inflicted on the enemy after the entrance to the Sikanderbagh was effected, was immense; more than 2000 of the enemy were afterwards carried out.[21]

There is no dispute about the part which Burroughs played in the first part of the action. Emerging from the narrow streets, his company was met by a hail of bullets from the walls of the garden. They wheeled right in columns of sections, a drill movement which steadied them under fire, and they took up a position behind a low earth wall separated from the Sikanderbagh by 80-150 yards of open ground. Here they sheltered while an occasional bullet whistled through the framework of their feather bonnets. 'Nae doubt the niggers think our brains are higher than they are,' remarked one unconcerned veteran.

It was with some difficulty that the guns had been brought forward, but eventually two 18-pounders were brought to bear on the walls from a position not far from where Burroughs was sheltering. The walls of the garden were only two and a half feet thick, yet the type of mortar used in their construction made them peculiarly resistant and it was an hour and a half before a small breach was opened in one of the bastions. Even then there was some doubt about whether it was large enough for a man to enter.

During this time while his men had been sheltering behind the wall, Burroughs was in a very exposed position some distance further forward despite the remonstrances of his lieutenant who passed up loaded rifles which Burroughs discharged at the loopholes. Owing to the trend of the sheltering wall, Burroughs' company were nearest the breach but Burroughs was ahead of his men. When the order to charge was given, his men had to climb up and over the earth rampart whereas he had several yards of a start. He was in a position where he ought to have been first through the breach.

All accounts agree about the ferocity, the noise, the smoke, dust and confusion of that wild Highland charge. Malleson's *History of the Indian Mutiny* described the assault:—

A Sikh of the 4th Rifles reached it first, but was shot dead as he jumped through. A similar fate befell a Highlander in his track. A young officer of the 93rd, Richard Cooper by name, outstripping the majority of his comrades, was more fortunate. Flying, so to speak, through the hole, he landed unscathed. 'His jump into it,' wrote the gallant Blunt who witnessed it, 'reminded me of the headlong leap which harlequin in a pantomime makes through a shop window, and I thought at the time that if he were not rushing to certain death, life would be very uncertain to those making entrance by that ugly blind hole.'

Malleson enumerated the next fifteen men to climb through the breach. There was no mention of Burroughs. It was this account which led to the correspondence in *The Standard* and prompted Alexander to give his own version of the events:—

> Burroughs (by being beyond the protecting wall) thus got a start of at least a dozen yards before any of No.6 Company, and we were directly opposite and nearest to the breach. I myself reached the breach immediately behind Burroughs, but rather out of breath, partly from running, and partly from shouting, I suppose, and well ahead of both Ewart and Lieutenant Cooper of No.5 Company. On reaching the hole, Burroughs had bent his head, and actually succeeded in jumping in, knocking his feather bonnet off in performing this harlequin's feat. Fortunately for him, as it afterwards turned out, I stopped and picked up his bonnet, and tossed it into the hole after him, before he had time to turn round or another man was in the way. Private Dunlay and two, or perhaps three, more men of No.6 Company were pushed up after Burroughs, when Cooper reached us, and, like the excitable Irishman he was whenever there was a fight on, pushed everyone aside and . . . scrambled in, followed by his own man . . . Lieutenant-Colonel Ewart now came up . . . I followed Ewart.

This is an entirely different version of the incident. There is the same harlequin's leap, but this time performed by Burroughs, not Cooper, and quite different *dramatis personae*. Ewart's account is less dogmatic about the facts, and he was prepared to admit the possibility of mistaken identities, particularly since the alpaca coats of the 93rd were difficult to distinguish from the brown uniform of the Punjab Rifles. Ewart himself was among the first to reach the breach but was hindered by his tight uniform trousers which he was wearing instead of the kilt and, incredibly, he was wearing spurs! Reaching the breach, he saw both Cooper and Burroughs inside but he afterwards heard it said that the first man had been neither of them but Sergeant-Major Murray of the 93rd or a Sikh named Subadar Gokul Sing. The memoirs of Sergeant Forbes-Mitchell, biased in favour of the non-commissioned officers as the other accounts were probably biased in favour of the officer class, named Lance-Corporal Dunlay as the first, followed by Sergeant-Major Murray and Gokul Sing, with Burroughs fourth or fifth, but the first officer.

Burroughs' own account first appeared in a personal letter he wrote to one of his sisters immediately after the event and which was published, much to his annoyance, in the *Ayr Advertiser*.[22] It contained little detail, only the claim that he had been first to enter the breach, but he later elaborated in a letter to Surgeon-General Munro when the latter was writing his memoirs. Burroughs described how, when he first reached the breach, he found it too small to permit entry and had to tear down some of the crumbling masonry before he could squeeze through. This is a different version again from the harlequin's leap which others described.

Other accounts speak of the breach being enlarged, but only after the first party was through. One cannot help feeling that the point of this version is Burroughs' small size and slim build. He is emphasising that, if he had to remove bricks to squeeze in, no one could possibly have entered before him.

What conclusions can one come to apart from the fact that a number of eye witnesses were inaccurate in their observations and that some were claiming for themselves what they must have known to be false? The truth cannot now be discovered but there are a number of pointers which suggest Burroughs as the most likely candidate for the honour. There is, first, the undisputed fact that he was in the position closest to the breach and had a head start over members of his own company. Cooper had twenty or thirty yards more to cover and the Punjabis considerably more. Second, Burroughs' build is consistent with his entering the breach easily. Most accounts agree that the hole was barely three feet square and about the same distance off the ground. Third, Alexander's account, which credited Burroughs with the honour, is the most detailed and based on notes and plans which he made at the time. But the fourth reason is the most compelling. After the action, a number of officers and men were recommended for the Victoria Cross, three of them for action at the breach. The citations were as follows —

Burroughs For individual gallantry in the Sikanderbagh and *being the first* who entered one of the breaches and engaged in personal combat with greatly superior numbers of the enemy in which he was wounded by a sword.
Cooper For gallant conduct in *being among the first* to enter the Sikanderbagh . . .
Dunlay entered the Sikanderbagh with Captain Burroughs whom he gallantly supported against superior numbers.[23]

It is therefore clear that the official view of the regiment at the time was that Burroughs was first. With so many witnesses to the action, a mistake or a false claim is unlikely to have been allowed to pass. Much of the later confusion stems from the fact that, although recommended for the Victoria Cross, he was not awarded one. Those writing after the event tended to assume that he had not received the V.C. because his story was untrue but, as will be seen, his failure to gain the coveted award had nothing to do with the truth or falsity of his version of the events.

Returning to the story of the storming of the Sikanderbagh, the point has been reached where a number of officers and men were clambering through the 'ugly blind hole' in an order which cannot now be precisely determined. They found themselves in a small, low room opening on to the broad walk which led round the garden. Driven back by a hail of bullets, Burroughs had to wait until about twenty-five men had crawled through the hole. He then led a sortie towards the main gate which was about seventy-five yards away, hoping to force it and so to admit the main body of the troops. The walls and platforms at the side of the gateway were lined with sepoys firing wildly, and the air was thick with smoke. Just short of the gateway Lieutenant Alexander saw the flash of a *tulwar* and Burroughs fell beneath the blow. His life was probably saved by the wire framework of his feather bonnet which was dented like a bishop's mitre by the force of the stroke.

At the same moment the main body of the army succeeded in forcing the gate from the outside and they swept into the Sikanderbagh. The sepoys retreated to the pavilion at the centre of the garden or into the many small rooms which surrounded the outside wall, and a general massacre followed. When the work of extermination was over there were very few of the defenders who had escaped from the garden. As the gory work was in progress, Sir Colin Campbell entered by the shattered gateway. There he found Burroughs lying wounded, bleeding profusely from a deep cut on his ear and face. He paused to speak and, having assured himself that Burroughs was in no danger, he continued into the garden.

About 2 p.m. the 93rd mustered outside the walls. Lieutenant Alexander had not seen Burroughs since he fell and believed that he had been killed, so he assumed command of No.6 Company. With the company on parade, he heard a voice behind him saying, "Thank you, Mr Alexander, you may fall in now.' Burroughs reappeared covered in blood, begrimed with dust and powder and with his feather bonnet bent double. It had not been the intention to use the 93rd again that day, but the enemy were strongly entrenched in the mosque of the Shah Najaf, a few hundred yards farther ahead. The regiment were given the task of clearing out the mud huts between the Sikanderbagh and the Shah Najaf mosque and, this done, they took refuge in the remains of the huts, sustaining a number of casualties from rifle fire penetrating the thatch, a more unnerving experience than meeting rifle fire in the open. As evening approached the firing slackened and the 93rd were moved cautiously forward to where a breach had been discovered in the wall surrounding the mosque. They found that their enemy had departed and the position was abandoned. As darkness fell, No.6 Company searched the mosque itself. They found the dim interior lit with lamps and the walls hung with banners bearing texts from the Koran, but the building was completely deserted. Then they noticed a sinister black trail leading out of the mosque, snaking across the courtyard and out of the back gate — a powder trail — and further search revealed enormous quantities of gunpowder stored in the mosque. Water carriers were brought up to dampen the trail and scatter the powder.

That night No.6 Company were assigned to guard duty at the rear gate of the mosque and their first task was to dig a series of trenches across the line of the powder trail. It was a cold night. A fire was lit at a safe distance and a search of the surrounding buildings produced a calf which was slaughtered and cooked. Burroughs lay down to sleep near the gate, ordering Alexander to waken him when the meal was ready but, when the time came, Alexander was unable to rouse him. Another officer was fetched but their combined efforts still failed. The exertions of the day and loss of blood had brought about total collapse. For Alexander it was an anxious night with little rest. It transpired that the mosque still contained a few sepoys who had been left behind and who now tried to escape under cover of night. The panic caused by these incidents resulted in sentries firing in all directions, risking injury to their own men or even the accidental firing of the powder trail. In the morning, when breakfast was prepared, Burroughs was still asleep. He then woke up 'but not in the best of tempers'.

No.6 Company were not involved in any action that day and the following afternoon they were pulled back to the Sikanderbagh to act as a personal guard to Sir Colin Campbell. They remained there for the next four days. Sir Colin had a bed set up in the open under the walls and he also had his personal bath. He and his staff officers ate in reasonable comfort at a trestle table but for his guard there were no such luxuries. Their three days' rations exhausted, they were reduced to begging scraps from Sir Colin's native servants.

The relief force had been barely strong enough to fight its way into the Residency. It was in no position to hold it permanently and it was planned to remain only long enough to permit its evacuation. This was no easy task since a thousand sick and wounded had to be brought out as well as six hundred women and children, a number of state prisoners, two hundred cannon and about £250,000 of treasure.

Preparatory to the women and children passing through the Sikanderbagh on their way to Dilkusha, Burroughs suggested that a fatigue party set about removing traces of the recent massacre. Carrying out the bodies proved to be a task beyond their powers. Some were heaped into the surrounding rooms out of sight and others were burned in great smouldering heaps. Over the whole place hung a nauseating smell of death and the fatigue party could only keep going with a double rum ration. Some rooms were prepared for the reception of the women and children for whom the men asked Burroughs' permission to save up their evening tea ration. They were disappointed when many of the women rejected the thick black army tea and indignantly asked for milk in it. However, as Alexander noted, the wives and widows of *officers* accepted it with grateful thanks!

After a bombardment to confuse the enemy into expecting an attack, the garrison of the Residency was withdrawn. The force, now numbering over four thousand, was pulled back under cover of darkness through the maze of narrow lanes without the enemy being aware what was afoot. By morning Lucknow had been successfully evacuated.

Although the main object had been accomplished in brilliant fashion, the position of Sir Colin Campbell's small force had become increasingly insecure due to the deterioration of the situation at Cawnpore where the British had again been forced to retreat into the Entrenchment and where the Bridge of Boats across the Ganges was in danger of being captured. Since this was the way out of Oudh for the Lucknow army, speed was necessary if the situation was to be saved. A forced march and a successful engagement with the enemy retrieved the position and then, for the next ten weeks, the 93rd was involved in some rather indecisive campaigning as Sir Colin built up his force in readiness for the final reduction of Lucknow. It was campaigning which took Burroughs to his birthplace at Fatehgarh where he saw the charred remains of his former home on the banks of the Ganges. By early February the British force at Cawnpore had been built up to 31,000. Sir Colin was ready to advance once more on Lucknow although he was still far outnumbered by the rebel army, reputed to be 120,000 strong.

During this second advance on Lucknow, Burroughs' company formed part of the escort to the huge siege train. It was slow, irksome work on crowded dusty roads congested by the advance of this long column. Off duty Burroughs was now living in some comfort, having assembled the large retinue of servants which was considered necessary in a well-ordered Indian household. His servants included the *syce* (groom), the *bhisti* (water-carrier), the *dobhi* (washerman), the *khidmutgar* (table servant), the *mheter* (sweeper), as well as a cook, grass-cutter and a number of bearers. In addition to the horse which he acquired early in the campaign, he had obtained two camels and a camel driver. As the temperature mounted with the onset of the hot season, he employed *punkah-wallahs* (fan operators) from time to time. This not inconsiderable household for an officer who was still only a captain was augmented by the arrival of three loyal sepoys who brought a present of a hill tent from his father in Benares.[24] With households of this size, it was not surprising that the road to Lucknow was congested!

On 26th February Burroughs had a particularly bad day. The heat was now intense and the normal season for campaigning was already past. To give some protection, the 93rd had been issued with 'uglies' — veils suspended from their bonnets which made the Highlanders look like 'a bunch of old women'.[25] It took five hours of heaving and shouting to get the siege train under way and, at the end of a twelve-hour day, Burroughs recorded in his diary that he felt tired and 'knocked up' with the heat. The following day thunder and rain, which seemed unable to lay the dust or moderate the heat, did nothing to raise his low spirits and, to make matters worse, he went down with an attack of 'intermittent fever'.

It was at this point that he received a further blow — the decision about his Victoria Cross. A number of recommendations had been made and Sir Colin Campbell, in the middle of a taxing campaign, had more to do than sort out points of honour among squabbling contestants for honours. He therefore decreed that three crosses were to be awarded to the 93rd, one for officers, one for non-commissioned officers and one for the private soldiers, and that these awards should be decided by the votes of each category. The officers accordingly voted between Burroughs, Colonel Ewart and Captain Stewart of Murthley. Their votes went to Stewart, a popular figure in the regiment, whereas Burroughs was not well-liked.

As Burroughs wrote later, 'The disappointment of those who had been recommended by their commanding officers, but who were not awarded the cross, was very great. They would have been happier had they never been recommended.'[26] On his return to London after having been wounded, he went on crutches to the Horse Guards to complain, feeling particularly aggrieved that Lance-Corporal Dunlay was awarded the V.C. for supporting him while he himself got nothing. The military secretary to the Commander-in-Chief agreed to write to Sir Colin Campbell to clear up the matter. The reply was shattering. Sir Colin remembered seeing Burroughs lying wounded at the gate and he had assumed that Burroughs must have entered along with the main body of the 93rd. He wrote that Burroughs must be under an hallucination to imagine that he had entered by the breach. Burroughs never gave up the struggle to vindicate himself, and when he later returned to India he collected evidence which he sent to Sir William Mansfield, Commander-in-Chief in India. His evidence was left to gather dust. Burroughs was right to be aggrieved for there is ample evidence that he did enter by the breach. But eventually Burroughs' persistence resulted in his becoming a bore and it was commonly believed that he was claiming more than he was entitled to do. In later years this was the belief of many of his tenants in Rousay.

Burroughs was back in action by the time Lucknow fell, recovered both from his intermittent fever and his disappointment. He was one of the last to be wounded in the campaign. As guard commander at the Barra Durri

Gate, he was called on to dislodge some sepoys who were firing from a neighbouring house. Although he observed that there was a good deal of gunpowder about the place, he ascended an outside staircase and gained the roof of the building. At the same time a party from the 97th had also been detailed to attack the enemy position and were at that moment preparing to blow it up, unaware that Burroughs was on the roof. An instant before the explosion, he observed the puff of smoke and realised what was going to happen. He made for the stair but it was too late. He was buried in the debris of the building and sustained comminuted compound fractures of both bones below the knee in his right leg.

Medical opinion was that amputation was necessary to save his life and that the operation should not be delayed. Dr Munro, however, refused to operate until the patient had recovered consciousness and could give his consent. The position was then explained to Burroughs — the dangers of an amputation which in a field hospital often proved fatal and the equally dangerous alternative of trying to save the leg. Burroughs decided to put his trust in Munro's ability as a surgeon and the limb was accordingly set under chloroform.[27]

Conditions in the field hospital were unpleasant in the extreme because of the high temperatures. The surgeon had ordered the tents to be pitched under the shade of trees and the ground was kept saturated with water. Coolies were constantly employed in fanning the wounded, yet the discomfort from heat and dust was hard to bear.[28] He was soon separated from his regiment but a move into a house overlooking the river brought an improvement and his household servants did their best to console him. 'They ought to be glad I cannot kick now,' he recorded in his diary.

Six weeks after his accident his leg was removed from its gutta percha splint and pronounced straight. Two weeks later he was able to make his first attempts with crutches and appeared before the Medical Board. The function of the Board was to grant sick leave but no provision was made for transport home. Some of Burroughs' fellow officers had trouble in making their way back through hostile country to Calcutta. Burroughs was luckier, for the Mutiny was now largely over. He was able to travel without too much difficulty, first by litter and then by river steamer to Benares where his father was stationed. He stayed there for eight weeks until he was more mobile and then went on to Calcutta, sailing for home in early October. The following summer, while still on sick leave, he paid a visit to his Rousay estate and received the Freedom of the Burgh of Kirkwall.

On his return to India, the regiment was posted to Peshawar, commanding the entrance to the Khyber Pass. As a contrast to the horrors of Lucknow, this was Indian army life at its best. The climate was delightful, there was a good hunt (jackals, unfortunately, instead of foxes), and life on the station was enlivened by dances, theatricals and parties. Yet Peshawar had a sinister reputation as an unhealthy place and so it proved to be when the regiment was attacked by cholera. Within the course of a week the two officers senior to Burroughs both died and Burroughs found himself in command. The hospital was disinfected and whitewashed but without results. The entire battalion was then moved into tents on the parade ground but still the cholera persisted. In desperation the station was abandoned and the regiment was kept moving in easy stages in search of better health. It was only when they had crossed the Indus that the cholera suddenly left them, but by then ninety-three officers, men and dependents were dead.[29] Burroughs had taken command for the first time in very difficult circumstances and acquitted himself well. The official report on the state of the regiment confirmed that:—

> Notwithstanding the adverse circumstances of the cholera and fever the drill and discipline of the 93rd Highlanders did not suffer in any way, a situation which reflects the greatest credit on Major Burroughs.[30]

In his final years in India he made a return visit to Lucknow when on leave. His two previous visits had seen him in the thick of the action and his return as a tourist saw him involved again. He made some sketches of the scenes of his former triumph (see Fig. 8) and, wishing to obtain a better view of the city, he entered a mosque and climbed up to one of the minarets. The former conqueror of Lucknow paid no attention to a notice at the bottom of the stair prohibiting entry. The *darogah* expostulated with Burroughs in tones which Burroughs considered offensive and, when he refused to withdraw, the *darogah* struck him with a stick. Burroughs was set on by a crowd of thirty or forty men and he received a severe beating before he was able to escape. For his part in the incident, the *darogah* received a one-month gaol sentence.[31]

In 1864 Burroughs was promoted to lieutenant-colonel and he commanded the regiment in hard campaigning on the North-West Frontier. In 1870, after thirteen eventful years in India, the 93rd returned to Britain, landing at Leith in a snowstorm. They crossed the Forth by ferry and made their way by train to Aberdeen where the welcoming crowds were fascinated by their leopard, tiger, monkeys and Indian birds. The regiment's little colonel provided an almost equal attraction.[32]

Thereafter he was, for a while, in command at Edinburgh Castle, but in his last three years he was able to spend a good deal of time away from his regiment and on his Rousay estate. In 1873 the 93rd sailed for Portsmouth aboard the *Himalaya,* the same ship which had taken Burroughs to the Crimea twenty years earlier, and it was from Aldershot that he finally retired. He had spent twenty-five years with the 93rd, the last nine in

Fig. 8. Two drawings of the Sikanderbagh made by Burroughs when he visited Lucknow in 1868. By that date the Sikanderbagh had been partly demolished but the drawings are a re-construction of its former state. The lower drawing shows the breach (directly under the palm tree) and the main gate beyond. The upper drawing from inside the garden shows the gateway with the bastion where Burroughs entered on the extreme left.

command, and he was given a great send off. Every person in the lines turned out and, no sooner had he taken his seat in the carriage that was to take him to the railway station than the horses were unyoked and the carriage was pulled by a number of the soldiers preceded by the regimental band playing 'Will ye no' come back again'. On reaching Farnham Road the horses were re-yoked and the band played 'Auld Lang Syne'. The men lining the road or perched in the branches of trees gave three hearty cheers as their colonel drove slowly away.[33]

That a special affection did exist is borne out by the many tributes paid to him by old soldiers when he was under attack for his crofting policies. The relationship was a complicated one, for Burroughs was not one of those officers for whom the men felt an immediate warmth. They disliked his French mannerisms, his fussy ways and his tendency to go by the book. They suffered too from his unpredictable temper. Dr Munro felt he drove the men too hard on the parade ground[34] and the general report on the regiment in his later years commented unfavourably on the large number of court martials.[35]

Yet his men found much to admire, particularly his undoubted courage. He had served through the great days of the 93rd. Events like the Thin Red Line and the Relief of Lucknow became legend, and Burroughs was part of that legend. They admired too his acts of personal kindness. When faced with what he saw as a threat to his authority, he was liable to explode violently and then to develop a special relationship with the culprit after the man had submitted to proper discipline. There was, for example, Patrick Doolan who had made Burroughs a laughing-stock before his French officer friends in the Crimea by saddling his pony the wrong way round. 'Sure, sir, you never told me whether you were to ride to Balaclava or to the front,' expostulated the bold Doolan. Later Burroughs made Doolan his personal servant and they remained together until Burroughs was invalided home from Lucknow. Another was Donald MacLean, a six feet three inch Highlander who objected when Burroughs made him kneel on the parade ground so that he could inspect his ears and who had called Burroughs a 'monkey'. After MacLean was killed at Lucknow, Burroughs remitted a small pension to his widowed mother for as long as she lived.[36] Yet another was Peter MacKay who had rescued Burroughs when he lay wounded in the rubble of the house at Lucknow and carried him to the surgeon. Burroughs assisted him when he was dying in a Belfast workhouse.[37]

What had appeared as unbearable behaviour in a young officer became splendid eccentricity as he became older. He was a great character, the subject of a fund of good stories. When he retired to his Rousay estate, a collision with his tenantry was perhaps inevitable. The autocratic military discipline which had ruled the 93rd, that tough body of men noted for drunkenness, courage and Free Kirk piety, was not suited to dealing with Orkney farmers. The management of a crofting estate required altogether more diplomatic methods.

7

Rousay Society in the Years of Prosperity, 1870-1883

'The colonel is quite at home, seeking relief from the adventures of a glorious life . . . as he guides the helm of his unique estate, and appears as a burning and shining light amid the traits of Scandinavian character so clearly recognisable in the manners and habits of the Orcadian.'   'A Scribbling Pedestrian in Rousay'[1]

ON leaving the army Burroughs looked forward to his new life in Rousay. His annual routine included a stay in either Edinburgh or London for part of the winter and a trip abroad in summer, perhaps to Switzerland or South Germany where he and his wife would reside in a fashionable hotel catering for an English military and aristocratic clientèle. The greater part of the year, however, was spent in Rousay where he enjoyed the shooting and fishing and involved himself in the running of his estate, fussing with details and ordering the lives of his tenants. It was a style of life more in keeping with a Highland laird or even an English squire than the type of proprietor Orkney was used to, but in happier times his tenants might have become accustomed to his habit of running the estate as if it were a regiment. He was autocratic in his ways but, although his style was different, he was no more domineering than many Orkney lairds before him and, indeed, no worse than several of his contemporaries. In the course of time the autocratic laird might have come to be regarded with the same affection and loyalty as the autocratic officer had been regarded by the men of the 93rd. Such affection was important to Burroughs. It was part of the prescribed background to the 'Highland' way of life he was trying to create in Rousay.

For the thirteen years up to 1883 life in Rousay was, at least superficially, something like that ideal. Burroughs was genuinely trying to provide a lead and to work for the betterment of the community. As long as agricultural prosperity lasted, relations between the laird and his tenants were generally good. On an individual level his tenants found him approachable and often more amenable than his factor. For example, strict estate regulations bound the tenant to a specified crop rotation but Burroughs would sometimes allow the tenant to vary his cropping when the reason for the change had been explained to him. He was also well liked by his household servants and even embarrassed the well-trained servant with his courtesy. At that time it was not considered proper for the master to recognise a servant girl should he meet her in the street but Burroughs, with the officer's habit of returning the salute of the other ranks, would always doff his hat. The girls at market time avoided embarrassment by dodging into Kirkwall lanes when they saw the General approaching.[2]

Of the more formal occasions, there was hardly a social function in which Burroughs was not involved in some capacity, organising, acting as chairman, making speeches or proposing votes of thanks. The typical island gathering ended with three cheers for General Burroughs. He had arrived in Rousay at a crucial time in the development of community life when traditional folk culture was rapidly being replaced by a more modern social life. In earlier times leisure activities had centred on the hearth with songs and stories accompanying the indoor tasks of spinning and straw plaiting. It was a culture in which much that was old had been lost with the final disappearance of the Norn language, yet there was lively social contact and occasions like the midwinter festivities provided opportunities for enjoyment. Alexander Marwick, a Rousay farmer, left a description of how Christmas was celebrated in his young days, early in the nineteenth century:—

> In the first of my minding, the Christmas was kept as follows; every house that grew crop brewed some ale for Christmas. On Christmas eve every house killed a sheep but they neither had white bread or tea; their bread was oat cakes and sowan scones. When they got cod in the Christmas week they baked a cake of bere meal and cod livers which was as good and as well liked as any shortbread of the present day. The young men then played football till dark, then went to a fiddler's house and danced until 12 o'clock at night. The Christmas day well spent, on New Year's eve a number of young men went from house to house singing the New Year songs where the door was quickly opened and the singers sat down to the best that was in the house. It was looked upon as a token of respect to those they visited but ill-loved neighbours were generally passed over.
>
> . . . In these days superstitions prevailed among the people to a great extent. But when home brewed ale was less used, the superstitions died away.[3]

It was a social life with few organised events apart from those connected with the church — weddings, funerals, the Sunday services and the high points of communion.

Coinciding with Burroughs' return, a more varied, more formalised and a more secular social life quickly developed. To a large extent this change was the result of the General's involvement and personal initiatives. Certainly the outside world impinged on Rousay to a greater degree than ever before; improved communications increased mobility; newspapers, the letter post and mass literacy made Rousay society open to new influences. Agricultural improvement involved the acceptance of modern farming practice as superior to traditional methods. It brought with it the wider assumption that ideas from outside were progressive and desirable in contrast to the traditional lifestyle which came to be regarded as outmoded and inferior. As surely as agricultural progress swept away the run-rig landscape, it abolished much of the traditional culture which, in a desire to be considered up-to-date, the farmer and his family were liable to dismiss as so much old-fashioned and superstitious nonsense. This view was reinforced by schools whose aim was to bring the island into the mainstream of a national culture. Transient schoolmasters, few of them Orcadian, suppressed dialect and had little sympathy with the old ways.

The very presence of Burroughs, a new type of laird, was the result of these improved communications. In earlier times it had been impossible to lead a fashionable life in Orkney when it could be reached only after a highly uncomfortable voyage of uncertain duration aboard a smack from the Forth or by means of a long and difficult journey through the Highlands. This was changed by the inauguration of the steamship service from Granton and by the building of the railway to Thurso. Orkney now had that degree of remoteness which lent a certain romantic charm, no longer the complete isolation which made contact with polite society impossible.

Although change may basically have been due to improved communications and the concomitant belief in the superiority of outside culture, Burroughs was at the very centre of these developments and in a position to influence every facet. Change was due to better communications — Burroughs was instrumental in obtaining an island steamship service, he built roads and campaigned for a regular postal delivery; agricultural progress brought new values — the laird controlled the land and invested in dykes, drains and farm steadings; increased literacy broadened horizons — the General was Chairman of the School Board and influenced the curriculum of the schools. External forces to a very large extent acted through the laird. Until his quarrel with the crofters in 1883, his tenants deferred to his opinions and accepted his judgments. The pace of social change in Rousay can be seen from the following list of events between 1870 and 1892:—

1870   Founding of the Young Men's Mutual Improvement Society.
1871   Building of Trumland pier.
1873   Founding of the School Board.
1874   First ploughing match.
       First Agricultural Show.
       Founding of Rousay and Viera Agricultural Society.
       First annual picnic of school children to Westness House.

Formation of Rousay Artillery Volunteer Corps.
Repairs to Established Church.

1875   Establishment of a public market.
New harmonium for the Established Church.
First daily arrival of mail.

1876   First daily delivery of mail.
Opening of money order office.
Opening of the new school in Sourin.
Opening of the new school in Egilsay.

1877   First award of prize for the best kept cottage.
Opening of the new school on Wyre.

1878   First annual Volunteer Ball.

1879   First steamship service, the *Lizzie Burroughs*.

1881   Opening of new school in Wasbister.

1882   First donation of annual sewing prizes to schools.

1883   Formation of Rousay and Viera Boat Club and first regatta.

1885   Opening of Wyre Post Office.

1887   Formation of Rousay branch of Scottish Girls' Friendly Society.
Burroughs' Orkney Roads Bill.

1891   Formation of the Medical Association.

1892   First resident doctor.

The one society which was already in existence when Burroughs returned to Rousay was the Young Men's Mutual Improvement Society, founded in 1870. It was a literary society whose members read essays to each other and conducted occasional debates. At one of their earliest meetings a member presented a paper on 'The Ten Virgans' (*sic*) and another read an essay on 'The Pleasures of Home', a programme which was fairly typical of the society's activities and which reveals a lack of sophistication and indeed an innocence which would be impossible in a later age used to more immediate entertainment. Debating societies have sometimes developed into a forum of public opinion, a kind of local parliament, but the Rousay society remained pretentiously literary. On only one occasion, and that in 1892 when the struggle was largely over, did they debate anything connected with the crofting question. Then, Frederick Burroughs Kirkness who, despite having been named after the laird, was being pursued for arrears of rent with a view to having him evicted, moved the affirmative to the question 'Should Parliament interfere between Landlord and Tenant?' It was a lively debate with crofters and farmers aligning themselves on opposite sides and the crofters eventually carrying the day. The society might have been more interesting if it had held more debates of this kind.[4]

G

Burroughs was keen to promote agricultural improvement and in February 1874 he organised Rousay's first ploughing match which took place in Skaill Park, Westness. It attracted twenty-one competitors and a large crowd of spectators who amused themselves by kicking around a football which Burroughs had provided and which was afterwards given to the scholars of the Wasbister school. In August of the same year the island's first agricultural show was held on the hillside above Trumland but was less of a success due to a gale accompanied by torrential rain which swept the show park. Nevertheless satisfaction was expressed at the standards of the entries and these events were put on a regular footing by the formation of the Rousay and Viera Agricultural Society.[5] The society's prizes tended to go almost entirely to a few big farms, but no doubt the example was beneficial and the events socially enjoyable.

Another of Burroughs' interests was inevitably the Artillery Volunteers. When he retired from the army there were Volunteer companies in most parts of Orkney with a total strength of nearly seven hundred men, but there was no company in Rousay. In 1874 he replaced Colonel Balfour in overall command of the Orkney Volunteers[6] and soon obtained permission to raise a corps in Rousay.[7] It was to have a maximum strength of eighty but, despite Burroughs' many efforts to persuade young men of the advantage of a few years in the Volunteers to teach them discipline, this figure was never reached. The Volunteers usually had a complement of between fifty and sixty including a regular soldier as a full-time sergeant. The Company had their battery at the Point of Avelshay, commanding Wyre and Rousay Sounds, and they mustered there for their first big gun practice in August 1875 when *The Orcadian* reported a very high standard of shooting.[8] However, in inter-company competitions Rousay did less well, the trophy regularly going to the Shapinsay company, which gave Colonel Balfour quiet satisfaction after having yielded overall command to Burroughs' seniority. Within Rousay there were also competitions between the Sourin and Wasbister batteries.

From 1878 Volunteer balls became a regular feature of the social scene. The first ball was held in Trumland House but thereafter it took place in the Sourin school. The volunteers had their own trumpeter who provided martial music and, when the guests departed there were usually a number who 'were on good terms with themselves' although, as the local paper was careful to emphasise, 'none were intoxicated'.[9] In other parts of Orkney the Volunteers sometimes ran into difficulties because of drink and the frivolous nature of the comic turns at their dances. The Free Church minister of Birsay, for example, threatened to obtain an interdict against the Volunteers using their own drill hall, but in Rousay there was no such opposition. Rousay was a temperate society and the General was a stern opponent of any kind of drunkenness. Later the drinking habits of the Free Church minister himself made it difficult for any of his congregation to criticise the Volunteers.

Another annual event was the picnic for the schoolchildren. In early years the picnic was held at Westness House and later picnics took place at Trumland, but they all followed the pattern set in 1874 when upwards of two hundred children assembled, accompanied by their teachers and three ministers. Tables had been arranged all round the croquet lawn, the children sang songs and then food was served by Colonel and Mrs Burroughs and their relatives, Captain and Miss Lillie, who were guests at Westness. After the meal the ladies took the younger children away to run races while Burroughs and Captain Lillie initiated the older boys into the mysteries of rounders, which was a new game to them. The picnic ended with the appearance of a masked man — in other years a ghoul or a negro — and after a glorious romp there was a well-filled bag of left-overs for each child to take home. *The Orkney Herald* commented:—

> Substantial manifestations — like this and others — of their interest and affection for the young on their estate cannot but win for our proprietor and his amiable lady the greatest love and respect from all their tenantry, and they may rest assured that there is no youthful heart on their property but beats with pleasure at the thought of having spent a happy day, and with gratitude to the providers of such an enjoyable treat.[10]

For the adults there were similar occasions. The return of the laird after an absence, a harvest home or a further step in his promotion — for after he retired on half-pay he was promoted to Major-General in 1880 and Lieutenant-General in 1881 — provided occasions for reciprocal celebrations. The tenants would entertain the laird and he would return the compliment. After a meal there would be innumerable toasts, to the Queen, to General and Mrs Burroughs, to the factor, to each of the churches in turn and to each of the schools and so on. Often one of the schoolmasters was expected to provide the humour or compose suitable verses to mark the occasion. Then Burroughs would invariably address the tenants as if he were chairman giving his annual report to a meeting of shareholders. His speeches were frequent but seldom varied. The theme he returned to again and again was the prosperity of Rousay farming and the great strides which had been made in recent years. While this was true, his underlying purpose was to justify his high rents and to answer the complaint that farmers were having increasing difficulty in meeting these payments.

His wife joined him in promoting the good of the community. Eliza (Lizzie) D'Oyley Geddes came from the same Indian army background as her husband. Her father, Colonel William Geddes of the Bengal Horse

Artillery, had served with George William Traill in the 1815 Nepalese campaign and had married into the D'Oyley family, influential and artistic leaders of Calcutta society. Lizzie's sister was married to Colonel William Dunbar who had served along with Burroughs in the Crimea and at the Relief of Lucknow. Colonel Dunbar was a Gentleman-at-Arms and this gave the Burroughs an entry into Court circles. Mrs Burroughs found the eighteenth century mansion house of Westness too old-fashioned and cramped. She persuaded her husband to build Trumland House, an imposing mansion in the Scotch baronial pepperpot tradition. She and her husband had many common interests and, although they argued furiously, the marriage was a happy one.

Mrs Burroughs played the new harmonium in the Established Church and started a circulating library[11] but her main interest was in the condition of the tenants' houses. She was keen to see them establish flower gardens in front of their cottages and offered to provide roots and cuttings from her own garden, but she did not meet with much response. Bellona Cottage, the home of the regular sergeant of the Volunteers, was always held up as an example of what might be achieved but, despite her efforts, the typical Rousay croft was more likely to look out on a midden than on a flower garden. At Mrs Burroughs' instigation a clause was included in the new estate regulations of 1876 that all buildings were to be whitewashed every three years, and supplies of lime for this purpose were supplied free of charge to the smaller tenants. From 1877 she offered a prize for the best-kept cottage 'within fifty yards of the public road'[12] — she evidently did not intend to inspect some of the more out of the way places. Prizes usually went to cottages in the Frotoft and Trumland areas, those parts of Rousay most under her influence and containing a large number of estate servants.

Another of her interests was the Scottish Girls' Friendly Society of which she was county president. It was a society for servant girls and its activities were an amalgam of religion, good advice and entertainment. Illuminated cards were presented to those girls who remained in the same situation for three years. The Rousay branch had a membership of about thirty servant girls and held its first meeting in the billiard room at Trumland House where Mrs Burroughs addressed them on the theme 'Woman, the Help-Mate of Man'. A musical evening followed her talk.[13]

She was also a competent artist, a trait inherited from her D'Oyley grandparents. A number of her water-colours of the Rousay landscape still hang in Trumland House, and she gave lessons and encouragement to any young servant who showed signs of artistic ability.

When George William Traill acquired property in Rousay there were no roads on the island[14] but, following the division of the run-rig lands of

Wasbister in 1842 and as part of the improvements, a road was constructed through Wasbister and Quandale.[15] As has often been the case in the Highlands and Islands, the improved communications came just in time to aid the removal of the population. The cost of the road was shared between Traill and the Earl of Zetland, but since it was constructed by statute labour, Traill's share amounted to only £4:13s:8½d. For next to nothing he had acquired a road linking the various parts of his estate. In 1846 there was again some considerable road-building activity. William Ross was paid £3:9s:8d for constructing two arched bridges and James Inkster was employed supervising the work of the tenants on 169 days.

From 1855 onwards there was regular expenditure on the roads and the work of constructing a road round the island began. It was financed by a 'voluntary' assessment on the tenant of one shilling per £1 rent and, since Burroughs was by this time virtually sole proprietor, having bought the Earl of Zetland's Rousay property, it was a levy he could collect without difficulty as an addition to the rent. The assessment was payable either in money or by the tenant's labour vouched for by a certificate from George Learmonth, the manager of Westness Farm, who acted as overseer of road works. Road building was undertaken by the estate, the assessment treated as estate income and the cost as estate expenditure. There was no separate account for road works nor was an attempt made to strike a balance between receipts and payments.

The method of financing the roads caused a good deal of discontent. It was said to be based on a vague agreement in George William Traill's time that the tenants would pay for the roads and the proprietor would bear the entire cost of poor relief. Nevertheless, as Burroughs later pointed out to the Napier Commission,[16] he had actually spent more on roads than he had levied either in money or labour through the assessment. Tenants were, however, suspicious of a system whereby they paid an assessment yet no accounts were ever made public. The estate had a good bargain, having built and maintained a road system for a net expenditure of £167 spread over twenty-six years.

Although island roads built by statute labour could be constructed cheaply, roads on the Orkney Mainland were much more expensive. Acts of Parliament in 1857 and 1867[17] had authorised the construction of certain roads and given the Road Trustees powers to acquire land and borrow money, but had expressly stated that islands were to be separate for road debt purposes. The Mainland debt could not be passed on to the islands. A further Act went through Parliament in 1878. In its original form it would not have applied to Rousay but, as it went through the Lords, it was amended to include island roads built by statute labour. The new Act had the effect of distributing the Mainland road debt, which now amounted to

£30,000, over the whole county. Rousay had been ahead of other areas in
road building and they now found that, having built and paid for their own
roads, they had to bear the cost of Mainland roads. Other islands more
backward in road building, like North Ronaldsay, discovered that they
now had a road debt but no roads. Burroughs calculated that the Rousay
share of the debt might amount to £125 per annum for the next fifty years.

He therefore combined with the proprietors of Eday, North Ronaldsay
and Papa Westray to promote a parliamentary bill to have this decision
reversed and to make each island responsible for its own road debt.
Opposition to his bill came mainly from Stromness, where the people were
already facing a steep increase as the result of the 1878 Act. It was in their
interest to see the burden of debt spread as widely as possible.

Burroughs' bill was first considered by the County Road Board.
Burroughs was chairman and he ruled that, since his bill dealt with the
allocation of debt, he was not going to allow elected trustees to vote. There
were strong, angry protests, particularly from Sheriff Mellis who was
amazed by this ruling, but despite the Sheriff's legal opinion, Burroughs
insisted on his interpretation. The Road Trustees, less the elected
members, then voted by 4 votes to 3 to support the bill.[18] For a measure of
this kind it was important to win local backing and thereby the probable
support of the Member of Parliament. However, a meeting of the
Commissioners of Supply was hurriedly called and by 9 votes to 7 they
decided to oppose Burroughs' bill.

So the bill went to parliament without local support and it was opposed
by Lyell, the M.P. for the county. When the bill came before the Commons
it failed by a single vote. One might have thought that this defeat would
have been the end of the matter but, encouraged by the narrowness of the
margin, Burroughs announced his intention of reintroducing his bill as
soon as possible. In February 1887 'the hospitable proprietor of Rousay
and Viera', as the *Court Journal* described him,[19] moved to London to
supervise arrangements, his hospitality aimed at winning friends for his
bill and easing its passage. It was once again opposed by the local Member
but passed its first reading by 219 votes to 139 — a vote which was not on
party lines and which was a surprisingly large one for this kind of issue.[20]
Thereafter the progress of the bill was easy. It was unopposed in its later
stages and received the royal assent in May.[21]

This legislation was estimated to have cost Burroughs £1200. Although
it had been initiated in conjunction with other landowners and indeed all of
the North Isles of Orkney benefited, he was left to bear the entire cost.[22]
When Burroughs felt that he was in the right, the principle at stake was
more important than profit. The same attitude was later to be found in his
quarrel with his crofters. In that dispute as well, other North Isles lairds

were quite content to let Burroughs fight the battles but were ready to reap the rewards of any victories he might win.

Another of Burroughs' ventures was the founding of the Rousay, Evie and Rendall Steam Navigation Company which first brought a steamship service to the islands of Rousay, Egilsay and Wyre. For thirteen years the company and its little steamer, the *Lizzie Burroughs*, struggled in the face of constant financial difficulties, mechanical trouble, shipwreck and the suspicion of many of the islanders. Like everything else in which he was involved, the steamer was controversial.

One of the first of his improvements when he came back from India was the building of the pier at Trumland, completed in 1871 at a cost of £573. Island piers are seldom built without controversy, and Trumland was no exception. Burroughs claimed that he built it at his own expense although he never charged pier dues, but his opponents claimed that he had used the road rate. There were also complaints about the location of the pier for, although it is a focus of the present-day community, this was not the case in 1871 when Trumland was still a fairly sparsely inhabited part of the island. It was said that Burroughs had sited the pier there only because it was convenient to the new mansion house he was proposing to build and would facilitate the bringing ashore of building materials.

Steam navigation had come to the North Isles of Orkney in 1865 when the *Orcadia* started operating, but she did not include Rousay in her itinerary. For a further fourteen years Rousay continued to rely on the uncertain service provided by two sailing packets.[23] The formation of a new company was discussed as early as 1876, but considerable doubt was cast on the economics of the venture since the two packets grossed receipts of only £400 per annum and it was calculated that the new steamer would have running costs of ten guineas a week or £546 per annum. It would be difficult to survive and indeed this would only be possible by capturing the entire existing trade, reducing costs to the absolute minimum and somehow increasing the volume of traffic. One solution might be to extend the service to Westray, which would bring more trade, but the crossing of the open water of the Westray Firth would need a bigger and more expensive vessel and the longer run would also result in a less frequent service to Rousay.

In 1877 it was decided to go ahead on the basis of a service terminating in Rousay. House-to-house visits were made by the factor, by now George Murrison, for the purpose of persuading farmers to take shares in the company. The collection met with some success and a number of Kirkwall people also invested in the venture,[24] but the factor's efforts had made a bad impression. With the recent financing of the roads in mind, many people were wary of taking on a new burden. They felt that someone as wealthy as Burroughs should be financing his own schemes, not cadging money from his poor tenants.

However, by December 1877 fund raising had been sufficiently successful for the new company to take the decision to purchase a steamer[25] which was to be specially built by Messrs MacKenzie at the Albert Dock in Leith.[26] She was 61 feet overall, with a beam of 15 ft 4 ins and a gross tonnage of 31 tons. On her trials it was reported that she made good speed with her 15 h.p. engine, but once in service she was notoriously slow.

After her trials on the Forth, she sailed north and was very nearly lost in a stormy crossing of the Moray Firth. She had been expected in Kirkwall on Saturday evening and, when she failed to arrive, there were fears for her safety, but she turned up the following morning and continued on her way to Rousay. On Monday she made a trial run to Kirkwall without passengers and was critically inspected by the public. The general verdict was that she was 'a handsome looking little craft' but there were doubts as to whether she would pay, considering the large sums of money the directors had laid out and the lack of piers or cargo-handling facilities at her various ports of call.

That afternoon, when she returned to Rousay, disaster was only narrowly averted. When she anchored off Trumland, water was discovered in her engine room and, despite constant pumping, the level continued to rise. By the time the captain decided that the vessel must be beached, the water had extinguished the fire. Without power, her anchor was raised only after a struggle and the stay sail set. With only minutes to spare she was run ashore near the pier. There was understandable relief that the trouble had not occurred two days earlier during the storm in the Moray Firth.[27]

The leak was traced to a faulty valve and the damage was easily put right. On Friday of the same week (11th April 1879) the *Lizzie Burroughs* made her first regular run to Kirkwall.[28] As well as calling at three points in Rousay, she also served the islands of Egilsay, Wyre and Gairsay and called at four points on the Mainland — Aikerness, Evie, Tingwall and Rendall. From time to time various alterations were made to her timetable in a constant quest for the most profitable route. In 1882 her schedule was as follows:—

Monday — Sourin 7.30 a.m., Egilsay 7.45, Trumland 8.00, Wyre 8.15, Hullion 8.45, Evie 9.00, Tingwall 9.40, Gairsay 10.00, Rendall Point 10.20 and then on to Kirkwall.

On Tuesdays she returned via the same ports of call, but on Wednesdays, Thursdays and Saturdays she made a round trip from Rousay, cutting out some of the stops. In the interests of economy, the service was later reduced to three days per week.[29]

In August 1879, at the first annual general meeting after the inauguration of the service, there was satisfaction with the progress made and Burroughs was reappointed chairman with George Murrison, his factor, as unpaid secretary. It was, however, decided to raise the fares to 9d steerage and 1/6 for a cabin ticket and to dispense with insurance, an economy measure which would save the company £80.[30] The following year the debt, far from being reduced, had increased to £430 and there was a motion that the vessel should be sold and the company wound up. However, this move was heavily defeated and there was optimism that, now the sailing packets had withdrawn from the run, there were better times ahead. It was decided to economise on running costs still further by reducing the crew and putting them on a profit-sharing basis instead of a regular wage. This arrangement was not acceptable to the existing crew who were consequently paid off and new men engaged[31].

The steamer was out of action for six weeks in 1883 for repairs[32] and suffered further damage in 1884 when she broke loose from her moorings and was driven ashore on Egilsay and badly holed. Her captain collected a large number of casks in an attempt to float her off but she was stuck fast and remained there for a fortnight until Burroughs succeeded in towing her off with his steam yacht, the *Curlew*. Six weeks later she was patched up sufficiently for the *Orcadia* to tow her to Stromness for repairs.[33]

The repairs cost £100 and put the service into serious financial difficulties once again. Another house-to-house collection was made by the factor but he was not very favourably received. As *The Scotsman* commented, the *Lizzie Burroughs* had certainly made enemies, 'why we cannot make out'.[34] The reason was not far to seek. By 1884 the community was polarised by the Crofting Question and there were large sections of the population ready to believe the worst of their landlord. There had always been the feeling that, since he controlled the company, he ought to put up all the money himself. There was widespread misunderstanding of the financial state of the company and even a belief that Burroughs was making a personal profit. In letters which his tenants wrote to the newspapers, the gross receipts of £500 per annum were mistaken for profit.[35]

In reality there was no money to be made from the company and the expenses were never-ending. In 1887 the company had to pay £138 for a new boiler[36] and in 1890 the Board of Trade inspector ordered extensive repairs which required the vessel to go to Hall, Russell and Co in Aberdeen at a cost of a further £116.[37] Then Burroughs decided to dispense with the services of a full-time factor and George Murrison, who had acted as unpaid manager since the company's inception, left to take a farm in Aberdeenshire. Burroughs insisted that Murrison receive an honorarium of £52:10s for his services over the years and, although other directors protested that the company was again in debt by over £300, the honorarium was paid.[38]

The company lasted only another two years during which it was managed from Kirkwall by William Cooper, then in April 1892 the decision was taken to cease trading and put the company's affairs in the hands of a liquidator. The *Lizzie Burroughs* was advertised for sale with an upset price of £250 but, after brisk bidding, she was sold to Robert Garden for £484 which enabled the company to pay 13/2 in the £1. It was a condition of the sale that she should be renamed within three months, and as the *Aberdeen* she remained on the Rousay run for a short time until finally driven off by competition from the Orkney Steam Navigation's *Fawn*.[39] In later years she was used to stock Garden's shops in remote communities in the north and west of Sutherland. In her last years her engine was removed and she was converted into a sailing smack.

One reason for the *Lizzie Burroughs'* lack of success was her failure to gain the mail contract. Mail continued to be brought across Eynhallow Sound in a small open boat which also carried a few passengers. It was a difficult and dangerous crossing through the tide rips, and in October 1893 the mail boat was lost in a south-westerly gale. She had taken aboard a Stenness mother with three young children and had just left the Mainland shore when she was struck by a squall. Another boat in the vicinity saw the passengers and boatmen clinging briefly to the upturned hull but could do nothing to help. Several days later the mail boat was washed ashore on Papa Stronsay.[40]

The mail boat had begun its daily crossing in 1875 but as yet there was no delivery of mail, and letters sometimes lay for months in the Hullion Post Office before they were collected. Burroughs organised a petition for a mail delivery which was signed by all householders. The request was successful and in May 1876 James Craigie, 'an active and obliging young man', began delivering letters on three days in the week.[41] At the same time the Hullion Post Office began handling money orders, a service which had long been desirable. By the 1870s even small farmers were thoroughly involved in a money economy, with cash receipts from cattle sales and with bills to pay. Handling coin could be inconvenient, as Thomas Reid, Clerk to the School Board discovered. He was travelling to Kirkwall to bank £83 of the Board's funds when he accidentally let slip the money bag which fell overboard from the *Lizzie Burroughs* into deep water at Trumland pier. Continuing his journey into Kirkwall, he obtained the services of a diver and later in the day the money was recovered, confounding the pierhead experts who had predicted that it would be swept away by the strong tides.[42]

One of the last organisations which Burroughs sponsored was the Rousay and Viera Boat Club, founded in 1883, which held its first regatta that year. It attracted entries from Kirkwall, and the yachts raced round Wyre. Burroughs, aboard the *Curlew*, was commodore and George Learmonth of Westness Farm was club secretary. Prizes were presented by Edith Dunbar, a niece of Mrs Burroughs.[43]

By the 1880s the pace of social development was less rapid than it had been in the years following Burroughs' return to the island. The passing of the Crofters Act curtailed Burroughs' activities. Not only was he less inclined to become involved but the Act, in the same way as it broke the laird's economic dominance, also challenged his assumption of leadership in the social sphere. Later developments were often initiated by other people. It was, for example, the Rev A. I. Pirie who was instrumental in securing the services of a resident doctor. In 1891 he organised a Medical Association with a membership fee of 2/6 per six months with half prices for children. Membership entitled patients to the doctor's services at a reduced rate. The following year the Association was able to secure the services of Dr. W. G. Inkster, the son of a Rousay man who had emigrated to Canada. The doctor was the first local man ever to return to the island in a professional capacity.[44]

In reviewing the social activities of nineteenth century Rousay, one cannot but be impressed by how much was happening, and yet this was only a small part of the life of the community. In a close-knit island society, informal contacts continued to be more important than organised events. One also inevitably contrasts the social life which was possible when the population was near its maximum with the level of activity possible at the present day with greatly reduced numbers.

8

Rack-Renting[1]

'The rent increases after each seven years separated those tenants who wanted to advance from those who were content to stand still.'   F. W. Traill-Burroughs[2]

FOR the first dozen years of Burroughs' residence on his estate and until his quarrel with the crofters in 1883, Rousay appeared to the casual observer to be a community where rapid improvement was leading to a prosperity, a standard of living and a way of life unknown to earlier generations. It was easy to be misled by this superficial impression into believing that all was well between landlord and tenant. Bitter memories of clearances and resentment caused by the high and ever increasing level of the rents were not so obvious. With some justification the smaller farmers felt that recurring rent rises swallowed up all the fruits of their efforts.

In 1840 the rental of the estate, then confined to Frotoft, part of Wasbister and the island of Wyre, amounted to a mere £286 and, of that, 30% was delivered in traditional payments in kind. That year, as well as money rent, George William Traill received —

35 poultry at 6d	17	6
31 geese at 1/6	2 6	6
86 $^{10}/_{16}$ bolls raw bere (converted from former malt rent) of 280 lbs Impl. per boll at 12/-	51 19	6
19 $^{12}/_{16}$ Bolls Oat Meal of 140 lbs Impl. per boll at 12/-	11 17	0
782 lbs Impl. of butter at 6d per lb.	19 11	0
	£86 11s	6d

While no tenant paid his rent entirely in kind, almost half paid part of their rent in this way, including all the tenants in Wyre. In the years that followed, the estate discouraged payments in kind and 1845 was the last year in which they were regularly made, although later a tenant in difficulty might occasionally still pay part of his rent in this way. The phasing out of rent in kind marked the end of the merchant-laird tradition.

The old lairds drew produce from their estates which they converted into a money income through trade, while the new lairds' income came directly from rent and they were interested in agricultural improvement as a means of increasing that rent.

The end of estate involvement in kelp-making was another feature of this same transition. During the kelp boom years from 1780 to 1830, production, shipping and marketing had been firmly controlled by merchant-lairds like the Traills of Frotoft. Profits from kelp had been much more important than rent. When prices collapsed in 1830, kelp-making rapidly declined, but the estate continued to be involved in a small way as a result of kelp-making obligations in some leases. The last of these was a lease which William Seatter of Saviskaill had entered into with Mr Ranken, a Kirkwall lawyer and former owner of the property. George William Traill inherited this agreement when he purchased Saviskaill but, due to the low price of kelp, such a lease was latterly more bother than it was worth. In 1841 the estate barely broke even. After paying the expenses of shipping, the laird received only £8:14s:5¾d for the sale of the kelp, but the lease obliged him to pay Seatter £3 per ton, which left him with a profit of only 5/9¾d for his trouble. For Seatter, kelp-making remained a good bargain since he was receiving the price which had been paid in the boom years, much more than was common in the depressed conditions of the 1840s. The estate cannot have been pleased when he increased his production to 9 tons 11 cwts the following year and, although they were again able to avoid an actual loss, Seatter was discouraged from making kelp in the last two years of his lease. Saviskaill is a good example of a farm where the abandonment of kelp was followed by agricultural improvement. The run-rig of Wasbister was divided in 1841-2[3] and Seatter was allowed a rebate on his rent until the division could be completed (possibly on condition that he gave up the expensive habit of kelp-making). In 1844 he was given a new nineteen-year lease which made no mention of kelp, his rent was increased from £70 to £86 and he was provided with a new steading which included a water-powered threshing and meal mill. An adequate head of water for the mill was obtained by raising the level of the Loch of Wasbister by several feet. An unusual feature of the improved farm was the large number of cottars who were allowed to remain. They were sub-tenants who had provided the kelp-making labour force and Saviskaill was one of the few large farms on which such holdings continued to exist in appreciable numbers after agricultural improvement.

In George William Traill's time the rental of the estate rose from £286 in 1840 to £1,005 in 1847, the year of his death. The greater part of this rise was due not so much to actual increases in rent as to further purchases increasing the size of his property. Improvements to Westness Farm also enhanced the value of the estate. Although there were increased rents to pay on many farms, these were moderate and as, for example, at Saviskaill, increases often followed substantial expenditure on improvement. Rousay was fortunate in having a laird who, because of his personal wealth, did not require to derive an income from his estate. The estate accounts included entries under the heading 'Payments to the Proprietor', but these comprised only odd payments which, for convenience, the factor had happened to make on behalf of the laird — donations, subscriptions, the purchase of a few shares and similar miscellaneous items. Quite literally, Traill drew no income from his estate but, on the contrary, subsidised improvement at the rate of about £1,000 per year. Since Balfour in Shapinsay was improving his even more extensive estate with a family fortune originally founded on his uncle's lucrative career in Madras, Indian capital played a very significant part in the development of the North Isles of Orkney. Unlike the traditional merchant-laird, the man with Indian money behind him could devote his entire rental to improvement and, when necessary, supplement it from his private means, or from low-interest loans to which the landowner now had access. But although Traill had no need to squeeze his estate for rent, the abolition of rents in kind and the end of kelp-making, combined with his policy of high investment, created a situation whereby rent might be expected to increase in the future, particularly if the next laird should be less affluent than Traill had been.

After Traill's death and until Burroughs attained his twenty-first birthday in 1852, the estate was administered on his behalf by a trust. Donald Horne, an Edinburgh lawyer who had an interest in the huge improved farm of Houseby in Stronsay, was judicial factor, and Sir Edward Colebrooke, Burroughs' guardian, represented the family. Sir Edward was painstaking and scrupulous in protecting his ward's financial interests and personally inspected the minutest details of the accounts. He also kept Burroughs permanently short of money. The young officer had, for example, only £15 when he visited his new estate for the first time in 1848. Appeals for an advance fell on deaf ears. If he was short of money, Sir Edward told him, it was time to terminate his visit and join his regiment.[4] Under this careful regime rent was increased only slightly (about 1% per annum) and about 90% of the rent was reinvested in improvement. The trust also invested money which Traill had borrowed but which was still unspent at the time of his death.

In 1853 Burroughs was able to buy the Earl of Zetland's lands in Rousay.

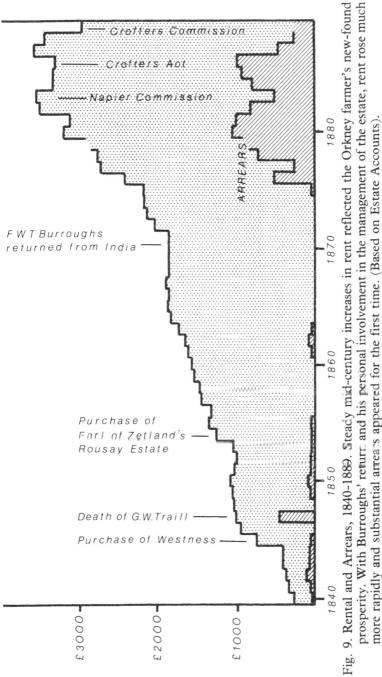

Fig. 9. Rental and Arrears, 1840-1889. Steady mid-century increases in rent reflected the Orkney farmer's new-found prosperity. With Burroughs' return and his personal involvement in the management of the estate, rent rose much more rapidly and substantial arrears appeared for the first time. (Based on Estate Accounts).

Thereafter he was owner of virtually the whole of the island and increases of rent, as shown in Fig. 9, are no longer complicated by further additions to the estate. Rent increased very steadily at an average rate of 3.7% per annum between 1855 and 1865 but thereafter remained steady until Robert Scarth retired as factor in 1873.

Aged seventy-five when he retired after managing the estate for thirty-three years, Robert Scarth was a powerful, competent and knowledgeable old man. He had inherited his father's financial business, transmitting deposits on behalf of the Edinburgh banking house of William Forbes & Co, and in 1855 he became agent for the Union Bank's first branch in Orkney.[5] From an early age he acted as factor to a number of estates including those of the Laings and the Traills of Woodwick. He was Chairman of the Harbour Trustees, a Town Councillor and Senior Baillie in Kirkwall.[6] From time to time he loaned money to the proprietors he served and he bought and sold their livestock on his own account. From 1852 until he retired, he was tenant of Trumland Farm, on which a new steading had been built and thorough drainage undertaken in 1848, and which he continued to occupy with much more modest increases in rent than on other farms. He was never resident in Rousay but lived in Papdale House on the outskirts of Kirkwall and latterly on the improved farm of Binscarth where his mansion house surpassed the houses of many of the proprietors for whom he acted as factor. On one occasion when Scarth was a guest at a dinner in Rousay he was described as:—

> . . . a hard, a very hard man, not to be driven from his purpose either by threats or by soft sawder . . . always keeping his promise though very chary of making one . . . yet there is luck under him, as every man finds means of paying his rents.[7]

This was true. Arrears hardly existed when he was factor,[8] although for much of the time there had been a steady increase in the rent. His formidable presence and his skill in pitching the rent just at the level that the tenant could reach, resulted in its being very exceptional for a tenant to fall in arrears.

After Scarth retired, rent rose very quickly from 1873 to 1883, the decade before the trouble with the crofters. It is difficult not to conclude that much of this was due to amateurish management of the estate, in direct contrast to the professional expertise of Robert Scarth. It was certainly unfortunate for Burroughs' reputation that the first major round of rent increases should have coincided with his gaining control of the estate on attaining his majority and that the second phase which precipitated the crisis should have come when he returned as resident laird and became personally involved in estate management.

The tenants had no great opinion of John MacRae, Scarth's young son-in-law, who acted as factor from 1873 to 1875. A native of Kingussie, he had little experience of Orkney conditions. Trouble also resulted from his dual role of Procurator Fiscal and Burroughs' personal lawyer, since it was not always clear in which capacity he acted. Following complaints about the rent, MacRae valued a number of farms, but Rousay folk who would have respected Robert Scarth's vast experience were amused by the antics of the new factor. They particularly enjoyed his habit of chewing small samples of soil to estimate the salt content. James Leonard, after his eviction, remembered with relish how the factor had broken his 'toy spade' on the tough soil of Triblo. According to Leonard's hostile account, the factor recommended blasting to break up the bedrock which lay just below the surface, a course of action which the tenant thought more likely to blow away what little soil there was.[9]

Previous factors had lived in Kirkwall, but in 1875 Burroughs appointed a full-time resident factor to manage the estate and George Murrison, an Aberdeenshire man, was chosen. Living in Viera Lodge, the former residence of George William Traill, and working in regular contact with a resident proprietor who took a keen interest in the day-to-day running of his estate, Murrison had neither the independence nor the status which Scarth had enjoyed. The rapid increase in rent was probably the policy of the landlord rather than the factor. In addition to increases each year, the traditional system whereby tenants paid rent for the previous crop was changed and henceforth they were expected to pay rent for the current year. This represented a once-and-for-all exaction equivalent to the entire rental of the estate. Arrears first appeared in 1875 and by 1880 amounted to about one third of the rental. These arrears were not due to the tenants' reluctance to pay the current year's rent, for they had appeared before the system of accounting was changed, nor were they the result of the tenants deliberately withholding rent in the hope of a reduction since arrears pre-date Irish rent strikes and all prospects of special crofting legislation. Rousay tenants had an exemplary record of payment but they now claimed that the estate was rack-rented to the point where they could no longer meet the landlord's ever-increasing demands.

There had certainly been a remarkable rise in the rent but this by itself does not prove the charge of rack-renting. An increase in rent may not necessarily be unjust if there is also an increase in the value of the property. It is obvious that Rousay farms had become more valuable due to the landlord's investments, the tenants' efforts and, above all, to better cattle prices from improved access to southern markets. Whether or not the new rents were justified depends on a comparison between the rents and the enhanced value of the property.

H

For his new rent the tenant had more arable land, much of it reclaimed by his own efforts. From less than 2,000 acres at the beginning of the century, the arable had increased to 2,268 acres by the time of the first available agricultural returns in 1866 — a modest growth. Thereafter extensive reclamation increased this to 3,327 acres in 1880.[10] With worsening economic conditions this expansion suddenly ended, and from 1880 until Burroughs' death in 1905 the arable acreage remained remarkably constant. The greatest expansion took place between 1875 and 1880, and during that five-year period there was an addition of no less than 571 acres. Although this was a remarkable increase, it by no means matched the rise in the rent for, while the area under cultivation expanded by 21%, the rent rose by a swingeing 47%. Such an increase, or indeed any increase, was particularly resented on the smaller farms where reclamation had been carried out by the unaided efforts of the tenant rather than by estate expenditure. Reclamation properly required a hill plough and a team of four heavy horses, resources beyond the reach of the crofter who still often used the flimsy Orcadian single-stilted plough drawn by a light horse or more often by oxen. Neighbours might co-operate, combining their horse power to attempt to plough the hill or, where this failed, undertake the work of reclamation with the spade. Despite these difficulties much of the reclamation was done by crofters some of whom had suffered eviction and been allowed to settle on former common, often high on the hillside at the limits of cultivation. With little or no help from the estate and by piecemeal reclamation over the years, many of these crofts had been built into little holdings of ten or twelve acres. The crofters bitterly resented a rent which outstripped their capacity to reclaim.

The second comparison which must be made is between the rent and the value of the farmer's produce. It was obvious that recent years had brought much better prices as steamships enabled Aberdeenshire cattle dealers to visit the islands regularly and convey their purchases to markets on the Scottish mainland. Table 8 shows that, over the whole period 1855 to 1880, the increase in the rent (136%) almost precisely matched the greater value of the cattle (135%). Nor was it the case that the farmer profited from keeping more cattle, since numbers were very steady at just over a thousand for the greater part, if not the whole, of the period. The farmer may have increased his income by the tendency to market beasts at a younger age, but the effect of this in the period under review was only marginal. But if, over the 25-year period as a whole, rent had matched the income from cattle sales, there had been an intervening period when the farmer was a good deal better off. In the 1860s cattle prices had been rising much faster than rent, but from 1875 to 1880 when the big rent rises took place under Burroughs' personal management, cattle prices were steady or

	1855	1860	1865	1870	1875	1880	1885
Rent	£1362	£1583	£1861	£1854	£2188	£3212	£3053
Percent of 1855	100	116	137	136	161	236	224
2 Year Old Cattle	£7:4:9	£9:11:3	£11	£16:13:4	£17:5:8	£17	£16:16:8
Percent of 1855	100	132	152	230	239	235	233
Oats per Quarter	£1:1:4	£1:0:10	£1:1:9	£1:3:9	£1:4:0	£1	18/1
Percent of 1855	100	98	102	111	112	94	85
Lambs	15/9	£1	£1:8	£1:4:6	?	?	11/3¾
Percent of 1855	100	127	178	156	?	?	72
Arable Acres	2000 (estimate)	?	2268	2522	2756	3327	3313
Percent of 1855	100	?	113	126	138	166	166
Number of Cattle	?	?	1097	1032	1077	1085	1010

Table 8. Was Rousay Rack-Rented? The rent the farmer or crofter had to pay has to be compared to the price he received for his produce. Until 1870 his position was improving, his income rising faster than his rent. After 1870 there was a rapid increase in rent but the prices the farmer received were beginning to fall. (Sources: Estate Accounts. Prices are the average obtained from Westness or Trumland Farm. Arable acres from Agricultural Returns include Egilsay and Wyre.)

even tending to decline slightly. The tenants resented having to meet new rent demands from a steady or declining income.

That this was, in fact, the case becomes clearer when other agricultural products are taken into account. Traditionally the sale and export of grain had been the mainstay of the Orkney economy and the spectacular growth of the cattle trade masks the fact that grain exports continued to be surprisingly important into the second half of the nineteenth century, increasing in absolute terms although now relatively less important than cattle sales. Grain prices were first to be affected by the onset of the Agricultural Depression when Free Trade, American railroads and large steamships combined to flood the market with cheap cereals. In Orkney, prices which had risen only slowly up to 1875 dropped to levels considerably below what they had been in 1855 and, although there was no falling off in the acreage of oats, there was a tendency for the greater part of the crop to be consumed on the farm rather than sold as a cash crop. Lamb prices by 1880 were showing a similar downward trend although for the smaller farmer this was less important. By that time he had been deprived of the common grazings and was unable to keep many sheep.

The loss of the commons diminished the value of crofts just at the very time when rents were rising fastest. The rent of many of the smaller crofts had been substantially increased in 1879 and, in the following year, crofters lost their last remaining rights to the common grazings. The Rousay commons at one time had been particularly extensive, comprising not only the whole hilly interior of the island but also a good deal of low ground lying interspersed with arable land. Actions in the Sheriff Court for the division of run-rig (Wasbister 1841-2, Frotoft 1844-5)[11] had established the legal ownership of such commons, and the subsequent work of enclosing and reclaiming had deprived the smaller tenants of any use and wont rights they may have had on the low ground.

On the high ground, although it was 1880 before they were entirely deprived of their common grazings, their rights had long been under attack. The importance of the commons to the smaller tenants has already been described (Chapter 4), and since the old *coogild* had fallen into disuse, grazing was unrestricted. For the croft with only a few acres of arable land, unlimited use of the commons was a large part of the available resources. Such uncontrolled use resulted in the accessible parts of the common becoming denuded of vegetation by over-grazing, and the scalping of turf to manure the arable land produced a sea of mud under the hooves of half-starved cattle and sheep, with haphazard, ill-drained peat banks lying half full of water. Yet it was only through access to such grazings that the smallest crofts could survive.

The earliest attack on the commons was the enclosure of the Head of Faraclett in 1817.[12] According to tradition, the farmers of Scockness, Faraclett, Pow, Bigland and Swartafiold co-operated in the construction of a dyke, and 'slaps' were left for each of the five farms. On its completion, however, the Baikie estate who owned Faraclett claimed the grazings as their exclusive property and ordered the slaps to be built up. For a time the Scockness men lifted their sheep across the dyke on to the grazings, where they were promptly rounded up and put back across by the Faraclett men.[13] The dispute went to law, not through any regard for the traditional rights of smaller tenants, but because other landowners considered that the claim by the Baikie estate infringed their property.

As part of a general settlement, it was soon afterwards agreed to make a division of the whole Rousay commons. It was one of the earliest divisions to be made in Orkney and was only possible because Rousay was one of those parts of Orkney where the issue was not complicated by the presence of Crown Estates. The procedure for division was liable to be expensive and the proprietors rejected an estimate from the land surveyor, William Mathieson, to measure and divide the commons at a cost of £100.[14] Instead of going through the courts as they would have been required to do had any one proprietor insisted, they entered into an agreement to divide the commons by mutual consent. Such a method was quite legal although it was usual, as the Rousay proprietors did, to have the agreement registered in the Sheriff Court. Two knowledgeable farmers valued and divided the commons in just over a week at a fraction of the cost of a proper survey, but cutting corners could lead to disputes. It was usual to divide commons in proportion to the valued rent of the proprietors concerned, but in Orkney the only available valuation was ancient and defective, hence a number of proprietors argued that they ought to agree to divide according to the actual rental. The matter was eventually referred to the arbitration of James Traill of Ratter, Sheriff Substitute of Caithness. Despite his involvement, however, the division which eventually took place in 1825 was a private agreement among the proprietors, not the result of a legal division carried out under the Act.[15]

Division of commonty concerns ownership but does not necessarily imply a change in the traditional use by tenants. In Rousay the division appears to have had no immediate results but, after 1825, the position of the small tenant was precarious and the landowner could make changes in the management of the grazings or exclude the small tenants at any time he chose to do so. The first inroads were made in 1845 when 2,000 acres of former commonty were attached to the newly created Westness Farm as sheep pasture. This part of the hill was not dyked off from the remainder, so tenants were served with a printed circular forbidding them to keep 'wild or Orkney sheep'. This prohibition later appeared in the official *Conditions of Leases* but, along with a ban on cutting turf from the common, it was widely ignored. The *Conditions of Leases* emphasised that tenants had no rights beyond the boundaries of their farms but this was included as a statement of the legal position rather than a rule which the estate intended for the moment to enforce.

Soon after Burroughs took up residence, he turned his attention to the profit which might be made from the hill grazings. Previously no charge had been levied for their use since it was assumed that rent included the payment both for the arable and for the privileges of common grazing. Now, however, wire fences opened up new possibilities for the better management of hill pasture. Farmers like John Gibson were pressing Burroughs to accept 2/- a head for sheep's grazing provided the farmer was granted exclusive use of the hill. Consulting his agricultural textbooks, Burroughs came to the conclusion that even this attractive offer was too low. He calculated that a charge of 7/6 for a sheep or £2:15s for a cow ought to be possible and, at these rates, he might augment his income by as much as £1,875 from the hill lands of Rousay. It was an attractive prospect. In the margin of this optimistic calculation the General wrote in large letters — 'Nota bene!!!'[16]

Being temporarily without a factor, Burroughs asked Marcus Calder of the Balfour estate to report on the contemplated changes. Calder endorsed the proposal to divide the hill grazings with wire fences. He delimited large areas to be attached to the farms of Westness, Trumland and Langskaill and others to be let by competitive offer. A portion was allocated to the Established Church minister as an addition to his glebe.[17] Some common grazings were to remain but Calder recommended that these should be mere 'breaks' of limited extent. Stocking of such commons ought to be rigidly controlled and the smallest crofters ought to be excluded altogether in order that they might devote their energies to fishing rather than agriculture.[18]

Thereafter the crofters' grazings were confined to three areas — one of limited extent serving the Frotoft farms and, for the Sourin crofters, the more extensive pastures on the north side of Knitchen Hill and on Kierfea Hill. However, Calder's proposals for controlling the grazings were never put into effect and the old free-for-all continued until these commons were finally abolished in 1880. The effect of this loss can be seen from the number of sheep in the possession of those tenants who applied for rent reductions from the Crofters Commission in 1888. Despite the fact that Rousay has some of the most extensive hill grazings in Orkney, none of these crofters had more than four sheep. Seventeen out of the forty-five crofters had no sheep at all.[19] Those who kept sheep could hardly have fed them had they not been able to 'slip them over the dyke' when neither the laird nor factor would notice.

The justifiable complaints of the crofters, therefore, are concerned with the period when Burroughs was personally involved in the management of the estate. They complained of massive rent rises, increases which far outstripped both their capacity to reclaim land and the prices they obtained for their produce. Rent threatened to erode advances they had made between 1850 and 1870 and these new increases coincided with their final loss of grazing rights. Yet although they were faced with rack-renting and a deteriorating situation, few crofters were reduced to levels of poverty common in Highland crofting districts. Rousay crofts were big by that standard, a great deal had been done to expand and modernise them, and the crofters hoped to do even more if only the policy of the estate could be changed.

9

Money Problems and the Financing of Improvement

'Since 1840, some £40,000 has been expended on improvements on this estate. The money was laid out with a view to improving the estate, and the social condition of all of it; and in the expectation of its returning a fair interest on the outlay.'   F. W. Traill-Burroughs[1]

BESIDES reflecting the ability of the tenant to pay, rent also reflects the need or the greed of the landlord who collects it. One has the feeling that the rise in the Rousay rents owed a good deal to Burroughs' financial difficulties. He was commonly regarded by his tenants as a rich man and, of course, he was, for there was an enormous gulf between the General with his rental of over £3,000 a year and the farm servant who might receive £10 and six bolls of meal, or the poor crofter who probably had even less. Between the owner of Trumland House and the tenant of a few acres of reclaimed common there was a difference in the standard of living which probably surpasses anything which could be found within the British Isles today. Yet Burroughs had some difficulty in maintaining himself in this style and was constantly beset by money problems. He had inherited the estate from George William Traill but not the Indian fortune to go with it, since Traill had disposed of £50,000 in separate legacies.[2] Burroughs had to live off his rents supplemented by his army pay. Whereas Traill had drawn no income from his estate, but had subsidised it by an average of £1,000 a year, Burroughs regularly drew an income averaging £1,500 and, when he was in financial trouble, sometimes much more.

When Traill acquired the estate it was unencumbered by debt and he financed most of his purchases of land from his personal fortune. He had, however, found it convenient to raise the money for Westness by means of a £3,500 loan secured by a heritable bond on the estate. At the time of his death, he was negotiating a further loan of £1,500 to be spent mainly on the improvement of the Quandale pastures.[3] Burroughs inherited these debts and, soon after he came of age, he added a further heritable bond to raise a loan of £3,000 for the purchase of the Earl of Zetland's property in Sourin and Wasbister. Sir Edward Colebrooke, his parsimonious ex-guardian, tried to dissuade him with the time-honoured advice that buying land with borrowed money was likely to be 'a losing affair'.[4] Yet Burroughs, although now in debt to a total of £8,000, was confident that he had made a good investment. It gave him ownership of nearly the whole island; he was still young and there was every prospect that such a debt could be paid off during his military career. For the tenant it was less of a bargain since ultimately it was he who had to bear the cost of borrowing. Sourin crofters who were paying increased rent for the privilege of exchanging the easy-going and absentee Earl of Zetland for the interfering and financially embarrassed Frederick Burroughs must have felt that they had made a particularly poor bargain.

Up to this point Burroughs' debts were not serious but about 1855 his father, who was serving in the Indian Army, became involved in problems of his own. Burroughs senior was a dashing figure, much in demand for polkas and waltzes, but he was an incompetent soldier and his personal finances were perpetually in a state of confusion. The more he sank into debt, the more he simply put off attending to business matters, even to the extent of neglecting to cash cheques he received. Muddle rather than deliberate dishonesty was at the root of his troubles.

His wife (from whom he was separated) described him as 'a testy touchy little man' with an unerring ability to quarrel with his superiors. He had the ambition to be 'a second Wellington', she told him, yet was annoyed when any of his commanding officers troubled him at unusual hours; he had been keen to become adjutant of his regiment but, when he did, he had grumbled at the duties and said that he would have given it up had it not been for his wife and children; he had then sought a post in the Adjutant-General's depot but had liked the work even less.[5] Now he was pinning his hopes on an appointment in the Finance Department. There was little in his past to recommend him for such a post.

On the death of Burroughs' grandfather in 1829 his father had inherited enough to provide him with a comfortable income, but it was rapidly lost as a result of unwise business ventures in Calcutta.[6] While his family of two sons and four daughters was young, he managed to survive on his army pay despite slow promotion. Later, when his three eldest daughters were being educated in London, debts began to gather. By 1855 these amounted to £1,200 owed partly to Sir Edward Colebrooke and partly to the estate of the late George William Traill of which both he and Sir Edward were executors.[7] On their return to India, these three marriageable young ladies had to be maintained in a separate household since their father was on active service.

His campaign in command of the Bhagulpur Hill Rangers during the Soutal Rebellion went disastrously wrong. Most of his poorly trained native troops deserted in the face of the enemy with considerable losses of supplies and equipment. The subsequent Court of Inquiry somewhat grudgingly exonerated Burroughs senior, but the sum of money he received in compensation fell well short of the losses for which he was held personally responsible.[8] These enquiries also revealed irregularities in his depot account and, to add to his worries, the other executors of George William Traill became increasingly concerned about discrepancies in the Indian side of the estate for which Burroughs senior was responsible. For example, a legacy to Traill's illegitimate son, Charles Traill, had not been paid although the money seemed to have disappeared.[9]

He had also to meet further expenses in connection with his wife, who returned to Europe in 1853 with the two youngest children, Charlotte and Charly. Mrs Burroughs was in poor health and, although outwardly remaining on good terms with her husband, she had no intention of returning either to him or to India. Living in hotels and rented accommodation, first in France and latterly in Germany with governesses for the children, she had great difficulty in keeping within her allowance of £440 a year (even when she was fortunate enough to receive it). Financial difficulties soured her relationship with her husband. He upbraided her with her aristocratic Peyron origins, accused her of expensive habits and told her she should have married into the French nobility. She complained that she was never allowed to interfere in financial matters but was told 'to take her allowance and go and attend to her puddings and pies'. She had never understood her husband, she said, 'and had often told him so'.[10] Her sharp tongue was believed to have contributed to her husband's slow promotion. When he was A.D.C. to General Littler at Lahore, his prospects had been damaged when she quarrelled with the General's wife 'on some very insane grounds'.[11]

Too poor to buy promotion and too incompetent and quarrelsome to gain rapid advancement by his own merits, Burroughs' position became increasingly awkward. Service on the North-West Frontier would bring an increase in pay, but there would be fewer 'eligibles' for his daughters, who were proving difficult to marry off. After thirty-six years' service, he was trapped by his debts and could not afford to retire on half-pay. Even to take leave was impossible, since he suspected the Delhi Bank would take action to prevent him leaving India.[12] Matters came to a head when, in 1865, his health broke down and the Medical Board insisted he return to Britain for at least eighteen months.

Strictly speaking Burroughs had no responsibility for his father's debts nor had Burroughs senior any claim on the Rousay estate, but it is to the son's credit that he took on this responsibility. Between 1858 and 1865 he repaid over £6,000, clearing what he believed to be the last of his father's debts in 1865 to allow him to return on leave. He received little thanks. His father was embarrassed by having to accept assistance and he hated revealing the muddled state of his finances to his more methodical son. His health restored, Burroughs senior returned to India where he accumulated a further debt of 5,546 rupees (equivalent to six years of his army pay) before he eventually retired from the army.[13]

In addition to providing direct assistance, Burroughs also had to take over expenses which his father would normally have borne. Until her death in Dresden in 1863, he paid an annual allowance of £360 to his mother. A further £200 a year had to be found for his brother Charly who was at school in Croydon. Failing to pass the Indian Civil Service examination, he then entered Sandhurst where his expenses were even heavier. Charly regularly overspent his allowance. His brother had to pay bills from tailors and shoemakers and rescue him from moneylenders and pawnbrokers. Charlotte received an allowance of £100 a year but she too had no compunction in running up other bills which she expected her brother to pay. Burroughs' care for his family was an honourable course of action, but one can understand the annoyance with which he wrote testy little comments in the margin of his factor's accounts to the effect that these expenses were properly the responsibility of his father.

By 1862 his efforts on behalf of his spendthrift family had landed him in difficulties and soon he was faced with further expenses of his own. Westness House came on the market and, being the principal mansion house on the island, it was a purchase which he was particularly anxious to make. He had also reached the stage in his career when he was eligible to purchase the next step in his promotion. In a scribbled calculation which has been preserved, he set out the courses of action open to him.[14] He could sell out from the army since his commission was a saleable commodity and might fetch £2,300. This, plus the money in his bank account, would pay off his father's debts, allow him to buy Westness, pay for his passage home and leave something to reduce the burden of debt on the estate. The alternative seemed impossible. If he bought promotion, he would be left with only £894. The purchase of Westness for £800 would leave him practically penniless and his father's debts would remain unpaid. After much heart-searching, he had in fact decided to sell his commission and quit the army when the cholera epidemic at Peshawar (see Chapter 6) suddenly altered his promotion prospects. By the death of officers senior to him, he rose in the course of a few days from senior captain in the regiment to senior major and was soon able to secure a lieutenant-colonelcy without purchase.

He had already borrowed £3,000 towards his father's debts, much to the annoyance of Robert Scarth who was constantly warning him of the danger of burdening the estate for such purposes. Rousay was being 'squeezed of its last farthing', the factor reported, to meet the remittances to Burroughs senior. In congratulating the laird on his lieutenant-colonelcy, Scarth expressed the hope that promotion would make further borrowing unnecessary.[15] Burroughs took the opposite view — his new income increased his borrowing capability. He now raised a further £4,000 to clear his father's debts and borrowed the entire purchase price of Westness House from the trustees who were selling it.

By 1864 Burroughs' indebtedness amounted to £14,650, but even this might have been cleared in the course of time. He gave up hope of an early return from India since, like his father before him, he was trapped by the need to meet repayments from his army pay. During his last years in the army he made a serious attempt to reduce the burden and managed to repay over £7,000 before he retired in 1873. His marriage brought him £3,000 which his father-in-law to be assured him would be immediately at his disposal, but it also brought him a twenty-year-old bride who found Westness House cramped and old-fashioned. She needed a more stylish setting to entertain house parties of friends and relatives. Before their marriage they called on David Bryce, the prolific Edinburgh architect whose country houses were much in demand and whose work marks a high point in Victorian gothic extravagance. Bryce arranged to visit Rousay the following summer and promised to build 'a very compact, complete and nice looking house' for less than £3,000.[16] The work at Trumland began in 1873 but by that time both the size of the residence and the cost had escalated considerably. It was an imposing mansion house with Burroughs' military medals carved in stone above the door (without, to his continuing chagrin, the Victoria Cross), and its high-ceilinged rooms provided spacious and comfortable surroundings for a household which could afford an indoor staff of a butler-valet, a cook, three maids and extra help at busy times. The first-floor drawing room looked out over the islands of Wyre, Egilsay and Gairsay, one of the most magnificent views in Orkney with that random scatter of smooth green islands which give the North Isles of Orkney their peculiar charm. Burroughs always hoped that the future Edward VII, then Prince of Wales, would visit Trumland and it was a setting in which he could have been entertained without disgrace. The impending visit of Prince Edward was used to keep servants up to the mark. 'What would Teddy say?' the laird would demand in mock anger when he found something amiss. However, a visit from Prince Henry of Orléans — deposed French royalty — was the most he was ever to achieve.[17] Despite its grandeur, Trumland was a gaunt building. The

Orkney landscape was too naked for such an extravagance. The house was surrounded by fifty acres of terraced gardens, gravel walkways and wooded policies but, even a hundred years later, the trees have not yet grown sufficiently to blend the house into its setting. In Burroughs' time, despite the attempts at landscaping, it must have appeared a monstrous pile on a bare hillside.

Such a house with its surrounding offices — coach house, kennels, joiner's shop, stables and gamekeeper's house — could not be cheap and indeed turned out to be a good deal more expensive than Burroughs had expected. During the building, plans for a tower were, perhaps fortunately, abandoned as was the west entrance with its second lodge. Even after these economies, the eventual cost of house, grounds and furnishings was £11,887,[18] a figure which contrasts sharply with the price of a cottar house which could be erected for less than £5. Trumland was financed by further borrowing, first a loan of £5,300 in 1873 and then, as costs mounted, a further loan of £4,000 in 1880. Nor was this Burroughs' only new debt. In 1876 he took out a new drainage loan of £10,000 and in 1881 he borrowed £1,000 for the purchase of the steam yacht *Curlew*. He was now in debt to a total of £24,600. Even in the best of times this would have been a heavy burden to carry but, by 1881, the days of agricultural prosperity were over, prices were beginning to fall and rents had already been screwed to the point where many tenants were seriously in arrears. Burroughs was in no state to cope with the long years of agricultural depression.

It was not just the amount of the debt which caused the trouble but also the purposes for which money had been borrowed. Loans against the security of the estate between 1840 and 1881 had been expended as follows:—

Purchase of land in Westness, Sourin and Wasbister	£6,500
Purchase of Westness House; building of Trumland House	£10,100
Clearing of father's debts	£5,600
Purchase of promotion	£1,400
Purchase of steam yacht *Curlew*	£1,000
Agricultural improvement	£8,826
Borrowed but as yet unspent	£2,674
	£36,100

Thus only about a quarter of the borrowing was spent on agricultural improvement and the rest was expended in ways bringing no direct benefit to the tenant. Drainage loans were, over the years, supplemented by other improvements financed directly from rent, but even so the total strictly spent on improvement was less than half the £40,000 which Burroughs, in a written statement to the Crofters Commission, claimed to have expended. That he took a rather broad view of what constituted an improvement to the estate can be seen from the inclusion under this heading in the estate accounts of such items as cleaning out the cesspool at Westness, beating carpets, and repairing a broken seat aboard the *Curlew*!

Even money which was genuinely spent on agricultural improvement was not always wisely invested. It is, nevertheless, difficult to over-estimate the importance of these drainage loans in promoting agriculture. An Act of Parliament in 1840 had allowed landowners to raise money for drainage by making it a heritable debt on the estate and this was followed by the Public Money Drainage Act of 1846 which made government money available at a low rate of interest. These measures had a great effect in Orkney, not just in the obvious way by providing capital, but because drainage was the key to improvement. Since the old hump-backed rigs were no longer required to provide surface drainage, fields could be levelled, encouraging the use of harrows, rollers, seed drills and reaping machines and even, on the most elementary level, scythes instead of sickles. It was now possible to square and enclose fields, enabling crops like turnips and sown grass to be grown and so allowing the farmer to improve the quality of his stock. Negotiations for a drainage loan began in George William Traill's lifetime and, after the Inspector of Drainage had visited Rousay twice in 1848 to view the proposed work, arrangements were concluded by Burroughs' trustees. The sum borrowed was £1,500 for twenty-one years and, since repayments of 6% per annum included both capital and interest, the loan was available at a very low real rate of interest. Perhaps Burroughs' indebtedness reflects the ease with which money could be borrowed in the nineteenth century.

In the earliest years the loan was described as 'for the lands of Quandale' and indeed the availability of cheap government money may have been the deciding factor in abolishing the crofting township and converting it into sheep pasture, a project which involved a heavy outlay on dyke-building, draining and reseeding. But from almost the outset, drainage money was used more widely to finance a variety of improvements on tenant farms. In these early years the work was done by the estate and specific additions were made to the rent to cover the cost of improvement. However, in 1852 a new set of *Conditions and Regulations* was drawn up and now a tenant with a lease was allowed a rebate of up to one third of his rent for improvements such as dyke-building and draining done by himself, provided the work was approved by the factor and satisfactorily completed. In future, work was to be done by the estate only when the tenant failed to maintain dykes and drains, in which case the cost would be charged to the tenant in the old way. Since there was a great increase in the number of leases at this time, a good deal of improvement was done in return for rent reductions. It was a popular system with tenants but the proprietor, however, had to repay the government loan and had an income reduced by rebated rents. He could only recoup his losses by an increase of rent at the termination of the lease. Scarth's leases were short, commonly seven years on the smaller places, and this system of financing improvement resulted in automatic rent rises every seven years. For the outgoing tenant unwilling to accept the increased rent there was no compensation for the improvements he had made and there were others who would willingly offer to pay the rent he refused.

Burroughs did not approve of rebating rent, which he considered led to haphazard and unsatisfactory improvements. As he told the Napier Commission:—

> When I was away every man got one-third of his rental back for improvements, and I found it did not answer, for I saw dykes were commenced and never finished, and the money was expended in an unsatisfactory way. I said then 'All improvements now I will do myself'. I said I would do it myself and make a rent charge.[19]

But very little improvement was in fact being done since the money from the drainage loan had been used up and, as Burroughs struggled to pay his father's debts, he had nothing to spare from the rent. From 1864 until a second drainage loan was negotiated in 1876 only trifling sums were spent on improvement or rebated from the rent, for example, in 1869 nothing and in both 1867 and 1870 only £3. But although the estate spent little, the work of improvement went on, financed and carried out by the tenant with no compensation should he quit, and still the inevitable rent rise at the end of each seven-year lease. When rents were increasing most rapidly, it is doubtful if more than a handful of farmers had benefited from estate expenditure in the previous fifteen years.

Burroughs therefore was not telling the whole story when, in an article he wrote for the *National Review*[20] after the Crofters Commission had reduced the rents of many of his tenants, he stated:—

> . . . for some twenty years of my military service, I returned one third of my rental to my tenants to be laid out, under the superintendence of my factor, in improvements on their farms and holdings. I did not do this out of purely philanthropic motives. I hoped, while bettering their condition, to reap a fair return in my old age for this outlay of capital. Old age has now come upon me; but, by a stroke of the pen, the Crofters Commission has robbed me and my heirs of the fruits of my prudence, and has handed them in perpetuity to my tenants and their heirs who have no just claim on them.

What Burroughs did not mention was that there had been a subsequent period, nearly as long, when the tenants through their labour and their outlay of capital had also hoped to reap a fair return in old age. Through increased rent and at the stroke of the factor's pen, they too had been robbed of the fruits of their prudence.

Investment in improvement began again after 1876 when the second drainage loan was negotiated. Unlike the first, which had been public money, the second loan was from a finance company, the Scottish Drainage and Improvement Company. The loan was to cover the period 1876 to 1901 with annual repayments of 6½% of the sum borrowed covering both interest and the repayment of capital. A total of £10,000 was borrowed and the cost of work on tenant farms was passed on as a specific addition to the rent. The loan was intended to be self-financing.[21]

About half of the loan was expended on substantial new steadings and the remainder was equally divided between fencing and drainage. The loan certainly allowed the work of improvement to be resumed but a closer examination suggests that the benefits of the loan were not widespread and that the money was not always wisely invested. Only 14 of the estate's 112 farms and crofts were improved under the loan and these tended to be the bigger places. Of the many crofts under £5 rent, only one received any drainage money and that was a croft where the tenant was the Free Church minister, hardly a typical crofter. Other loans went to the Established Church minister and to the ex-farm manager. One's standing in Rousay society mattered when it came to securing a share of the loan. To a very large extent it was a loan to General Burroughs personally, and the £2,608 he spent on Trumland Farm (which was in his own hands) was more than was spent on all other farms put together. Nor was the money wisely spent on Trumland, for despite an ambitious programme of building, draining, reclaiming and fencing, there was never a time when the farm operated at a profit as long as it was under Burroughs' management. The loss on Trumland Farm was regularly about £180 a year.[22] He spent a further £1,320 on non-agricultural improvements, largely houses for his servants including his yacht master and a cottage for the drill sergeant of the Volunteers.

A further criticism concerns the amount of the loan. It was a large debt which was undertaken on the confident assumption that agriculture would continue to prosper. It was not just in Rousay that the proprietor and farmers looked on falling prices as a temporary setback, the result of poor seasons, and failed to recognise the danger signals of the approaching depression. Most of them, however, were never to know good times again.

In many cases it was the crofter who had improved by his own efforts rather than the farmer burdened by interest charges on costly improvements who was best placed to survive the years ahead.

A factor which is perhaps not sufficiently recognised as contributing to the financial difficulties of estates was the increasing level of public burdens. The neglect of this is not due to any failure of the lairds to draw attention to the payments they had to make — they were constantly complaining about taxation and other expenses — but rather that later generations hostile to big estates have concentrated on the niggardly and grudging way in which proprietors met their obligations and have dismissed their complaints about the burden of payment as special pleading. Yet public burdens which could occasionally amount to a third of the rental, although normally less, were certainly not insignificant. At the very least, it is important to recognise that General Burroughs' rental was not his income. In an estate like Rousay, where a single landowner was in a monopoly position in the parish, many public functions which would now be undertaken by local, or even national, government were run simply as a department of the estate and managed by the laird and his factor.

These burdens were many and may be divided into three groups. The first comprised the various taxes on the land which included the original Norse land tax, the skat, supplemented over the centuries by teinds, feu duties and, most recently, income tax. The total amount payable was tending to increase — from £195 (c.1855) to £284 (c.1882). The second group of burdens was connected with the provision of local services and included statutory obligations such as providing for the poor, paying the minister's stipend, supporting the parochial school, occasional repairs to church, manse and school, and the construction and maintenance of roads. Third, public services of this kind were supplemented by voluntary contributions to a number of good causes. The laird was obliged to support the parochial school but also gave donations to the Free Church school in Wasbister and to the school in Wyre. These were less than generous and, despite rising costs, the annual donations were never increased. Private charity to individuals tended to decrease over the years and ceased entirely when Burroughs quarrelled with the crofters. The laird, anxious to keep expenses to a minimum, was sometimes reluctant to meet even his statutory obligations. It took the combined efforts of the minister, the North Isles Presbytery and a lawsuit which went to the Court of Session, to force him to undertake repairs to the manse.

The most controversial service which the estate had to provide was support for the poor. In parishes which were assessed for Poor Relief before the 1845 Act — and Rousay was not one of these — the assessment was equally divided between heritors (landowners) and tenants. Rather than accept a formal assessment, Traill was said to have come to an agreement with the tenants that they would bear the entire cost of the roads and he would be responsible for poor relief. This arrangement continued after the 1845 Act and since, as has already been seen, the tenants had indeed borne nearly the total cost of the construction of the road system, they were always anxious to ensure that the laird kept his side of the bargain. The tenants did not lose out by the arrangement since, although the roads and poor relief were never explicitly balanced, the costs were nearly equal and, if anything, slightly in the tenants' favour. But it was understandable that they should contrast the excellent road system with their laird's miserly attitude to any claims for assistance.

Before the 1845 Act the poor had been provided for by means of church collections, help from the estate and assistance from their neighbours. In 1841 the church collections for the poor amounted to only £4:15s and, since there were twenty-eight persons receiving aid, this sum was clearly quite inadequate.[23] Neighbourly assistance, the traditional system by which the old and infirm went from house to house and were fed and boarded for a time in each, was undoubtedly the main way of helping the poor. It was a system which was regarded as quite acceptable and 'not accounted beggary'.[24] Increasingly, however, the estate was expected to play a part. It seldom did so by direct money payments but might assist by allowing paupers to occupy houses rent-free or by remitting part of the rent of tenants who supplied meal to the poor. Money was also given to the Free Church minister (despite his denunciation of the laird's clearance policy) to be distributed among the deserving in his congregation.

The 1845 Act put relief on a more formal footing by the establishment of the statutory Parochial Board. The Board in Rousay, however, had no real independent existence but from the outset was administered as part of the estate machinery. Although at that date the Earl of Zetland still owned property in Rousay, the Board's entire income came from the Traill estate and it was the estate, not the Board, which reclaimed the proportion due from the Earl. The first Inspector of Poor was George Lyall, Traill's farm manager in Westness who, since the factor was resident in Kirkwall, regularly acted on behalf of the estate. After Lyall's departure, Robert Scarth himself became Inspector of Poor although still an absentee. Scarth tried to collect voluntary contributions for poor relief but, since the estate simply deducted any such donations from its own payments, such gifts were few and soon ceased altogether. Tenants could hardly be expected to support a system whereby gifts did not increase the income of the Board but merely reduced the liability of the laird.

After Burroughs made his home in Rousay he was, almost as of right,

Chairman of the Parochial Board, and he personally made all decisions as to whether poor relief should or should not be granted. Since this relief came from his own income and since he had money troubles enough, relief was not particularly generous. When the Napier Commissioners asked Burroughs how paupers could survive on the £4 per year he allowed them, he could only reply that they had always managed.[25] It was obvious that they still relied on a good deal of neighbourly assistance. Such was Burroughs' control of the Board that no decision could be taken in his absence. In 1883 Mrs Georgina Inkster applied for assistance when her husband was in hospital and her family destitute but, since the General was on holiday in Germany, nothing could be done until his return. It was believed that even the doctor, who was not resident in Rousay, would not certify that the family was in need of assistance since, without the laird's prior approval, such an action might 'hurt him in his situation'.[26]

Despite efforts to keep poor relief to the minimum, the annual cost was regularly between £80 and £120 and this expenditure was at a time when there were none of the major famine crises which Rousay had known in earlier years. From 1859 onwards there were usually two or three people being maintained in lunatic asylums, asylums for the blind and other institutions. Costs could be heavy — as much as £28 a year for transport and board of a single patient at Morningside Lunatic Asylum, more than twice the annual wage of a farm servant. From 1865 there were also payments for paupers living in Wick, Montrose and Glasgow who had not fulfilled their five-year residential qualification and were thus a charge on their native parish of Rousay. Rather than meet these payments, it was sometimes preferable to have the paupers shipped home in which case their 'freight' had to be paid. Burroughs was anxious to prevent paupers becoming a direct charge on the Parochial Board and, to avoid making money payments, he preferred to remit arrears of rent or to help in other ways. Occasionally he even provided a new house for a pauper but since one such dwelling, Windbreck in Sourin, cost only £3:19s:8d to build, it is obvious that the standard of housing was minimal.

Despite the laird's penny-pinching attitude and reluctance to meet even his statutory obligations, the various public burdens took quite a large proportion of his income. Whereas George William Traill had paid 20% of his income in the period 1840-44, the proportion rose to 32% between 1855 and 1865. Thereafter, although the total cost of public burdens continued to rise, particularly after the Education Act when new schools had to be built and staffed, Burroughs' income from rent increased even faster so that the actual proportion of the rental spent in this way fell to only 17% in the period 1880-84. It was still, nevertheless, a not inconsiderable amount.

The last two chapters have dealt with the financial difficulties of the estate between 1840 when Traill acquired property in Rousay and 1883 when a crisis was precipitated by the visit of the Napier Commission. It is possible to understand Burroughs' problems and even to sympathise with him, yet the record as a whole is a damning one, not just for Burroughs personally but for the whole system of Orkney landlordism.

There had never been such a period of agricultural prosperity and yet the estate had become increasingly over-burdened by borrowing. Due to the amateur management of the laird, much of the investment had been misplaced. Tenants who had never before been in debt were subjected to rack-renting until they fell into arrears, and this at the very time that prices were beginning to fall. With tactless timing, many had suffered a round of rent increases just prior to the loss of the traditional common grazings. When rents were rising fastest the estate had ceased to spend much on improvement. The tenant had to pay an increased rent for the fruits of his own labour or, alternatively, leave without compensation. The paupers, struggling for survival on the hill margins of Sourin and Wasbister, understandably compared their lot with that of the laird, living in his new mansion house in a style never before seen in Rousay. They saw something sinister in a system whereby the laird who caused their distress through the level of his rents should also have control of the whole system of poor relief. It was these complaints, hitherto unformulated and unvoiced in public, which were to find an outlet with the visit of the Napier Commission to take evidence in Orkney.

10

The Napier Commission[1]

'Is the property mine, or is it not mine? If it is mine, surely I can do what I consider best for it? If these people are not contented and happy, they can go away.' F. W. Traill-Burroughs[2]

THE complaints of the smaller tenants might have resulted in little more than endemic grumbling against the laird and his policies had not a spark from outside Orkney lit the tinder of their grievances. Despite a long history of exploitation, there had seldom been effective opposition or outbursts of revolt. Far from being sturdy rebels, the Orkney crofters were seen by their superiors as being 'in a high degree indolent; wedded to old customs; averse to every improvement; dark, artful, interested; respectful to their superiors, as much from fear as from love and suspicion; sometimes endeavouring to undermine and slander one another'.[3] Thoroughly downtrodden, the crofters might complain, but they did not hope to succeed.

The spark which fired the Crofters' Movement came from outside Orkney, even from outside Scotland, for it was Gladstone's Irish land legislation which led to the hope of similar protection for the small tenant in Scotland and in Orkney. The disastrous harvest of 1879 caused widespread distress in Ireland, and the following spring brought the eviction of many tenants unable to pay their rent. The formation of Parnell's Irish Land League precipitated a major crisis which threatened to overthrow the whole fabric of Irish landlordism. With mass support from a desperate tenantry using the traditional tactics of rural outrage, the maiming of livestock and the destruction of agricultural implements, to which they added the new weapons of rent strike and boycott, the League created the impression of a countryside in revolt. This was a situation which was beyond the power of the government to contain by coercion alone. The Irish Land Act of 1881, although failing to meet all the League's demands, was a signal victory. The small tenants in Ireland gained security of tenure, they could have their rents judicially determined and could also sell their tenant right, a measure which virtually gave them a share in the ownership of their farms. Such legislation could not fail to be attractive to crofters on the other side of the Irish Sea.

The Irish origins of the Crofters' Movement had particular relevance to Rousay where the laird came of an Irish family. Burroughs' relatives were now to be found in Cheltenham rather than County Cavan but he retained all the prejudices of an Irish landowner. He was strongly anti-Catholic and a bitter opponent of Gladstone's land legislation. He followed with close attention the progress of Irish affairs, collecting in his scrapbooks all the newspaper articles he could find which dealt with Irish atrocities or with the progress of the Land Act through Parliament. Events in Ireland were also watched closely by his tenants since the activities of the Land League received a good deal of prominence, not only in national newspapers, but also in *The Orcadian* and *The Orkney Herald*. These local newspapers, founded in 1854 and 1860, and the increase in literacy among crofters, created an awareness of the outside world unknown among previous generations of Orkney folk. There were conflicting reactions to events in Ireland. Many found the programme of land reform attractive but others, the people Burroughs called 'the respectables', regarded it as self-evident that agitation would inevitably lead to outrage and disorder after the Irish pattern. The blaze of publicity which followed the Phoenix Park murders intensified this attitude. Hence the advocacy of crofting reform was never entirely respectable and the authorities were often quite unnecessarily jumpy at the prospects of disorder.

Poor harvests in 1881 and 1882 combined with a drop in wool and cattle prices and the failure of the east coast herring fishing resulted in the spread of agitation to the Highlands. By the winter of 1882-3 the distress in the crofting areas resembled the destitution of the 1840s, although Orkney escaped the worst effects in both periods. Reacting to this distress and to outbreaks of disorder which were affecting Skye, the government yielded to pressure and appointed a Royal Commission to investigate the conditions of crofters and cottars in the Highlands and Islands. Although the Napier Commission was to institute a new system of land tenure and although we may see its appointment as a major turning point in the history of the North of Scotland, the Commission was at first viewed with distrust. All Royal Commissions are open to the criticism that they are created to delay legislation, indeed an excuse for doing nothing. It was also at first widely believed that the Napier Commission was grossly biased in favour of landlordism. Neither criticism was justified. It began to take evidence in May 1883 in those areas which had been most affected by rent strikes and resistance to the law, and it proceeded with quite remarkable speed to issue a radical report only eleven months later in April 1884.

The effect of collecting evidence from the crofters themselves is well illustrated by events in Rousay. The Commission did much more than merely report an existing situation. The very process of collecting evidence generated completely new circumstances.

Crofters had always harboured grievances but they lived in a society where the laird was liable to construe any open expression of discontent as a crime, supported by the church which called it a sin. Since the spread of United Presbyterian and Free Church congregations, the church no longer spoke with one voice, but there were still powerful forces preventing any overt opposition to the landlord's policies. Now for the first time, and by the authority of Parliament and the Queen herself, crofters were encouraged to hold public meetings to discuss their grievances and to elect delegates who would act as spokesmen for their districts. Whereas disaffection had previously earned the combined disapproval of laird and minister, it was no longer so easy to brand dissidents within the community as troublemakers and those from outside as cranks and agitators.

The Commission's visit to Orkney was brief. They arrived aboard the *North Star* and began hearing evidence in Sanday on Friday 20th July 1883 when they learned that, although the Orkney crofter was incomparably better off than his Highland counterpart, he was burdened to a greater degree by compulsory services — the *on ca'* work in agriculture and kelp-making. The following day they took evidence in Harray, a parish exceptional in Orkney for its high proportion of owner-occupied crofts. Since one solution to the crofting problem might be a scheme of land purchase, the Commissioners were particulary interested in these 'peerie lairds'. Monday was their last day in Orkney and they spent it taking evidence in the Sheriff Court, Kirkwall before a large audience which listened spellbound to six hours of sensational evidence from General Burroughs' Rousay estate.

It is probable that not only the evidence of his own tenants but also the attitude of the Commission came as a great shock to Burroughs. The credentials of its chairman, Francis Napier, Lord Napier and Ettrick, could hardly have inspired greater confidence. Following a long and distinguished diplomatic career, Napier had been Governor of Madras for six years and had proved to be a vigorous administrator, combating famine by means of irrigation schemes and public works. After Mayo's assassination in 1872, he had temporarily acted as Viceroy of India. Burroughs obviously felt that, with a chairman of such authority who shared his own Indian background, it would be sufficient to point out that 'respectable' people in Rousay were not mixed up in any of this agitation. Having been on holiday in South Germany, he had probably had little chance to follow the progress of the Commission up to that time. Thus it was with amazement that he listened as Lord Napier granted a courteous hearing to and even appeared to side with those people whom Burroughs dismissed as agitators.

Rousay was one of the few parts of Orkney where crofters had organised and prepared a case for the Commission. This political awareness owed much to the radicalism of the Rev Neil P. Rose, George Ritchie's successor in the Free Church at Sourin. In 1880 Rose had left the island to take a church in Edinburgh, but in the summer of 1883 he returned on holiday and was active in urging crofters to put their case to the Commission.[4] Accordingly a series of meetings had been held in the Sourin school to draw up a statement of grievances and to elect delegates to give evidence. The chairman of these meetings was James Leonard of Digro. Burroughs was to find him an implacable opponent, a powerful and able man, not to be cowed into submission as most crofters could be. Although he might waver under pressure from the laird, he was ultimately determined to defend his principles even when this led to his eviction and having to leave the island. When work was available, he followed his trade as a mason and at other times he turned his hand to weaving. He was precentor in the Free Church and had founded a choir which occasionally gave public performances. Hitherto his relationship with the laird had been good. Burroughs' building schemes provided opportunities for employment and, from time to time, Leonard's choir was invited to Trumland to sing for the guests. He had a family of nine children, six of them still below school age in 1883. Two years earlier, three of the older children had died within a fortnight, carried off by diphtheria, and this tragedy had a lasting effect. After this loss, he ceased to take any pleasure in secular music and he became increasingly serious, even melancholy. He was a good public speaker, sometimes lecturing on Temperance topics and occasionally acting as a lay preacher.

Leonard was a sub-tenant on his father's eight-acre croft of Digro which lay on the very margin of cultivation, high up on Kierfea Hill, commanding a view over the whole wide sweep of Sourin. Four hundred feet above sea level in Orkney's cool and windy climate is a considerable altitude. The land was poor and the soil shallow and stony. This was one of the crofts carved from the commons, and Leonard's father had originally settled as a squatter a year or two before the division of commonty in 1826. Digro lay in the part allocated to the Earl of Zetland and, under that estate's easy regime, Leonard senior was allowed to continue to occupy his croft rent-free. When Burroughs purchased Sourin in 1853, a rent was put on Digro for the first time. With confused memories of lost udal rights, it was widely held that a croft reclaimed from the common ought to be the property of whoever reclaimed it but, whatever the merits on the grounds of traditional practice or equity, Scots law decreed otherwise. At first the croft was held

on a year-to-year basis at a rent of £1:2s, but in 1856 Leonard was given
one of Scarth's seven-year leases. In 1863 the lease was renewed at £1:10s
and in 1870 at £3, but when the third lease expired, the croft was put back
to a year-to-year basis. The rent, however, was increased to £4 and soon
afterwards Digro, like other crofts, lost access to hill grazings. Digro was
typical of the crofts Burroughs intended to abolish, depriving the tenants
of their land but allowing them to stay on as landless labourers. It was of
limited agricultural value and, with two households and a total of fifteen
people, it was grossly overcrowded. The houses, however, were good and
are still standing today. The well-built walls and neat flagstone roofs are a
testimony to James Leonard's skill as a mason, as is a miniature water-mill
standing behind the original house and supplied from a small dam farther
up the hillside.

As the Crofters' Movement centred on the Sourin Free Church
community, it was inevitable that the minister, the Rev Archibald
MacCallum, should be drawn into the conflict. Although at first lukewarm
and evasive, he too became Burroughs' bitter enemy, a man capable of
being just as unreasonable and autocratic as the laird. He was a native of
Glasgow with family connections in Islay and Arisaig which made him
naturally sympathetic to the crofters' cause. In 1883 he was aged thirty and
had been in Rousay for only three years, during which time his relationship
with the laird had been fairly normal. He had spoken to Burroughs about
one or two cases of hardship but, when he found the laird unsympathetic,
he had not pursued matters. It was the Napier Commission which turned
MacCallum into a determined opponent and revealed him to be a leader of
considerable ability. If Burroughs was the Rousay czar, it was MacCallum
who was the Lenin of the crofters' revolution, a master of power politics at
parish level.

MacCallum played no part in the crofters' first meeting and he was, in
fact, away from Rousay at the Free Church Assembly in Edinburgh.
However, by invitation he attended the final meeting two days before the
Napier hearing. Only crofters were to be admitted and the factor, who
attempted to gain entry, was turned away. MacCallum, however, rented a
small croft near the manse and so it could be argued that technically he was
a crofter. He was brought in to give an acceptable literary form to the
statement which the crofters had already discussed and which James
Leonard had drafted. At this final meeting MacCallum attempted to exert
a moderating influence at least on the language of the crofters' statement.
As those present went over the document line by line, the minister objected
to such phrases as a reference to Burroughs' 'wanton and inconsiderate
inhumanity'. His efforts met with little success although this particular
phrase was replaced by a criticism of 'the utterly inconsiderate and

unrighteous manner in which we are treated by the proprietor'. The minister had not won much of a modification but it was as far as the crofters were prepared to go.

The General was also preparing his case. He was in Germany when word reached him of impending trouble and he hurried home at once, arriving in Rousay only four days before the hearing. Although accompanied by his factor, he intended to present his case personally.

Despite these preparations in the rival camps, there was as yet no open breach between the laird and his crofters. Early in the morning on the day of the hearing, the crofters' delegates set sail for Kirkwall in an open boat. The day was sunny with little wind and they were debating whether to take to the oars when the *Curlew* came puffing out from Trumland. The General hailed them in friendly fashion, offered them a tow and threw them a line. MacCallum was invited aboard the *Curlew* but declined the invitation. It was typical of Burroughs' very personal view of the situation that he should particularly resent the crofters' evidence after this act of kindness on his part.

The proceedings opened with MacCallum's evidence and he began by delivering the long statement which the crofters had prepared. Using facts and figures drawn from the *New Statistical Account*, it made detailed comparisons between the condition of the estate when it had been acquired by George William Traill and the present state of affairs. Rents were three times more than they had been and the crofters related this to a decrease in the population and to a decline in ancillary occupations such as fishing. At the same time the decline in the number of proprietors from thirteen to three, of whom two held only small owner-occupied properties, had created a dangerous monopoly of power. MacCallum went on to describe the 'harsh and needless evictions' in Quandale and Westness and more recent cases of evictions at Nears and Hammer. He described the loss of the commons and asked the Commission to investigate the commonly held belief that the treaty which had pledged Orkney to the Scottish crown had vested ownership of common land in the whole body of the people of Orkney, an ownership later usurped by illegal feudal tenures. The statement contained the crofters' five demands. These were:—

1. The land should be revalued and a fair rent fixed.
2. Crofters should be given security of tenure.
3. Crofts should be increased in size.
4. Hill pasture should be restored to the crofters.
5. The Commission should inspect the condition of the houses.

It was not the nature of these demands which caused the trouble, for these were the very points which the Commission listened to day after day wherever they took evidence, and Burroughs was familiar enough with the crofters' programme to expect something of the sort. It was the language rather than the content of the crofters' evidence which shocked the laird. Burroughs resented insult more than he feared injury. He found it particularly galling that the bitter words and biting criticisms directed against him were contained, not in bumbling and inarticulate evidence, but in a lucid statement delivered with all the authority of MacCallum's pulpit voice. Lord Napier set about exploring the origins of this remarkable statement:—

> The memorial you have read is written in a style very superior to that in which most of the memorials we have received are composed, and I can hardly imagine that it is entirely the spontaneous natural composition of persons in the position of crofters or small tenants. Can you tell me who actually wrote or composed the document?

James Leonard broke in to say that the facts were furnished by him and Mr MacCallum had assisted in putting them together. MacCallum, very uncomfortable in the presence of Burroughs, was not prepared to admit even this much. It had been dictated to him almost in its entirety, he said, and he had done little more than correct the grammar. He had not wanted to have anything to do with it but had been asked to help. Since the crofters had gone over the statement sentence by sentence, it should be regarded as their work, not his. The minister was being evasive but there is, nevertheless, no reason to doubt that he had played little part in drawing up the document. Immediately before the Education Act, Orkney had already a higher level of literacy than perhaps any part of Scotland. This was in striking contrast to other crofting areas and, although Lord Napier might not have met a well-educated crofter before, men like James Leonard were quite capable of putting such a statement together without significant help from the minister. Indeed, judging from their later writings, the crofter from Digro could express himself more clearly and more logically than the Free Church minister. Lord Napier, however, was not prepared to let MacCallum evade all responsibility for what he had read. As the document had, at least, been partly composed by him, did he substantially agree with its contents? MacCallum could hardly avoid saying that he did. He had at last committed himself!

MacCallum also appeared evasive when he tried to draw a distinction between a personal attack on General Burroughs and more universal complaints against the whole system of crofting landlordism:—

> The movement is not at all concerned with personal feelings against our distinguished proprietor, General Burroughs, or his factor, but entirely against the system and manner in which they use the powers the law gives them ... The proprietor encourages many good things in a moral and social way in the island; his example is in many respects a model to proprietors. We have no complaint against General Burroughs, as I have stated; it is against the system and the law and the powers in his hands.

Lord Napier set about exploring the inconsistencies of this distinction:—

> You personally state that it is the system which is complained of, and the law, and not the character of the proprietor; but in the memorial, there is the strongest indication of personal maladministration with which the law has nothing whatever to do, because the law does not consolidate land, does not turn out tenants, does not prevent the proprietor giving compensation. The whole memorial seems to be a direct incrimination of the proprietor . . . What do you mean by that?

Driven into a corner, MacCallum had to admit that, insofar as the statement he had read was an attack on Burroughs personally, he stood by what he had said. Yet despite his discomfiture at the hands of Lord Napier, there is a good deal to be said for the distinction MacCallum was trying to make. A century after these events, one still has to decide whether to interpret the trouble in Rousay in terms of Burroughs' character or in terms of impersonal economic forces acting without the restraint of the law. Given Burroughs' background and financial circumstances, was it reasonable to expect him to act other than he did? It is most unusual to find the individual who steps aside from the path bounded by the confines of his class, to act in an altruistic way against his own financial interests. Most people find it easier to discover principles to justify attitudes ultimately determined by emotional reactions and financial considerations. That is not to say that Burroughs' principles were a sham — he obviously believed them sincerely — and, to be fair, the crofters were equally motivated by alternative principles which likewise coincided with their interests.

MacCallum had, however, committed himself a good deal further than he intended. He had been driven to admit that he agreed with the crofters' strongly worded statement and that this was a direct indictment of Burroughs' maladministration of his estate. It cannot have been comfortable being forced to take up this position in the General's presence. Burroughs made no recorded intervention, but it would have been out of character had he not made his presence felt and his feelings obvious.

After MacCallum stood down, the atmosphere cooled a little while George Leonard of Triblo gave straightforward evidence. George Leonard was not closely related to James Leonard, the crofters' chairman. He was an old man, a survivor of the Quandale clearance, and he had been brought forward, not so much to advance the crofters' present claims, as to provide a first-hand account of past injustices. As the evicted tenant of Stouramira, the last of the Quandale crofts (see Chapter 5), it was he who had carried his few belongings and his daughter, an infant in arms, through the hills of Rousay to settle on a bare twenty-acre square in Sourin. His later history was typical of the Sourin crofters. Like James Leonard, he had held three of Scarth's seven-year leases before being reduced to a tenant-at-will, and during that time his rent had increased from £2 to £6 and he had lost access to the commons. Now aged sixty-seven and unable to undertake work outside the croft as he had once done, he again faced an uncertain future. Land surveyors had been active on and near his croft and he had heard rumours — which Burroughs admitted were true — that his land was to be taken away from him and attached to a neighbouring farm. The Commission tried to question him on the relative merits of oxen and horses for ploughing but, for a crofter like Leonard, the question was irrelevant. He could not afford to keep a horse for a week, he said, and he used one of his cows together with a neighbour's cow for ploughing. The immediate outlook was grim since recent seasons had been 'cruelly bad' and he proposed to sell stock to survive. One of his beasts was nine years old and he cannot have expected to get much for it at 1883 prices.

The Inkster family of Hammer were one rung further down the ladder since they had already lost their land. Mrs Georgina Inkster appeared, not as an official delegate, but with a personal complaint about the difficulty of obtaining poor relief. Until 1878 she and her husband who had been in poor health for many years had lived with Hugh Inkster's mother but then Hugh, rather unwisely, had taken the tenancy of Hammer in Wasbister, a fifteen-acre croft with a house in poor condition. The stock had been provided by Mrs Inkster senior who gave up her own croft and moved in with them but, because of Hugh's ill health, he had never been able to work the land very effectively. A sister who also lived with them provided the only real income. In 1881 their land was taken away from them but they were permitted to stay on in the house. Burroughs had built a steading on the neighbouring farm of Innister but discovered it was too big and consequently decided to enlarge Innister at the expense of Hammer and two other crofts. The plight of the Inksters became increasingly desperate. Inkster was unable to work, his mother was elderly, his wife was encumbered by a family of young children, but for two years they survived on the money they received from the sale of their stock. In 1883 that money was exhausted, the last being spent in sending Hugh to the infirmary in Edinburgh. Left destitute, Mrs Inkster had applied for relief only to discover that no one was willing to make a decision while the laird was away on holiday.

The loss of the lands of Hammer caused feelings to run high and the whole district took sides. A row between the wives had ended with Mrs Inkster throwing a pail of dirty water over the farmer's wife from Innister and the incident led to a Sheriff Court appearance. Ploughs and scythes were broken at night, sheep belonging to one of the farmers disappeared and there were other violent incidents. MacRae, Burroughs' personal lawyer, ex-factor and Procurator Fiscal, paid a visit to Wasbister to collect evidence for further charges but found the people sullen and unco-operative. Both the General and his factor had visited some of the troublemakers and, with tensions running high, the unfortunate schoolmaster had chosen this moment to visit the destitute Inksters with a demand for the payment of school fees. This resulted in the Sheriff having to deal with another case of assault!

James Leonard, the crofters' chairman, concluded the crofters' case and, with his evidence, high drama returned to the hearing. Brushing aside Lord Napier's opening question, he made a request on behalf of his fellow delegates:—

> Being a delegate of the Crofters of Rousay, I have been asked to make a special request for them, and that is that our proprietor will injure no person for giving their evidence before the Royal Commission.

It was quite a normal request. Many Highland delegates had asked for a similar assurance and such a request had invariably been granted although sometimes reluctantly or grudgingly. The unusual feature in this case was that the request for immunity came, not as it should have done at the beginning, but only after three witnesses had already given evidence. If the request had come at the proper time, it would have been difficult for Burroughs to refuse and that morning when, at least superficially, he was still on good terms with his crofters, it might never have occurred to him to do other than agree. But he had now been sitting in enforced silence for the greater part of the day listening to the bitterest attacks on his personal management of his estate and he was no longer in any mood to comply.

Lord Napier put the question. Would he agree not to take any retaliatory action against those crofters who gave evidence? Burroughs replied:—

> I am not prepared to do so. It is contrary to human nature that I could treat a man who spoke of me so inimically as one or two have done here, in the same way as other men who are fairly disposed. Whatever I might say, my feelings could not be so after the people have vilified me as they have done today.

Napier pointed out that he was not concerned with Burroughs' feelings, but with his future intentions, and he reminded him that there was a right to reply to any of the allegations the crofters had made. Other proprietors had given this assurance and the Royal Commission would be hampered in its investigations unless crofters had freedom to speak without threat of retaliation. But whatever argument he tried, Burroughs remained adamant. He was prepared to give no such assurance:—

> 'Is the property mine, or is it not mine?' he demanded, 'If it is mine, surely I can do what I consider best for it? If these people are not contented, they can go away.'

The question which Burroughs saw as purely rhetorical was really the heart of the matter. Burroughs was a nineteenth century capitalist, seeing ownership in absolute terms and managing his property for personal advantage and maximum profit. Yet nineteenth century society still retained an older belief that the proprietor should manage his property for the benefit of all the people, assuming many of the functions which would now be undertaken by local or central government. The real question at stake was the very nature of ownership. What rights did it confer and what obligations did it present? Could there be power without responsibility?

Meanwhile Lord Napier had to warn Leonard that Burroughs had not given him the assurance he asked. He pointed out that Leonard was at liberty to continue to give evidence or to stand down. Leonard had become considerably heated during the exchanges between Napier and Burroughs and he had no hesitation in continuing. He began, almost incoherent with anger, but was soon in full flow and launched into an impassioned speech:—

> I challenge anyone to say that I have been acting unlawfully in anything; and with regard to the statements made here today, why should they be angry with us for making our statement to the Commission sent down by the Government? We are only telling the truth; and because we do that we will be evicted from our places and holdings. Certainly there is much need for change in the law and security of tenure. I think you have the strongest evidence before you that you have had, perhaps since you left London; and although I may have to leave the land, I am prepared to speak the truth and will not be cowed down by landlordism. I consider as Burns says — A man's a man for a' that.

Lord Napier interrupted to warn him to alter the tone of his evidence and immediately Leonard cooled down, dealing factually with his own personal circumstances. It was only towards the close of his evidence that he again became roused when asked to justify the charge of 'wanton and unrighteous conduct' against the proprietor. A 'thrill of sensation' went round the court room as he described the eviction of an old woman on her death bed. According to Leonard, she told the laird that she would never leave until she was put into a house from which no man could remove her. 'What house is that?' Burroughs had asked, and when she told him that it was the place where she would be buried, he had lost his temper, stuck his stick into the earthen floor and demanded to know whether she wanted to be buried right there under her own floor. Then, with a final denunciation of 'the despotism and terror of the landlord', James Leonard stood down.

Two delegates still had not been heard. One, William Robertson, was not present and perhaps had decided at the last moment that it was safer to stay away. The other, James Grieve, was asked one question only — did he agree with the statements made by MacCallum and James Leonard?

Grieve, who had recently returned from the colonies, married a housemaid from Trumland and settled as a sub-tenant on his brother's croft of Outerdykes, was another crofter of an independent stamp. He replied in two words only — 'I do'. They were the only words he uttered to the Commission, but by now he must have fully realised that they would be sufficient to result in his eviction.

The Commission turned from Rousay to hear some general evidence about South Ronaldsay, and then General Burroughs exercised his right of reply. He was the only Orkney landlord to do so, although some other estates had been represented by the factor:—

> I have heard with the greatest astonishment what has been said. I have seen myself in a light in which I never knew myself before, and I cannot believe that what has been stated is the opinion of the people of Rousay generally. I think the delegates must represent Rousay much as the three tailors of Tooley Street represented Great Britain on a former occasion. I don't think the respectables in Rousay are mixed up with this movement at all.

His evidence, a rather rambling rebuttal of the various points raised by the crofters, was interrupted several times by Leonard and MacCallum. The whole argument seemed likely to degenerate into a wrangle about whether or not James Leonard's children were dressed in the height of fashion when they attended church and whether Orkney farmers' wives and domestic servants had collectively spent over £500 for flowers to decorate their bonnets at the Lammas Fair in Kirkwall. Lord Napier did his best to maintain order and keep the evidence relevant. By skilful questioning he ascertained that much less than the £40,000 Burroughs claimed to have spent on the estate had been of direct benefit to the tenants, and he explored Burroughs' view of the obligations which he, as a landowner, had to his tenants. It was on this note that the hearing ended. Would Burroughs be glad to get rid of those people who had involved themselves in the Crofters' Movement?

'Decidedly,' Burroughs replied, 'I want a contented people round me.'

'Even if the land were to become void of inhabitants, except the farmers and the four footed animals?' asked Napier.

'I should be sorry if that were so,' Burroughs replied, 'I thought I was on the best terms with the people, and I should think the case you state is impossible.'

For an ex-interim Viceroy of India to suggest that his policies would depopulate his estate and to imply that he, who had always prided himself on promoting the good of the community, was lacking a proper sense of responsibility to his tenants, was a shattering experience. It was an unpleasant end to a difficult and trying day. As MacCallum later remarked, the crofters were not offered a tow home!

11

Trouble in Rousay

... there-shall be Blood Shed for if I meet you Night or day or any where that I can get a Ball to Bare on you Curs your Blody head ... ' Anonymous letter received by F. W. Traill-Burroughs[1]

IT is instructive to draw a parallel between Rousay before the Napier Commission and British India before the Mutiny. In both, the superficial impression was of a pleasant, even an idyllic society with a good relationship between the ruler and the ruled. Each exhibited a general air of progress and an expectation of increasing prosperity. Yet the gulf between the general and his crofters was in reality as unbridgeable as that which separated the Raj from the native population. Secure in a sense of his own superiority, a superiority stemming from his social position, wealth, knowledge of the world and habits of command, he was as unaware of the currents beneath the placid surface as his fellow officers had been in India. Both made the tacit and unquestioning assumption that what benefited the ruling class also benefited the peasantry. In India the retinue of obsequious servants, the scarlet-coated well-drilled ranks of sepoys and the band playing outside the mess in the cool of the evening, had created the facade of a paternal relationship between the superior yet benevolent officers and the childlike natives. In Rousay the picnics for the children, dinners for tenants, agricultural shows and regattas, had created the same false picture of mutual affection. Both societies were based on an illusion which made real communication and understanding impossible. No officer believed that his own sepoys were disloyal, and in regiment after regiment officers trusted their men right up to the moment when these same sepoys turned and cut them down. In the same way Burroughs was genuinely surprised and grieved by his crofters' attacks and it offended his military code of loyalty and discipline. Like the sepoys, his tenants were ignorant, unruly children who could not be expected to know what was best for themselves, but it hurt him when they made a public display of their lack of affection. His children had behaved badly in public and — what made it much worse — they seemed to be getting away with their bad behaviour.

K

Although Burroughs had to face the opposition of his crofters, not all his tenants were hostile. There was a group whom Burroughs always referred to as 'The Respectables', a term which he used as if it was a political party, which basically it was although lacking any formal organisation. The community was now polarised between 'Respectables' and 'Crofters', with few remaining neutral. The two parties struggled for control of local positions of power such as the School Board and conducted propaganda campaigns through the local and national press. The 'Respectables' included all the big farmers, not only because they were the people who benefited from agricultural change, but also because many of them were suspicious of any special concession being given to their smaller neighbours through crofting legislation. To these farmers could be added others, usually Tory in national politics, who were opposed to Gladstone's Irish measures or who had a general fear of radicalism and of the disorder which land reform had brought to Ireland. Such people were likely to be members of the Established Church, and since the Free Kirk minister was a leading 'Crofter', the division was partly on denominational lines. To the 'Respectables' can be added Burroughs' personal servants, the indoor staff, the factor, the gardeners and yacht master and a further category of those who owed an official position to his patronage, the Volunteer drill sergeant, Clerk to the School Board, Inspector of Poor, and the schoolmasters. Then, finally, since Burroughs himself, some of the farmers and senior farm servants were incomers, an element in the conflict between the two groups consisted of the latent hostility between native-born and immigrant. Thus Burroughs always commanded a considerable following, although not often a majority of the population.

Since the 'Crofters' had demonstrated their power at the Napier Commission hearings, the 'Respectables' now decided to mobilise. Ever since Burroughs had retired to Rousay, it had been the annual custom to invite the schoolchildren to a picnic at Trumland and many came accompanied by their parents. It happened that the picnic was due to take place a day or two after the hearings and, although Burroughs had considered cancelling it, he eventually decided to carry on as planned. John Gibson of Langskaill who made the speech of welcome when Burroughs first arrived thirteen years earlier was again active in guarding 'the connection . . . betwixt landlord and tenant'.[2] He happened to be attending a Roads Meeting in Trumland House and he took the opportunity of circulating a memorial which he tried to persuade the tenants to sign. Gibson's memorial repudiated MacCallum's claim that he spoke for all the tenants and alleged that the crofters' delegates were not representative and had distorted the true position on the estate. It was an embarrassment to those parents who had accepted an invitation to a purely social event, but although they were at the picnic as the General's guests, few could be found who were willing to sign. In the next few days efforts were made to collect more signatures. Gibson himself devoted a whole day to going round the Wasbister houses but gathered only two more names. Frotoft produced one supporter but no one could be found brave enough to take the memorial into the Free Kirk 'Crofters' stronghold of Sourin,[3] for by this time the news was out that the crofters' delegates were to be evicted.

It was at this stage, with the community divided and feelings running high, that Burroughs began to receive anonymous letters. The first, from 'A Friend of the People' and posted in Edinburgh, was abusive but relatively harmless.[4] The writer showed little knowledge of Rousay and the letter appears to have been a city radical's immediate response to newspaper reports of the Napier Commission. 'Man's inhumanity to man makes countless thousands mourn,' he proclaimed. A second letter which Burroughs received five days later was less literary in style but potentially much more explosive. It was postmarked Rousay 1st August, the handwriting was juvenile, the spelling uncertain and the use of capital letters erratic. It read:—

> Sir, I havee Noticed in the Papers that you are determined to Remove these men that give Evidance to the Commission in Kirkwall, well if you do as sure as there is a God in Heaven if you remove one of them there shall be Blood Shed for if I meet you Night or day or any where that I can get a Ball to Bare on you Curs your Blody head if it does not stand its chance. thire is more than me intended nail you. you are only a divel and it is him you will go and the sooner the Bitter. and if you leave the Island if it should be years to the time you shall have it. O Curs your Blody head, if you dont you devel, the curse of the poor and the amighty be on you if he does not take you away you shall go So you can persist or not if you chuse but be sure that you shall go. I state No time but the first Conveniance after their removal.[5]

If Burroughs had had sense — and in this kind of affair he showed little — he would have put such a letter in the fire. He decided instead to treat it seriously and to use it with maximum publicity to discredit the 'Crofters' by showing that agitation for land reform led to threats of violence. Menaces and midnight ambushes were standard features of Irish rural terrorism and, although there was never any real likelihood of such incidents in Orkney, the possibility of violence was the subject of much idle speculation. Indeed, only a few days before, some of the Rousay crofters had been present when William Norquay, the bank manager from St Margaret's Hope, had told Lord Napier that the government would have paid more attention to Orkney if the tenantry had been 'more of a landlord shooting and outrageous class'.[6] It was a remark which Lord Napier considered dangerous and so did Burroughs. Some of his tenants, however, took a more lighthearted view of such threats. 'Would you shoot me?'

Burroughs somewhat dramatically asked a farmer whom he was visiting. 'Yes certainly,' the tenant replied, deliberately interpreting the rhetorical question as a request, 'Just wait there till I get my gun!'

Burroughs personally visited the three island schools, examining scholars' copybooks and asking the schoolmasters if they could identify the writing.[7] From his investigations, he believed that he had discovered the culprit — fourteen-year-old Fred Leonard, son of James Leonard of Digro, the crofters' chairman. His next step was to inform the authorities in Kirkwall and to make an official complaint. The events which followed, the sending of a gunboat, no less, to deal with the schoolboy letter writer, were partly accidental and appear in retrospect as pure farce, a ridiculous over-reaction to a letter which should never have been taken seriously. But these events had a more sinister aspect. They illustrate how easy it was for someone of Burroughs' standing to summon the full force of the law to his support.

It happened that the fishery cruiser *Firm* was in Kirkwall at the time and that the Sheriff Principal was just about to sail for Shetland aboard her. Unrest in crofting districts could be a serious matter, as some of the Sheriffs in Highland counties had already discovered. Accordingly it was decided to divert the *Firm* to Rousay and see the situation there at first hand. Thus it came about that the case of the anonymous letter was investigated by Sheriff Principal Thoms, Sheriff Substitute Mellis, Procurator Fiscal MacRae, Mr Grant the County Superintendent of Police, and the clerk to the Fiscal, Mr Spence. Landing in Rousay, the Fiscal, his clerk and the Police Superintendent made their way to the Sourin school, while the two Sheriffs and some of the *Firm's* officers paid a social call on General Burroughs at Trumland House. There could have been no more obvious or tactless way of demonstrating which side authority supported. This lack of impartiality was even more serious in the case of the Fiscal. Like many country lawyers, MacRae combined his public duties as Procurator Fiscal with a private law practice. When he was investigating the disturbances involving the Inksters at Hammer, this dual role had already caused difficulties: it had not been obvious whether he was acting in his public capacity or whether he was acting as lawyer on behalf of a client.

Mr Moyes, the Sourin schoolmaster, had just taken the afternoon attendance when the Fiscal arrived. On the Fiscal's instructions, the children were dismissed and 'after a good deal of shuffling' the school room was cleared.[8] At the time Mr Moyes was principally concerned with his register, that nineteenth century holy of holies, which was wrongly marked since pupils had been recorded present for an attendance which would not now take place.[9] Had he known it, he had much more to worry about — the events which followed were to cost him his job. Fred Leonard was no longer a pupil, having recently left, so the Fiscal's clerk and the Superintendent of Police went off to search for him, eventually finding him herding cattle on Essaquoy. He was brought into the school where he was given pen and paper and made to write out certain phrases — doubtless including 'Curs your Blody head' — to check his spelling and handwriting. The investigation continued until Fred complained that he was tired, and presumably it proved negative since no charges were made and the investigation switched to another boy.

The new suspect was Samuel Mainland whose father had also played a leading part in the crofters' meetings. By this time the boy was out of Rousay, accompanying his father at the herring fishing in Stronsay, but he was arrested there the following day by the Superintendent and brought into Kirkwall for questioning. He was examined in private for three hours by both the Sheriff and the Fiscal and a somewhat disturbing aspect of the affair was that they seemed more concerned about the crofters' meetings than with the anonymous letter. They wanted to know who attended, what was said and what was decided. Eventually young Mainland was also released without charges being made against him, but it was a cause for complaint that the boy was released in Kirkwall and had to make his own way home.

A week later MacRae was back in Rousay, still accompanied by his clerk and the ubiquitous Superintendent of Police, and they went to Trumland to listen to rumours from the servants. They also visited the Free Church manse but got short shrift from MacCallum who threatened to report the whole business to the Lord Advocate. The minister had already been in touch with his lawyer about Burroughs' possibly libellous remark that he had traced the origin of the letter to 'the vicinity of the Free Church manse'.[10]

Burroughs was anxious to make all the capital he could out of the letter and, in particular, to use it to discredit those witnesses who had appeared before the Commission. He sent a copy of the letter to Lord Napier with his comments:—

> The letter will show . . . the style of witnesses who appeared before you, and of their friends; and that they are endeavouring to establish a reign of lawlessness and terror as in Ireland.[11]

It was a calumny which caused MacCallum to contact his lawyer once again and, indeed, he had every reason to feel aggrieved. There is not the slightest reason to suppose that the anonymous letter was in any way connected with the leadership of the Crofters' Movement or that it was anything more than the work of a youngster over-excited by the actions of his elders. Equally ridiculous was the belief held by some crofters that the letter had originated among the 'Respectables' as a devious means of discrediting their opponents.[12]

Burroughs' spectacular reaction to the anonymous letter encouraged others to write in the same vein. *The Orcadian* received, but did not publish, a letter thought to be in the same handwriting.[13] The 'Friend of the People' wrote again from Edinburgh describing the Sheriff and his entourage as 'all toadies'.[14] A third letter, addressed to Mrs Burroughs, purported to come from Mrs Grieve, her former maid, and contained threats against Burroughs and also against 'all Caithness men and strangers'.[15]

If there ever had been any real doubt about Burroughs' intentions towards those crofters who had given evidence, the affair of the anonymous letter made their eviction certain. His anger was directed against James Leonard and James Grieve, although the latter had uttered only the two words 'I do' when asked whether he agreed with Leonard's evidence. No action, however, was taken against either George Leonard of Triblo whose evidence about the Quandale evictions was mainly historical, or against Mrs Georgina Inkster whose evidence, although bitter, was on behalf of her husband rather than herself and whose family had, in any case, already lost their land. At the end of September James Leonard received the following letter:—

> As you have expressed yourself as very dissatisfied with the management of my estate and as your friends have threatened to shoot me, I wish to remind you that you are not a slave and bound to the estate, but a free man and that the world is open to you to suit yourself where you can.
> As to the threat of shooting me, I have been shot at before and am not to be intimidated by such a menace.
> But in order to prevent some of your foolish friends from coming to the gallows, I think it is high time and for our mutual advantage that we should part. I hope you will find a landlord more to your liking.
> My factor has received instructions to serve you with the usual legal notice to quit.[16]

It was only now that Leonard began to realise what his brave words to the Commission were to cost. He wrote back asking the factor to call, expressing the hope that matters might yet be settled in a peaceable way. He must have been encouraged when he received a summons to call at Trumland three days later. His enemies were to claim that he visited the laird under cover of darkness to beg forgiveness but notes on their meeting in the General's handwriting make it clear that he was at Trumland by invitation and that the time was 5 p.m. on an evening in late September.

According to Burroughs' minute, Leonard began by asking if he really was to be evicted. When assured that this was indeed the case, he protested that he had no ill-will against Burroughs but had attacked the system of landlordism. Burroughs replied that for his part he had always believed that they were on friendly terms apart from some minor differences on School Board matters; he had never been so astonished in his life as he had been by Leonard's evidence to the Commission; filling four columns of the newspapers with abuse was a strange way of showing friendship; he was now convinced that Leonard had always opposed him and would oppose him to the death — a phrase which had taken on added meaning as a result of the recent threatening letter. Leonard asked if he was suspected of having written it. The laird was non-committal. 'It is impossible for us to dwell together,' he replied. He insisted on shaking hands with Leonard, then they parted.[17]

In desperation Leonard made two final attempts by letter to persuade the laird to change his mind.[18] Faced with the agonising choice between his principles and his responsibility for a numerous family and pregnant wife, he stopped just short of an abject apology. Burroughs left these final appeals unanswered and in early October took steps to secure the removal of both Leonard and Grieve. The Sheriff issued a decree summarily to eject Leonard from Digro and to interdict him from the croft 'at all times coming'. A decree in similar terms was obtained against his brother, Peter Leonard, the actual tenant of Digro, but it was made clear in court that this second decree would not be enforced providing he adhered to estate regulations forbidding sub-letting. Like many decrees of ejectment, this was not an actual eviction but was rather a threat for the purpose of securing the tenant's good conduct in future. Similar decrees were obtained against James Grieve and his brother, Malcolm. Again the decree against the brother was not to be enforced provided he obeyed estate regulations.[19]

To add insult to injury, the Sheriff granted Burroughs his expenses in these actions for removal. He had, in fact, no option but to do so since the cases were undefended. Perhaps the Sheriff's recent visit to Rousay had suggested the futility of appealing to his sympathies but there were, in any event, no grounds on which the crofters could defend themselves. The removal of a tenant-at-will or his sub-tenant was quite legal and easily accomplished before the passing of the Crofters Act. It is on moral grounds only, not on the grounds of legality, that these evictions may be criticised.

Grieve was reasonably well placed after his eviction. He had been twenty-five years in the colonies and had returned to Rousay fairly affluent by local standards. Before the trouble, Burroughs had approached him with a view to his taking the tenancy of one of the Rousay farms, but Grieve had boasted that he intended to buy a farm of his own and that he would not consider paying the rent Burroughs was asking. When he was evicted from Outerdykes, he was given refuge on one of the few small pieces of land which did not belong to the estate. Temporarily accommodated in the 'end of a house', he was able to acquire a site at Mount Pleasant, so remaining in Rousay to cause Burroughs more trouble in the future.[20]

James Leonard and his numerous family, shortly to be augmented by a further addition, were not so fortunate. His father had died the previous year, aged eighty-three, but for the last twenty years Leonard, although technically only his father's sub-tenant, had worked the croft and had built new houses at his own expense. On his father's death, however, Burroughs ensured that the tenancy passed to an elder brother who was a cabinetmaker in Kirkwall. On his eviction, Leonard found no refuge in Rousay but had to move in with his brother in the town.[21] Later he was able to secure the post of precentor in the Established Church in the parish of Firth.

Further controversy resulted from Leonard's claim for compensation for the houses he had built. It was only as a result of the Agricultural Holdings Act of that same year that compensation became obligatory, but the laird, in the circumstances, was still determined to concede as little as possible. It was agreed that both sides were to appoint valuers, and a date and time were arranged for a meeting at Digro. The factor, however, failed to keep the appointment but, two hours late, the gamekeeper arrived to deliver a letter from MacRae (in his capacity as lawyer) ordering the valuation of fixture woodwork only. Puzzled by this instruction, the valuers persuaded Leonard against his better judgment to see the laird again and ask for an explanation. Burroughs refused to meet him, but the factor was able to confirm the decision.[22] Eventually Leonard received compensation amounting to £20.

Immediately the evictions became known, there was a storm of protest, not just in Orkney, but nationally and even overseas. This was the first case of crofters being evicted as a direct result of giving evidence to the Commission and their removal caused a sensation. Burroughs might try to justify his action by arguing that neither Leonard nor Grieve were tenants but were in illegal occupancy since estate regulations forbade sub-tenancy, yet even he did not try to deny the connection between the evidence and their eviction.[23] Both *The Orkney Herald* and *The Orcadian* condemned the evictions, as did Scottish and English newspapers. An outspoken attack even appeared in *The Boston Daily Evening Traveller*,[24] apparently written by one of the crofters who had emigrated after being evicted from Quandale in 1846. This added to the anonymous mail for Trumland since the unknown author posted a copy of the paper to Burroughs. Both Leonard and Grieve argued the justice of their case in the local papers, the nationals copied their stories and Burroughs, supported by the

'Respectables', kept the controversy alive with a stream of letters and articles.

With support for the crofters gathering, Rousay itself was brought to the very brink of violence. Even before the Royal Commission there had been some unrest, but during the winter of 1883-4 there were frequent cases of damage to crops and agricultural implements. One of the 'Respectables', writing to *The Scotsman*, described how some of the Sourin crofters who had refused to attend the original meetings had damage done to their boats, and the writer warned the culprit that he 'would not, if detected, guarantee him against a thorough lynching'.[25]

The main trouble, however, centred on Mr Moyes, the Sourin schoolmaster, who was widely criticised for the part he had played in the investigation of the anonymous letter. It was felt that he had been too co-operative with the authorities and had cast suspicion on boys who had recently been his pupils. He had, indeed, been too ready to lend his premises for the Fiscal's investigation, yet it is easy to sympathise with the young schoolmaster faced with this overwhelming visitation by the law and having to make a quick decision. The interrogation of Fred Leonard can also be faulted on the grounds that it was wrong to apprehend and question a fourteen-year-old boy without informing his parents, but to do so was the responsibility of the Fiscal rather than the schoolmaster. At the best of times, country schoolmasters were often unpopular. Moyes' duties included the unenviable task of collecting school fees from impoverished parents and compelling the attendance of children deliberately kept from school to assist on the croft. To this end he sent out Burroughs' gamekeeper, who acted as Attendance Officer, to round up recalcitrants. Many were ready to believe the worst of the schoolmaster, and the Sourin crofters did not let matters rest until they secured his dismissal. Life for Moyes became increasingly difficult. Shortly after the Fiscal's visit he went south to get married and arrived back in Rousay with a new wife and a boatload of furniture. He was met by a crowd of 'roughs' who jeered and hooted at him and he could find no one willing to transport his belongings to the schoolhouse. The farmer who eventually came to his assistance was threatened with vengeance and at night youthful vandals, now unrestrained by their parents, prowled round the school creating a disturbance and doing a certain amount of damage.

George M'Crie of Curquoy, Inspector of Poor, was another target and, under cover of darkness, a section of his dyke was pulled down. He was disliked for his office and the niggardly amount of poor relief commonly given. He was also a leading 'Respectable' and a frequent writer of letters to the newspapers attacking the 'Crofters', sometimes under his own name but more often using various *noms-de-plume*. He encouraged Burroughs in the belief that unrest on the estate was the work of agitators. When Burroughs was in London for his customary winter visit, M'Crie wrote:—

> I trust that, by the date of your return, at all events, the present 'wave' of carefully fostered discontent will have passed away from the island. Nothing will give me greater pleasure than to see it subside — I am certain it will — for *artificial* sentiment never lasts long.[26]

However, when Burroughs returned in April 1884, the disorder still continued. He did his best to restore peace, personally visiting the homes of some of the more unruly youngsters and telling their parents that he would hold them personally responsible for the actions of their children. He also wrote warning letters to some of the older people whom he suspected might be involved.[27]

It was always Burroughs' contention that it was the Napier Commission which had created the trouble in Rousay and set neighbour against neighbour. It was a rather superficial view since it glossed over the tensions which had been building up on the estate ever since 1840. Nevertheless, the Commission had acted as a catalyst. The facade of paternal concern had been stripped away and for the next six years there was to be continuous warfare between 'Crofters' and 'Respectables'.

12

Support for the Crofters

'It is a moral issue, a question of right and wrong, a holy war.' Rev Archibald MacCallum[1]

IN earlier times those tenants who had fallen foul of their landlord could do little but suffer in silence since acts of petty tyranny were local matters about which the country at large neither knew nor cared. The evictions of Leonard and Grieve were different. They were removed because of evidence given to a Royal Commission and so inevitably their plight was a cause of national concern. The struggle of the Rousay crofters did not happen in isolation but was part of a wider movement for crofters' rights throughout the Highlands and Islands. It was a cause which evoked the sympathy of both romantics and more radically minded liberals, attracting also the not wholly welcome support of Irish Parnellites. There was, therefore, a considerable body of opinion which the unfortunate Rousay crofters could rally to their support.

The Orkney Herald, in its first reaction to the eviction of Leonard from a croft which his father had reclaimed from common land, suggested a fund to investigate the legal ownership of the commons and, if necessary, to contest the assumed rights of the landlords. This suggestion was taken up by James Grieve and in November he announced that such a fund had been established with himself as secretary and MacCallum as treasurer. The original purpose of the fund was now to be extended since, as well as obtaining a legal opinion on the commons, some of the money was to be used to relieve the distress of James Leonard. Grieve himself was more comfortably placed and had obtained alternative accommodation in Rousay, so he disclaimed any personal interest in the fund.[2] The 'Respectables', no doubt glad to see Leonard out of Rousay, were quick to attack the whole idea as unnecessary[3] — Leonard was in good health, he had a job in Kirkwall, his older children were working, and he had just received £20 compensation for the houses he had built. As Burroughs rather unfortunately phrased it, 'he is an able-bodied man and so is his wife'! The original idea had been to build a new house for Leonard on the

145

Free Church feu,[4] but this ran into difficulties with the presbytery, and the scheme had to be abandoned.

From time to time there were comments that, although there had been a promise that the accounts of the fund would be published, this had never been done. It would be dangerous, the crofters argued, to publish a list of supporters, thus exposing them to the risk of victimisation. It appears that quite substantial donations were received from Orcadians in Glasgow and Edinburgh and that some support came from overseas, but there was a suspicion that very little was contributed locally and that this was the real reason for secrecy. In the absence of accounts, there is no means of knowing how the money was spent. If it was used to obtain a legal opinion on the commons, it was money wasted since unwritten rights of tenants, whatever their ultimate validity, stood little chance of being upheld in law. It would seem likely that the greater part of the money raised was used to send Leonard south to meet the influential leaders of the crofters' movement in Glasgow and Edinburgh.

There was little natural feeling of solidarity between Orkney crofters and their counterparts in Gaelic-speaking areas but, although contact was infrequent, a common feature was the adherence of the majority of the population to the Free Kirk. It was through the Free Kirk and through the Rev Archibald MacCallum's personal connections that the Rousay crofters were brought into the mainstream of the crofters' movement. Free Church leaders, and particularly the divinity college professors, provided the movement with an influential, middle-class, urban leadership. The attitude of Free Church ministers actually serving in crofting parishes was more variable.[5] The Disruption was a generation in the past and, in the intervening period, many Highland ministers had developed a comfortable relationship with their proprietors. However, this was seldom the case in Orkney where MacCallum's radical views were by no means unique among the Free Church clergy. Goodfellow of the South Parish in South Ronaldsay was well known for his ultra-radical views and he hastened to invited Leonard to preach, the presence of the ex-mason lay preacher evoking complaints about political preaching and snide comments about 'sermons in stones'. Armour, the Free Church minister of Sanday, was equally radical and on one occasion he was arrested and gaoled for creating a disturbance at a Tory political meeting.

Burroughs, who was seldom able to attribute disinterested motives to his opponents, saw this Free Church involvement in a particularly cynical light. In a letter to *The Times*[6] he accused these ministers of acting from purely financial considerations. Free-will offerings were declining, he argued, as were any genuine differences between the Established Church and the Free Church, so these ministers had been enlisted as agitators to create artificial divisions by fomenting opposition to landlords. Their apparent concern about emigration was likewise due to self-interest since 'even a pauper was worth 5/- a year to the Free Church'.

MacCallum's family connections were of equal importance in forging links with the Highland crofters. Another member of the family, the Rev Donald MacCallum, an Established Church minister, was even more deeply embroiled in crofter politics. He had already given evidence to the Napier Commission regarding the Parochial Board of Arisaig's neglect of paupers and, when he moved to Vaternish in Skye, he found himself in the very heartland of the crofters' movement. It was a struggle in which, unusual though it was for an Established Church minister, he identified himself totally with the cause. As 'High Priest' of the crofters, he presided over crowded meetings advocating such measures as rent strikes and the forcible expropriation of land. These radical policies contrasted with the more cautious approach of the divinity college professors but were much more in touch with the feelings of the crofters themselves. These were the activities which, in 1886, were to lead not only to a presbytery charge that he 'incited crofters to class hatred',[7] but also led to his arrest on a civil charge of 'prompting an unlawful agitation'.[8]

The Rousay crofters' opening move was to contact the Napier Commission and to submit a long supplementary statement describing the investigation of the anonymous letter and the evictions of Leonard and Grieve. They also approached the Rev Dr Oliver Flett, Baptist minister in Paisley and one of the most consistent champions of the crofters' cause. Son of an Orkney crofter, Flett had been apprenticed to a shoemaker in Glasgow but, with his Latin and Greek grammar beside him on the work-bench, he had prepared himself for the ministry. His marriage into the wealthy Coats family brought him influence — he was something of an establishment figure — but it did little to temper his radical views on land reform. In 1881, following the Irish land legislation but before there was any widespread movement for reform in either the Highlands or in Orkney, he addressed a public meeting in Westray and argued for a bill similar to the Irish Land Act.[9] Dr Flett now called a meeting of Orcadians resident in Glasgow. The meeting was well attended and it proceeded to pass a series of 'enthusiastic and unanimous resolutions' expressing sympathy with Leonard and Grieve, resolving to aid the cause of land reform and to test at law the landlord's right to seize houses built on the former common. A 'large and influential' committee was appointed and it was instructed to bring the case to the notice of Lord Napier and Mr Gladstone and approach Dr Charles Cameron, the Glasgow Liberal pro-crofter M.P., with a view to having the matter raised in Parliament.[10]

A few weeks later broader organisations to fight the cause of land reform were launched almost simultaneously in Edinburgh (The Highland Association) and in London (The Highland Land Law Reform Association). At first the Rousay crofters worked through the Edinburgh Highland Association and, at the inaugural meeting, their case figured prominently. The Highland Association was Free Church dominated and, although other leaders were brought in to create the impression of an inter-denominational movement, *The Scotsman,* consistently hostile to crofters, was able to comment sourly that 'The Highland Association is known to be as much part of the Free Church and Disestablishment machinery as any of the committees under Principal Rainy's direction'.[11]

Principal Rainy was not one of the those present at a crowded meeting in the Music Hall which launched the Association, but other Free Church professors played leading parts. After the formal business of resolving to form the Association, Dr Carment delivered a long speech describing the Rousay evictions, a speech interrupted by hisses and cries of 'Shame' when Burroughs' name was mentioned. He went on to describe the repressive combination of laird, factor, Procurator Fiscal, Sheriff and Moderate minister and demanded an enquiry by the Home Secretary.[12] Obviously the crofters had been in close contact with the professors, since Carment had Grieve's rent receipts from the factor in his possession while Professor Lindsay, another speaker, had those of James Leonard.[13] Within two weeks the Association's chairman was able to report that he had been in touch with the Home Secretary and had urged other land reform associations in the north to make representations on behalf of the Rousay crofters.[14]

Meanwhile the Glasgow Orcadians had been successful in enlisting the assistance of Dr Cameron who asked a question in Parliament about the Rousay boy, Samuel Mainland, whom he claimed had been arrested without warrant. The Lord Advocate replied that the arrest was in order and the warrant could be produced, but he refused to reveal the precognitions of either Mainland or Fred Leonard on the grounds that the matter was still under investigation. The following month Cameron returned to the attack and asked to see, not only the warrant, but also the phrases which Fred Leonard had been compelled to write in the Sourin school. The Irish M.P., Donald MacFarlane, Parnellite member for Carlow but a Highlander by birth and a supporter of the crofters, pursued a more profitable line by attacking the dual role of MacRae as personal lawyer and Procurator Fiscal. The Lord Advocate, however, replied that this was quite a usual arrangement and indeed one which was necessary in sparsely inhabited districts where there was insufficient work to justify a full-time Fiscal.[15] The crofters' friends in Parliament achieved little. Their questions had been mere sniping at side issues since the unpleasant fact remained that by evicting tenants because he disliked their evidence Burroughs had done nothing illegal.

Eventually, like their Highland counterparts, the Rousay crofters came to deal through the Highland Land Law Reform Association and its successor, the Highland Land League, which became the main vehicles of crofter opinion. As a reward for his martyrdom in the crofters' cause, James Leonard was employed at an annual salary of £52 as one of only two full-time agents working for the Association.[16] The other agent was in Skye and, since Orkney was very much peripheral, Leonard's appointment was due to his publicity value rather than to the amount of work there was for him to do in Orkney. It is difficult to gauge his success as an agent since both membership and the very existence of branches were kept secret, but it seems certain that the Association's support in Orkney was limited. To Burroughs, who had long seen paid agitators where there were none, Leonard's appointment provided confirmation that all the discontent in Rousay was being deliberately created from outside. One of the Associations' leaders whom he particularly disliked was Surgeon General MacLean, an ardent Caithness Liberal who had served with the 42nd Highlanders in many of the campaigns in which Burroughs had been involved, including the Crimea and the Relief of Lucknow. Added to his dislike of MacLean as a traitor to his class was the fact that he had been one of the group of young surgeons who had recommended that Burroughs' leg be amputated when he was wounded at Lucknow. He had as little confidence in the Surgeon General's crofting policies as he had in his medical abilities.

The Napier Report (April 1884) was more thorough-going in its proposals than perhaps the crofters had expected. However, by recommending that security of tenure should be granted only to crofts paying more than £6 a year in rent and that smaller crofts should be phased out, the Report ultimately found favour with neither the Highland Land Law Reform Association nor the landowners. Since it pleased nobody, the government were in no hurry to introduce legislation, and the hope which the hearings had generated began to evaporate. It was in this atmosphere that the Association met in Dingwall in September 1884 with MacCallum, one of the delegates to the conference. He delivered an impassioned speech in favour of the policy eventually adopted — the use of the newly enfranchised power of the crofter to elect M.P.s specifically pledged to a programme of land reform. The events of the preceding year had brought about a change in MacCallum. Gone was the tentative, rather apologetic tone he had used in his evidence to the Commission. He urged crofters not to vote Liberal just because a candidate called himself a Liberal, since many of them were just as obstructive as Tories. There was as much chance of getting reform from the present Liberal government as from a peat stack, he said. He urged crofters to follow the example of Ireland where success came only when members pledged to land reform were elected. It was a moral issue, he concluded, it was a question of right and wrong, a holy war.[17]

From Kirkwall, James Leonard campaigned for the Dingwall Programme, urging the new voters in Orkney and Shetland to make use of their power and criticising the local M.P.s, Laing and Pender, for their inertia. The extension of the franchise in 1884 had more than doubled the electorate in the constituency and it could be expected that the great majority of those voting for the first time would be sympathetic to land law reform. These expectations were borne out by events. With the election of Leonard Lyell, the crofters obtained an M.P. sympathetic to their aspirations and, when the need arose, willing to act quickly for their protection. Lyell was a Gladstonian Liberal and a strong supporter of Irish Home Rule, and he justified his support for the Irish by drawing analogies with Orkney and Shetland. Since he supported the crofters, it was right, he argued, that he should support Irish land reform and therefore also the cause of Irish Home Rule. Since he was a supporter of Irish Home Rule, he also had to advocate a degree of Home Rule for Orkney and Shetland in recognition of their special status.

Burroughs was as ready to question the motives of Gladstonian Liberals as he was to cast doubt on the sincerity of the Free Kirk. It was his view that:—

> ... a crofter may be curtly described as a newly enfranchised agricultural voter, whose vote it has become of great importance to 'certain old Parliamentary hands' to obtain, at whatever cost, other than their own.[18]

Although Burroughs perhaps saw Gladstone's commitment to land reform in an over-cynical light, his analysis was basically correct. With growing tensions in the Liberal Party and a large block of unpredictable Irish members, it was important to Gladstone that he should control the Highland constituencies and it was this consideration, more than the findings of the Napier Commission or the unrest in the Highlands, which finally persuaded him to introduce the Crofters Act of 1886. Legislation was indeed obtained by crofters using their new political power.

As long as Burroughs remained in the army he was strictly non-political. Indeed he took so little interest in politics that it was not even known whether he favoured Liberals or Tories. But in the 1880s it was becoming increasingly difficult for landowners in the North of Scotland to be Gladstonian Liberals. Measures like the Ground Game Act (1880), the Irish Land Acts (1881 and 1885), the Agricultural Holdings Act (1883) and finally the Crofters Act (1886) ensured his opposition. He became increasingly right-wing in his views. He was an active member of the Liberty and Property Defence League, an organisation intent on imposing limits to state interference and noted for its dislike of state education and income tax.

Lairds, who were accustomed to dominating the politics of the constituency, found themselves increasingly without a voice. It was not only Gladstonian Liberals who courted the crofting vote. The split between Gladstonian Home Rulers and Liberal Unionists resulted in Orkney and Shetland being contested in 1892 by rival Liberals, deeply divided over the question of Irish Home Rule, but often broadly agreeing on other issues. It was not necessarily the Gladstonians who offered the more radical policies and indeed Younger, the Liberal Unionist, attempted to outbid Lyell for the crofters' votes. His policies were deeply influenced by Oliver Flett, the Paisley minister who had rallied the Glasgow Orcadians at the time of the evictions. For Flett the Crofters Act was a halfway stage only. The crofters had gained security of tenure and this had given them freedom of speech since threats of eviction could no longer be used to silence them. As well as freedom of speech, they had gained the right to vote and hence the power to alter the system by democratic means. Flett advocated a land purchase scheme similar to that introduced in Ireland by the Ashbourne Act. He looked forward to the break-up of the big estates and an end to all landlordism.[19] These policies were little to the liking of landowners, yet they reluctantly gave their support to Younger despite his endorsement of Flett's land purchase scheme. The crofters, on the other hand, remained solidly behind Lyell, who was returned with a comfortable majority.

Many of the urban leaders of the Crofters' Movement were prominent in Gaelic scholarship and in promoting traditional culture. This essentially romantic support in Norse guise is represented by the activities of A. W. Johnston's Reform League of Orkney and Shetland or, as it was later called, the Udal League. Johnston's interests and abilities were antiquarian rather than political and the League's programme tended to be concerned with historical niceties rather than with the realities of the nineteenth century. Johnston is now remembered for the founding of the Viking Club and its publication of Orkney and Shetland records rather than for his eccentric Udal League. But in 1886, when Irish Home Rule was a major issue, Johnston's proposals for legislative and fiscal independence for a combined Orkney and Shetland gained some temporary support. He envisaged each parish with its elected council or *Herad* presided over by a *Lawrightman* appointed from the landowning classes. Each *Herad* would send representatives to the two *Lawtings* of which there would be one for Orkney and another for Shetland. They in turn would send members to the *Althing,* the supreme legislative body chaired by the *Lawman.* The crown was to be represented by the *Governor* and, in strict observance of the proper status of the old earls, this post was to be restricted to princes of the royal blood. The League's land programme held some attractions. Johnston proposed that Commissioners be appointed to supervise the break-up of big estates and to arrange the transfer of land to owner-occupiers who would then be confirmed in their udal status. Rights to common land ought to be restored and Orkney and Shetland should receive proper compensation from the British government for the Bishopric estate, sold off by the Department of Woods and Forests to finance the creation of parks in central London.[20]

It can be seen that the League was essentially a conservative and backward-looking organisation and, indeed, it is a great misfortune that the serious business of campaigning for a measure of autonomy for Orkney and Shetland ever became mixed up with this mumbo-jumbo. Its connections with land reform were almost incidental, the League advocating only those changes which coincided with Johnston's idealised version of the past. For a time it gained sufficient prominence for Lyell to chair some of its meetings, but efforts to win other supporters were less successful. Johnston had great hopes of involving Colonel Balfour whose book, *Odal Rights and Feudal Wrongs,* contained many of the arguments on which the League's programme was based. Johnston wanted to persuade him to become the first *Lawman,* but Balfour was horrified by the offer, protested that his interest was purely antiquarian, and dissociated himself from 'any radical change or revolution'.[21] In rejecting any connection with the League, Balfour was more clear-headed than Johnston. Balfour's book and the League's programme were based on the seventeenth and eighteenth century struggle between lairds and their feudal superior. Neither had much relevance to the nineteenth century struggle between lairds and their small tenants.

This chapter, in looking at the support which the evicted crofters could evoke, has dealt with the years 1883 to 1892. It has carried the story beyond the passing of the Crofters Act. It is now necessary to return to 1886 to examine the passing of the Act and its impact on Rousay.

13

The Crofters Act

'Happy are ye if ye suffer for righteousness sake.'   Rev Archibald MacCallum[1]

THE bill which Gladstone eventually introduced, The Crofters Holdings (Scotland) Bill of 1886, more commonly known simply as the Crofters Act, differed substantially from the recommendations of the Napier Commission, but since it offered security of tenure to all crofters, not merely those paying more than £6 a year in rent, it was much more acceptable. In one important respect, however, it fell short of the crofters' demands, since it made no provision for the return to crofting use of former common grazings or land which had been engrossed by big farms. It therefore did nothing to satisfy the land hunger of the Highlands and for this reason the bill was opposed by those M.P.s pledged to the programme of the Highland Land Law Reform Association and their Parnellite allies. The bill, however, had the support not only of the government but also the Tory opposition which had reluctantly come to the conclusion that reform was a prerequisite to restoring law and order in the Highlands. The passage of the bill was therefore rapid and it was opposed only by those who felt it did not go far enough. Landlords found themselves without friends and they felt betrayed.

Although the Act fell short of satisfying the crofters, it did meet many of their demands and it must be regarded as a turning point of supreme importance in the history of the Highlands and Islands. Subject to certain conditions (the most important being that he paid his rent regularly), the crofter could no longer be evicted but had security of tenure. Moreover, this security extended beyond one lifetime since tenancy could be bequeathed to an immediate relative. Should he leave, the crofter was entitled to compensation for suitable improvements made either by himself or by his forebears. Rack-renting was ended as the croft was held at a 'fair rent', independently determined. The Act established a Land Court, the Crofters' Commission, whose function it was to set fair rents, determine the value of improvements and administer the other provisions of the Act.

There was a good deal of discontent in the Highlands as a result of the Act's failure to provide new land for crofters, but in Orkney there was a different and more immediate cause for concern. It was intended that the Crofters Act would apply to the 'crofting parishes' in the counties of Shetland, Orkney, Caithness, Sutherland, Ross and Cromarty, Inverness and Argyll, but it was left to the Crofters Commission, subject to the approval of the Secretary of State, to gather evidence and decide which parishes were 'crofting parishes' within the meaning of the Act. So different was Orkney from the rest of the crofting region that it remained to be seen whether the Commission would exclude some parishes, or possibly the whole county. In many respects the crofting system in Orkney had much more in common with farming in Aberdeenshire than with the true crofting zone[2] The Crofters Act has created the impression that there was something unique about the system of agriculture in the seven crofting counties but, as a result of freezing the landholding patterns of 1886, the crofting counties are now more distinct than they were when the Act was passed. The Orkney system of farms with cottar pendicles on the moorland edge, supplying labour and tackling the work of reclamation by acting as a moving pioneer fringe advancing up the hill, was also the system in the north-east of Scotland and, at the time of the Act, the proportion of very small crofts was about the same. In both Orkney and Aberdeenshire approximately 20% of holdings were under five acres. In both, there was a farming 'ladder' of small, medium and large farms by which the ambitious farmer might hope to advance. This was in sharp contrast to the unbridgeable gulf between the fragmented crofts and the large sheep farms of the true crofting zone. Orkney owed its inclusion as one of the crofting counties to the fact that characteristics of an older style of farming persisted in Orkney when they had disappeared from most of the rest of arable farming Scotland. The kelp boom years had helped to maintain the traditional system of cottar labour; commons remained undivided long after they had disappeared from most parts of Scotland and, above all, farming remained backward until the coming of steam navigation. Thus Orkney, basically an old-fashioned arable area, came to be included with the crofting districts of the Highlands.

Fortunately the Crofters Commission had to decide the question of Orkney's inclusion or exclusion, not by an analysis of the farming system, but by a strict interpretation of the Act. A 'crofting parish' was defined as one in which, either at the time of the Act or within the previous eighty years, there were tenants holding land on a year-to-year basis and paying a rent of less than £30 for crofts which consisted of both arable and common grazing. Quite obviously there were many tenants-at-will in Orkney and equally obviously many farms rented at less than £30 a year. It was only the matter of the tenant's 'right of common pasturage' that could be disputed. By 1886 the commons were divided and this right had gone, but had it existed within the previous eighty years? If it had, Orkney consisted of 'crofting parishes'.

The Commission called for information to aid them with their decisions and, in response, the Orkney proprietors met in August 1886 to draw up a common submission. Colonel Balfour was called to the chair and, after discussion, the following statement was agreed:—

1. That the commonties or pasture lands of Orkney are of small extent as compared with commonties or pasture lands in the other counties specified in the Act.
2. That these commonties, previous to their being divided, belonged to a large proprietary, as will be seen from the decrees of division.
3. That these commonties have all been divided — some of them before the year 1820.
4. That previous to the division no individual proprietor could give his tenants a right of pasturage in the common. Such right could only be given with consent of co-proprietors which consent was in no known instance asked or obtained.
5. That since the division no right of pasturage has, so far as known, been given by a proprietor to his tenants.
6. That any grazing or pasturage by tenants either before or since the division has merely been by tolerance on the part of proprietors.
7. That, therefore, in the opinion of the conference, no parish in Orkney is a crofting parish within the meaning of the Act.[3]

The proprietors' case was simple. Unable to deny that there were tenants-at-will and farms rented at less than £30 in every parish, they were also forced to admit that commons had existed in every parish within the previous eighty years, the earliest Orkney division being in Stenness in 1815. They were forced to base their case on one argument — that tenants seldom if ever had a *written* agreement allowing access to the common. It ignored the fact that an unwritten right had undoubtedly existed by use and wont from time immemorial.

The crofters were also preparing a submission with the assistance of Andrew Thomson, a young Kirkwall lawyer. Born in Kirkwall where he received an elementary education in the Subscription School, Thomson had worked his way up through the Town Clerk's office and an Edinburgh legal firm before entering Glasgow University. In 1884 he returned to Kirkwall and, until his early death in 1894, a large part of his business consisted of acting on behalf of crofters in Orkney and Shetland. He was an ardent Liberal and served as election agent for Leonard Lyell. A passionate supporter of the Crofters Act, he was always ready to oppose any attempt by landlords to circumvent its intentions.

Due to the representations of the proprietors, Orkney was one of the last places where the question of the 'crofting parishes' was decided by the Commission. At the end of November 1886 it recognised all Orkney parishes with the exception of St Ola and Stromness, for both of which it required further evidence. The following year they were also designated 'crofting parishes' and thus it was decided that the Act applied to the whole of Orkney.

It was a decision widely welcomed. Both local papers were at this time hostile to landlords and devoted considerable space to crofting affairs. *The Orkney Herald* published a parish by parish account of the crofters' grievances and *The Orcadian* ran a weekly 'Crofters' Column'. Reporting the Commission's decision, *The Orkney Herald* commented:

> Orkney is overwhelmingly a county of crofters . . . a position of penury and hardship — of toil and moil to pay the rent and, where possible, to make ends meet. The land which they occupy is very frequently the scraps of the parish and these, in a majority of instances, reclaimed by the holders or their immediate ancestors from the hillside, the links and the bog. On these holdings houses have been raised, enlarged and improved as the reclamations proceeded and the land increased in productiveness, but all the work has not only been done in almost every case at the sole expense of the crofters, but their rents have been raised in something like relative proportion. It is no wonder, therefore, that after all their labour, and planning, and pinching, very many of the crofters are today not only in arrears with their rent but are dependent on the forebearance of their tradesmen and friends for being kept afloat.[4]

It was hardly surprising that, when the lairds held a further meeting to consider the implications of the Commission's decision to include Orkney, the local press was not admitted. It was rumoured to be a dispirited gathering, with the proprietors divided about the wisdom of further resistance. Some like Mr Gold, the Earl's factor, argued that the law must now be accepted, while others, the 'more tyrannically minded' as *The Orcadian* described them, were in favour of trying to do something. The conference failed to agree on any future joint action and it was left to individuals such as Burroughs to make further protests if they wished.[5]

As soon as the decision was announced that Rousay was a 'crofting parish', the celebrations began. At the close of the morning service in the Free Kirk in Sourin on Sunday 28th November, the Rev Archibald MacCallum announced that the harvest thanksgiving would be held the following week. The decision to designate Rousay a 'crofting parish' was, he said, a further cause for thanksgiving, comparable to the redemption of Israel out of Egypt and out of the house of bondage. The importance of the change was great and it would be deep and lasting. He was particularly gratified when he considered his own district of Sourin where about 46 of the 55 households would receive the protection of the Act. Although the Act applied to other districts, they would not benefit to the same extent since, for example in Frotoft, only two or three holdings were likely to qualify.

He harked back, quite erroneously, to a time when wicked men had plotted to make Sourin a desert by driving the people from the land of their fathers. He recalled how the late Rev George Ritchie, who had led his congregation out of the Church of Scotland at the time of the Disruption, had protested at this unspeakable cruelty, and when the laird had answered that the land was his to do as he pleased, the 'venerable old minister' had answered him with the text, 'The Earth is the Lord's and the fullness thereof'. The words of the minister had been unable to deflect the laird from his wicked purpose, but before it could be accomplished, the mysterious but holy and adorable providence of God had swept utterly from the land of the living the man who had thought to make others homeless wanderers on the face of the earth. 'So let all thine enemies perish, O Lord!' MacCallum declaimed, and the congregation must have known that he had the present laird in mind.

MacCallum's facts were somewhat confused although, no doubt, his oratory had a certain symbolic truth. It seems almost pedantic to point out that the district which George William Traill threatened to clear was Quandale, not Sourin, the greater part of which he did not even own. Nor did death thwart the plans for clearance since the eviction of the Quandale tenants went ahead, uninterrupted by the death of the laird. It should also be recorded that the 'venerable old minister' was only forty-eight at that time.

Although the majority of those present must have known these things, the large congregation was visibly moved and deeply affected as MacCallum reached the climax of his peroration. Many were moved to tears as, speaking with great solemnity and impressiveness, he described how he alone of the ministers of Rousay had fought against a cruel and merciless system 'wet with tears and reeking of the blood of the poor'. At this time he singled out James Leonard for particular mention and coupled his name with the text, 'Happy are ye if ye suffer for righteousness sake'.[6]

The following Friday, MacCallum gave a lecture in the Free Kirk on the subject of the Crofters Act. The ministers of the other denominations had been invited to attend, but Spark of the Established Church declined, and Pirie of the United Presbyterians sent a dry little letter advising crofters to take proper legal advice on how to make their applications. The implication was that they should consult a lawyer instead of listening to MacCallum. The lecture was consequently a second Free Church celebration consisting of a heady mixture of reminiscences, apocalyptic texts, doggerel verse on the subject of clearances and solid facts about the Crofters Act and how to take advantage of it. James Grieve acted as chairman and the proceedings were punctuated with enthusiastic applause.

MacCallum's views on the shortcomings of the 1886 Act are of particular interest. He had three main criticisms to make, the first being that the protection of the Act was restricted to those tenants paying less than £30 a year in rent. He felt that this figure was too low and ought to be increased to £100. In Orkney, where the distinction between crofts and farms was blurred, this was a point of some importance. In those areas which the Napier Commission had studied in detail, such as the Parish of Farr in Sutherland, crofts and farms were quite distinct types of holdings. In Farr there were 293 crofts of which the largest paid a rent of £7:16s, while the smallest of the seven farms was rented at £290. In Rousay there was a much more regular farming ladder and the Crofters Act created a somewhat arbitrary distinction between large crofts and small farms. The second criticism was that MacCallum would have liked the Act to contain powers to break up farms rented at more than £100 a year such as Westness, Langskaill and Saviskaill, and thus create new holdings for the landless. He advocated, therefore, a system of small and medium-sized farms, all subject to a 'fair rent' procedure, but still owned by the laird. His final criticism was the failure to right old wrongs, to restore to crofting use land at one time cleared and to return commons which had been expropriated.[7]

It is difficult for us who are accustomed to government intervention in the economy to appreciate the revolutionary nature of the 1880s land legislation. We have come to think of manipulation of prices and incomes as normal and, indeed, one of the most important functions of government. Landowners such as Burroughs, brought up on the *laissez faire* doctrines of the nineteenth century, viewed almost with incredulity any attempt to interfere with their rents. As Burroughs wrote, intending to pour ridicule on the whole idea, a Prime Minister might equally well appoint a Royal Commission to compel shopkeepers to reduce their prices or to order landlords to let private houses in towns at rents fixed by the government.[8] The sarcasm is rather lost on later generations grown used to exactly this kind of governmental action. For Burroughs, ownership of land was absolute. He often compared owning land to owning clothing — the crofters had no more right to his commons than they had to his hat, they had no more right to his farms than they had to his coat. It was a view of ownership which implied that the landlord need consider no interest but his own. The tenant had no rights beyond the agreement of his lease, if he were lucky enough to have one, and the landlord was under a moral obligation only when the tenant had earned it by good behaviour. Since property was absolute, any action by the government which diminished its value by reducing rents or cancelling arrears was morally wrong — it was theft. He objected to the Crofters Act, not just because it affected his pocket, but because it infringed the fifth commandment — 'Thou shalt not steal'.

Yet few people, no matter how strongly they hold to a principle, can be entirely consistent. An illuminating story is told of Burroughs when he commanded the regiment in India. After a long, hot and dusty march the men were given permission to fall out near an isolated village store. The lucky shopkeeper found himself in as strong a monopoly position for the sale of beer as any crofting laird ever was with regard to the supply of land. Colonel Burroughs was horrified to learn that the man was charging a shilling for a glass of beer. Summoning the shopkeeper, Burroughs forced him to hand back the excess money he had taken, telling him that the proper charge was sixpence and, should he try to charge more, he could expect to have his store pulled down.[9] When it suited his purpose, Burroughs too was capable of fixing fair prices and cancelling arrears.

The Crofters Act was passed in 1886 and before the year was out it had been decided that the Act applied to at least most of Orkney, yet it was a further two years before the Commission made its first visit and began the work of fixing fair rents. The three-man Commission found that the task of holding courts throughout the Highlands and Islands and investigating hundreds of individual crofts was work which taxed their limited manpower.

The visit of the Commission was eagerly awaited and the factor, collecting rents in January 1888, found the crofters hostile and reluctant to pay. Again and again he was told that the land was the people's, that they had paid rent long enough and now they intended to pay no more. Extremists were trying to persuade crofters to withhold their rents until after the Commission's visit, arguing that the greater the arrears, the greater the rent reduction they could expect. Rent arrears rose to £1,014, or nearly a third of the rental, and much of this was due to the rent strike.[10] Yet not all of the arrears should be attributed to this. Arrears had been growing ever since 1876, long before there was any prospect of legislation, and there is little doubt that falling prices were making it difficult to meet the rent. Elsewhere in Britain, not just in the crofting counties, farmers were encountering hard times and the average level of rent throughout the country fell by between 10% and 20%.[11] Burroughs, however, made no reduction until compelled to do so by the Crofters' Commission and, indeed, the rental of the estate reached an all-time high in 1888 on the eve of the Commission's visit.

The applications from the Burroughs Estate were among the first Orkney batch which the Commission considered in September 1888.[12] There were 45 cases from Rousay, 38 of them from crofters holding land directly from the laird, and the remaining seven were from sub-tenants, most of them on Langskaill. Working against constant pressure on its time, the Commission dealt with all 45 cases in two days, most cases taking about ten minutes including the formality of administering the oath. There was some justification for Burroughs' criticism that the Commission based their decisions on a very superficial knowledge of the property with which they were dealing. They lacked the time and staff to do otherwise.

The Rousay crofters were represented collectively by Andrew Thomson and the story told was the now familiar one of successive rent increases, the loss of the commons and the unrewarding struggle of reclamation. Nearly half of the land cultivated by these 45 crofters had been reclaimed by them or their immediate predecessors. In nine cases the crofters had originally settled on hill land and had reclaimed all their arable land. Since they had lost the common grazings they kept few sheep — 17 of these crofters had none at all and no crofter possessed more than four sheep. Yet nearly all the crofters had several cattle, one man possessing as many as twelve beasts.

The Commission made one or two half-hearted efforts to find out about the crofters' income from the sale of eggs. By the time they heard the Rousay cases, the Commissioners had been long enough in Orkney to know that questions on this subject caused merriment but elicited absolutely no information. Hens were the preserve of the womenfolk and men were not supposed to know anything about them. Even if they did, they had no intention of divulging a secret income. In the same way as a crofter today may feel it is iniquitous that he is expected to pay income tax on his wife's earnings from a knitting machine or from bed and breakfast visitors, his forebears believed that egg production, since it was an ancillary enterprise conducted by their wives, should not be taken into account in fixing the rent of a croft. Although egg production was on a much smaller scale than it grew to be in the present century, it was already a significant element on many small crofts. The fall in grain prices had not resulted in a decline in the acreage of cereals, but there was a tendency to export less and consume more on the farm, particularly by feeding grain to poultry. When the rest of agriculture was stagnating, the poultry business continued to expand and egg exports from Orkney topped the million dozen mark in the 1880s. The price — around 8d per dozen — held up well at a time when other agricultural prices were falling.[13] Sheriff Brand, the Commission's chairman, first tried to draw James Craigie of Braes on the subject of hens. Craigie, who had been very exact in his evidence up to that point, suddenly became vague. He admitted owning poultry but was unsure of the number and would express no opinion when asked whether the sale of eggs helped him to pay his rent. Having tried another crofter with no more success, Sheriff Brand gave up. 'We will not say much about hens,' he said, 'It is a rather delicate subject.' Burroughs, however, often had a good deal to say and on many occasions he argued that egg sales provided crofters with an appreciable secret income from which they could easily afford to pay proper rents.

Inevitably those families who had fallen foul of Burroughs over evidence to the Napier Commission had lodged applications for rent reductions and cancellation of arrears. George Leonard of Triblo, the survivor of the Quandale clearance and now aged seventy-two, was at last free from the worry that any activity by land surveyors meant that the laird was intending to incorporate his croft in a neighbouring farm. He had his rent reduced from £6 to £4, and all of his arrears, which amounted to £4, were cancelled. Others were not so fortunate and for those already evicted there was no redress. James Leonard's former croft of Digro was now occupied by his sister and her husband, William Louttit, and when his case was heard the Commission, pressed for time and unwilling to open old wounds, resisted Andrew Thomson's attempt to introduce the subject of Leonard's eviction. However, since a claim for proper compensation for the houses Leonard had built was lodged with the Commission and since Leonard's status as crofter or sub-tenant was at issue, the commissioners had to listen wearily to long quotations from the Napier Commission evidence. Surprisingly Louttit was given neither a rent reduction nor were any of his arrears cancelled. Delaying the Commission had not improved its humour.

Of the 45 cases before the Commission, 37 resulted in a rent reduction, one, a sub-tenant on Langskaill, actually had his rent increased, and in the remaining seven cases the existing rents were continued. Thirty-two of the crofters had been in arrears and in all but four cases at least part of the debt was cancelled. Although Burroughs had a reputation as a bad landlord and his estate was always thought of as high-rented, it is interesting to note that the decisions of the Commission suggest that it was no worse than others. Rousay crofters had their rents reduced by about 30%, which was about the average for all Orkney estates. In Rousay, 54% of arrears were cancelled, which is only slightly above the average of 49% for Orkney as a whole. On some estates the Commission made much greater reductions than it did in Rousay. On the Kirbister Estate in Westray, for example, rents were reduced by a full 50%, and 80% of arrears were cancelled. By this measure there were estates where crofters were even harder pressed than they were in Rousay.

Despite the depressed state of agriculture and the example of most landowners, Burroughs held out to the last against any reduction in rent. A draft of a letter to tenants dated May 1887 shows that he had considered an abatement the previous year[14] but he had evidently decided to wait until the Commission had done its work. Now he had to consider what was to be done about the other tenants including those crofters who had not applied to the Commission. He decided to reduce their rent for 1888 by 10% (provided they paid promptly) and in characteristic fashion he represented this as a reward for their loyalty. Since the recent hearings had reduced rent by an average of about 30%, they would almost certainly have had a better bargain from the Commission. These loyal crofters also received a long letter explaining the worldwide nature of the depression, expanding on the many advantages which Orkney possessed and including some recent statistics on egg production!

Although Burroughs complained bitterly about the Commission robbing him of his income, the actual effect of these reductions was not great. The Commission's decrees diminished his rental by only £158 and his own abatements to crofters cost a further £60. It was not a big reduction on a rental of £3,449. Abatements to farms and the fall in rent which he could obtain on the open market reduced his 1889 income from rents to £2,987. Even so, this merely brought the rental back to its 1879 level. Despite the activities of the Commission and despite the fact that agricultural distress had resulted in countrywide rent reductions, he had succeeded in maintaining his rental at a higher level than was to be found in other parts of the country. Whether the tenants could pay the amounts now set was another matter.

14

The War Against the Crofters

'General Burroughs considered that, his tenants having done everything the law would allow, he would give them nothing which the law did not demand. He did not wish to deny it.' D. J. Robertson, Burroughs' lawyer[1]

ALTHOUGH his crofters might have been surprised to hear it said, General Burroughs was in many ways a kindly man. As he grew older he took an interest in the fate of soldiers retiring after a lifetime in the ranks. He was an advocate of better pensions for them and argued for the provision of an asylum for old soldiers in each military district.[2] Whenever he heard of any man from the 93rd who had fallen on hard times, he was ready to help with private charity or willing to promote a subscription from among his fellow officers. But kindly feelings towards crofters was another matter. He had reached that dangerous point where he ceased to think of them as individuals and began to hate them as a class. It was a matter of principle, and for that principle he would eventually have driven away every crofting tenant from his estate had not the Crofters Act prevented him from doing so. It was principle, not greed, which drove him on, for he was prepared to pursue his vendetta even when it cost him money and he had no hope of financial return.

The first round of his war against the crofters was fought even before the visit of the Commission to fix fair rents. Since the Act was law and could not be ignored, Burroughs carefully examined its provisions and he thought that he had discovered two loopholes by which its intentions might be thwarted. The security of tenure which the Act provided was not absolute since crofters might still be removed if they were in breach of any one of eight statutory provisions. One of these clauses allowed the eviction of a crofter who became bankrupt, and another permitted his removal if he allowed the buildings on his holding to become dilapidated. If a crofter were removed for either of these reasons, he lost the right to assign his tenancy to a relative and the croft reverted to the landlord. Both clauses appeared to offer possibilities, but if he was to take advantage of the bankruptcy clause, it would be necessary to act quickly and have the tenants removed before the Commission had an opportunity to visit Orkney and cancel arrears of rent. The first cases from Sutherland strengthened his resolve. It became clear that, far from being insufficiently radical and too pro-landlord as many crofters had feared, the Commission was actually decreeing substantial reductions and cancelling a large part of the arrears.

The procedure for bankrupting a tenant was not only simple, it was quick, and there seemed no way an action of this kind could be prevented. In early February 1888 Burroughs brought a motion for the payment of arrears before the Sheriff with regard to five crofters, William Work, John Craigie, James Grieve, William Louttit and Robert Grieve,[3] and the following week he pursued four more, Simpson Skethaway, James Cowper, Thomas Gibson and Alexander Leonard.[4] The result of these actions was eagerly awaited, not just in Rousay but throughout Orkney, for it was a test case and other landlords had indicated that, where Burroughs led, they intended to follow. Just as many in the 93rd must have been quite content to allow Burroughs the honour of being first through that dangerous breach in the walls of the Sikanderbagh, Orkney landowners were willing to let Burroughs have the notoriety and the expense of leading the way through the loopholes of the Crofters Act.

The procedure for removal ought to have been automatic. Since it could not be disputed that the tenants were in arrears, the Sheriff granted decrees for payment. The next step was for these decrees to be officially served on the crofters and, if the debt remained unpaid after ten days, this constituted bankruptcy and the crofters, without any further procedure, lost the protection of the Act and were liable to eviction. It seemed that it was impossible to do anything in the time available. Andrew Thomson, as usual, was acting on behalf of the crofters threatened with eviction and he hurriedly contacted G. B. Clark, the M.P. for Caithness who was one of those members pledged to the programme of the Highland Land Law Reform Association. He obtained Clark's ready support and sent off a telegram alerting Leonard Lyell to the situation:

> General Burroughs, Rousay, having obtained decrees against number of crofters for arrears of rent, has followed same by charging, which on lapse of ten days, constitutes notour bankruptcy within meaning of Crofters Act. Charges in my possession. Unless Act at once amended as proposed by Dr Clark, will not confer intended benefits on Orkney crofters of whom 400 in the county. Arrears sued for small, crofters doing utmost to pay. Other proprietors have intimated proceedings.[5]

Dr Clark took up the matter immediately and asked the Lord Advocate if he was aware that Burroughs and others were taking action to make their tenants bankrupt and that there was considerable alarm in Orkney as a result of these cases. The Lord Advocate replied that the government were indeed concerned about the threatened evictions and intended to introduce a bill which would be pushed through all its stages to prevent this happening. Gladstone's Liberal government had by this time fallen, but their opponents were equally unwilling to see the Crofters Act circumvented, having themselves supported the bill on its passage through Parliament. A short bill, the Crofters Holdings (Scotland) Bill of 1887, was quickly passed and had the effect of allowing a crofter threatened with bankruptcy proceedings to appeal to the Commission which was given power to halt the action until it had considered the cancellation of arrears.[6] The new procedure was soon tested when Burroughs brought a further fourteen crofters to court. The cases were duly sisted until the Commission could consider the arrears. Affairs in Rousay had reached a sorry state when it required a special Act of Parliament to thwart the laird's attack on his own tenants.

The amendment to the law did not prevent a crofter being evicted for bankruptcy if, after the case had been considered by the Commission, there were still arrears which the crofter was unable to pay. This might well be so since the Commission only occasionally cancelled all arrears. In 1892 Burroughs made one final effort to remove a crofter for bankruptcy. The crofter concerned was called Frederick Burroughs Kirkness, but even being named after the laird provided no immunity. His farm of Quoyostray in Wasbister had originally belonged to the tenant's grandfather. It was one of several small owner-occupied properties which George William Traill had been able to acquire and in which he left the former owner as tenant. Frederick Kirkness's father, as the naming of the son suggests, had been a strong supporter of the laird. One of the original Free Church deacons, he had quarrelled with Ritchie when rebuked by the session for fishing on the Saturday before communion instead of attending the preparatory service. Refusing to admit that he was at fault, he transferred his allegiance to the Established Church and for many years acted as their precentor.[7] At the time of the purchase of Quoyostray in 1840, it was undrained and unsquared, with its 24 arable acres in scattered, irregular rigs. The estate undertook the work of draining, its arable land was increased to 51 acres and a few years later 130 acres of adjacent hill land were added. At the time of the Crofters Act, as well as the farm there was a flourishing blacksmith's business run by the tenant's brother and a shop managed by his sister. The holding was a substantial one and the rent of £30 placed it at the very upper limit for a croft. Kirkness was not one of those crofters who appeared before the Commission on its first visit. He did not apply for a rent reduction and was not at that time in arrears with his rent. Thereafter he rapidly fell behind and by 1892 his debts amounted to £52. Burroughs took Kirkness to court, whereupon the tenant applied to the Commission to have proceedings halted. When the Commission heard his case, it was decided to cancel all his arrears and to reduce his rent from £30 to £19.[8] The attempt to bankrupt Kirkness failed. Following this generous reduction in his rent, Fred Kirkness spoke for the affirmative in a debate organised by the Young Men's Guild on the question 'Should Parliament interfere between landlord and tenant?'[9] and, in a crowded meeting, carried the motion with a triumphant majority (see Chapter 7). Burroughs, however, felt particularly bitter about this decision, which reduced the rent of Quoyostray to the level it had been at more than twenty years previously.

The crofters' rent strike at the Candlemas term in 1888 was followed by a further dispute at Martinmas which also resulted in legal proceedings against a number of crofters. This was the first term after the Commission's visit and the crofters understandably expected to pay the new reduced rent. They were surprised to discover that Burroughs and other Orkney landowners were still demanding the old rents and were claiming that the new arrangements should take effect only from Whitsun 1889.[10] Since most crofters would pay only their new rent, Burroughs brought eight of them before the Sheriff for rent arrears. The dispute stemmed from an ambiguity in the Crofters Act where two clauses appeared to be contradictory. In these circumstances Sheriff Armour would have preferred to remit the case to the Court of Session for a decision. As the sum involved was less than £25, this could only be done with the agreement of both parties, and Burroughs refused to give his consent.[11] The Sheriff therefore had to make a decision and he found in favour of Burroughs;[12] thus the new rents were to apply only from the summer of 1889. This was a test case, and once again Orkney lairds were quite content to let Burroughs fight the battle but were ready to reap the fruits of his victory. Although others gained as much as he did, it was Burroughs who attracted the opprobrium for staging the confrontation.

Burroughs was also blamed for serving crofters with rate assessments based on their old rents. As *The Orcadian* pointed out, he could not do otherwise since he was obliged to base assessments on the Valuation Roll which had not been revised, yet this is another instance of Burroughs acting ahead of his fellow landlords.[13] *The Orcadian* advised crofters to appeal against their rating and printed a standard letter which they could use.

The battles of 1888 widened the breach between laird and crofters. Until then it had been Burroughs' custom to give every tenant a Christmas gift of half a pound of tea. That Christmas there was no present for any crofter who had appealed to the Commission.[14]

However, the most autocratic and unpleasant side of Burroughs' character was revealed in his attempt to remove his tenants by using what he saw as a second loophole in the Crofters Act. The Act laid an obligation on the tenant to keep his house in a good state of repair and permitted his removal if he allowed his buildings to become dilapidated. At the same time, the Act explicitly reserved all mineral and quarrying rights to the landlord. Burroughs proposed to use these clauses. He would deny building stone to his tenants in the hope that they would be unable to repair their houses, and thus he would be able to repossess their land. Seldom can the power of a landlord have been used in a more despicable way.

The idea of using his quarrying rights as a weapon against his crofters may have sprung from Burroughs' amateur interest in geology and his constant hope that money could be made from mineral deposits on his estate. In 1877 he had discovered what he took to be a fossil foot print and he corresponded with Archibald Geikie, the eminent geologist, whose book he had recently read.[15] Geikie was noncommittal about the mark on the rock which he described as a 'print', but Burroughs, who had a habit of annotating and correcting everything he read, had no such doubts and wrote '*foot* print' in the margin of Geikie's letter.

His interest in geology aroused, Burroughs found what he believed to be a vein of lead near Westness and a deposit of iron ore near Quham in Outer Westness. He corresponded with his relative and former guardian, Sir Edward Colebrooke, whose Lanarkshire estate was near the mining village of Leadhills. Colebrooke urged caution but promised to send an expert to examine the deposits. Burroughs, however, was in a hurry and, without waiting for the Leadhills expert, he engaged the services of John Laity, a Cornish miner, who came to Rousay with two assistants and worked the lead seam for three months in the summer of 1878. During the next ten years Colebrooke repeatedly advised Burroughs against rash mining ventures, or at least to turn his attention to flagstones, which were likely to be more profitable than gold, lead or copper, but it was 1888 before the Leadhills man arrived to conduct a proper survey. Burroughs was absent at the time but John Williamson (whom Colebrooke described as a good surveyor although no gentleman) wrote to tell Burroughs that he had enjoyed his stay at Trumland and had caught 27 trout. The result of his survey was less satisfactory. The vein of lead was of good quality but far too thin to work profitably. An adjacent vein of copper was poor, the supposed iron ore at Quham was actually trap rock and quite valueless, and even paving stones were unlikely to be profitable when quarried in a location so remote from cities. This report ought to have put an end to all thoughts of mining but, within a fortnight of receiving it, Burroughs had an offer from the Egremont Iron-ore Company for the purchase of mining rights and in

M

1891 a similar offer from Brown How of Patterdale, both of which he turned down.

Estate regulations had originally made no mention of mining or quarrying but in 1881, when Burroughs was optimistic about the mineral potential of his estate, a clause had been added reserving the right of the landlord to open a mine or quarry on a tenant's land. Later a second clause was added prohibiting mining or quarrying by tenants. The Crofters Act with its explicit reserving of mineral rights to the landlord coincided with Burroughs' interest in mining ventures and it was perhaps not surprising that he saw his rights under the Act as a weapon he could use against his enemies. There was a further reason for his action. Estate regulations had previously required crofters to obtain the proprietor's permission for any new building they intended to erect but, under the Act, this was no longer required. Burroughs was incensed that crofters who had recently been pleading poverty should now be busily engaged in putting up new buildings over which he had no control. On an estate liable to rack-renting, it was never wise that a croft should appear more conspicuously prosperous than its neighbours and tenants-at-will had hitherto been unwilling to invest in a doubtful future. The new security, however, had unleashed a flurry of building activity.

The matter came to a head over the re-roofing of a house occupied by Robert Inkster, a seventy-six-year old crofter living at Swartafiold in Sourin. Both house and barn had stood unaltered for forty years and both were in a very poor state. In the summer of 1890 Inkster took up residence in the barn and, with the help of a relative, stripped the old flagstone roof from the house and set about the work of repair.[16] He had not consulted Burroughs about his intentions and indeed had no legal obligation to do so. The laird first heard about the repairs in a report of what he described as 'a triumphal procession of some ten carts' taking stone from a quarry to the house site. Although estate regulations had for some years forbidden quarrying, this clause like a number of others had not been enforced and tenants had always been in the habit of opening small quarries whenever they required stone. In Rousay good building stone was plentiful and seldom far below the surface. Burroughs, however, angrily resenting this display of independence, sent his ground officer to warn Inkster and, in a heated exchange, Inkster declared he would continue to take as much stone as he needed.[17]

The laird's next move was to have a lawyer's letter sent to Inkster warning him that, unless he gave an undertaking that he would remove no more building stone, Burroughs would obtain a legal interdict against the 'theft' of his property. A similar warning letter was sent to Peter Yorston who was also improving the house and steading on his croft of Oldman in

Sourin. The crofters immediately contacted Andrew Thomson who was
again called on to defend Rousay crofters from their laird. The lawyer,
however, realising that, no matter how unreasonable the laird's action
might appear, he was acting within his legal rights, informed Burroughs
that the veto would be strictly adhered to, but at the same time asked if
there was any quarry where Inkster would be permitted to take stone.
Would he be permitted to buy building stone or could he open a quarry on
his own land? Burroughs was quite open about his intentions. The Crofters
Act, he replied, obliged the crofters to keep up their houses but the
proprietor was within his rights to prevent quarrying and that was exactly
what he intended to do.[18]

Andrew Thomson thereupon published the whole correspondence in
the press and both local papers were forthright in their condemnation of
Burroughs. *The Orcadian* commented: —

> He sets himself deliberately to defeat the most manifest intention of an Act of
> Parliament because, forsooth, it trenches upon his conception of the divine rights of
> landlords.[19]

The leader went on to compare the plight of the crofters with that of the
Israelites, captive in Egypt and forced to make bricks without straw. It
quoted Exodus: —

> And the taskmasters of the people went out, and their officers, and they spake to the
> people, saying, Thus saith Pharaoh, I will not give you straw. Go ye, get ye straw
> where you can find it; yet not aught of your work shall be diminished.[20]

It was a comparison which captured the fancy of the national press and
the story of the 'Rousay Pharaoh' received a good deal of publicity.

No legal action was taken against Peter Yorston of Oldman who
reluctantly accepted the veto, although protesting vigorously in a letter to
The Orcadian.[21] But because Inkster had told the grounds officer that he
intended to continue to take stone and was reported to have claimed a right
to quarry on his own croft, an action for interdict was brought against him
and was granted by the Sheriff.[22] At the same time, a further interdict was
sought against Betsy Craigie of the appropriately named croft of Falldown.
In September her son-in-law, William Grieve, was quarrying building
material when he heard that other crofters were in trouble. He immediately
abandoned the stones he had already cut but, two months later, thinking
the fuss was over, he brought them home. In this case the Sheriff dismissed
Burroughs' application for an interdict on the grounds that, although
quarrying was contrary to estate regulations, Betsy Craigie, like other
former tenants-at-will, had never been given a copy of the regulations nor
had she been warned that the traditional freedom to quarry was being

withdrawn.[23]   Burroughs, in seeking these interdicts, had won the first case and lost the second, yet it would be wrong to think of the honours as having been equally divided. As Sheriff Armour said in granting the interdict against Inkster:—

> It may be that a landlord who so chooses to act inflicts great hardship on his tenants, and, perhaps in certain cases, he may defeat the Crofters Act and get rid of a crofter by this indirect means. It appears to me, however, that as the law at present stands, he is within his rights.

The second case had merely established that, before a landlord could obtain an interdict, he had to make sure that the tenant knew the estate regulations or had received a proper warning. The Sheriff's decision was confirmed by the Lord Advocate when Burroughs' affairs were once again raised in Parliament by the member for Orkney and Shetland. The Lord Advocate considered that there was no need for fresh legislation since the abuse was not widespread and the landlord was not breaking the law.[24]

With the onset of winter, the plight of seventy-six-year old Inkster was becoming increasingly desperate. He had moved out of his house in the summer thinking that the repairs would soon be completed but he now had ten cartloads of stone at his door which he was interdicted from using. In November, while carrying a *caizie* of peats into his makeshift quarters in the barn, he accidentally stumbled against the doorway of the ancient building, causing the collapse of the whole precarious structure and damaging his household effects.[25] He is reputed eventually to have repaired both buildings using a cargo of building stone purchased in Westray.[26]

The dispute dragged on for years, with Burroughs remaining adamant in his refusal to allow crofting tenants access to quarries. The law having been unable to protect them and Parliament having refused to consider a change in the law, the crofters' only redress now lay with the Commission. But even the Commission was precluded from immediate action since the fair rents already determined had by law to run for seven years before they could be reviewed. In 1897, when this period had elapsed, seven crofters applied for a reduction in rent on the grounds that the action of the proprietor put them to additional expense in building and repairing houses, steadings, dykes and drains.[27]

Two of the crofters who applied to the Commission were Simpson Skethaway and John Gibson, the joint tenants of Knarston, and their story as told to the Commission is a good illustration of the difficulties being put in the way of crofting tenants. A joint tenancy was a very unusual arrangement in Orkney, but Knarston had been held on this basis for over a century. The two tenants each had their own houses and each paid half the rent directly to the laird, but the farm was worked as a single unit and the crop in each field was divided between them. Animals, although individually owned, were housed together. The farm was a sizeable one, with 50 acres of arable land and 27 of pasture, and in 1888 the rent was £60, double the limit for a croft. On its first visit, the Commission had accepted the argument that Knarston ought to be considered as two crofts rather than a single farm. It was a decision which Burroughs deeply resented, and the tenants of Knarston had a particularly difficult time in the years which followed. Like other crofters, they used their new security to improve their buildings, and Skethaway had approached Burroughs for permission to quarry stone. When this was refused, he had taken stone from a traditional quarry which lay below high water mark at Scockness, but on receiving a warning letter he desisted. Despite these difficulties and his age — he was seventy — he succeeded in building a new stable using stone which Spark, the Established Church minister and no friend of Burroughs, allowed him to quarry on the neighbouring glebe. He was also able to re-roof two outhouses with flagstones given free by the owner-occupier of Hullion. Traditionally a flagstone roof was covered with a layer of turf, but when Skethaway began to cut turf on his own croft, he received another letter from Burroughs ordering him to stop on the grounds that he was damaging the agricultural value of his holding. Again Spark came to the rescue and Skethaway was allowed to take what he needed from the glebe. His co-tenant, John Gibson, told a similar story. He had been unable to obtain roofing flags in Rousay and had been forced to buy them at 12/6 a hundred in Westray, hiring a boat to transport them.

Burroughs' lawyer did not dispute the facts. As he told the Commission, the crofters were taking everything that the Crofters Act allowed them and it was now the General's policy to give them nothing that the law did not demand. The Commission gave Burroughs fourteen days to reconsider his prohibition on stone quarrying before it made a decision on the crofters' application for a rent reduction. Burroughs, however, confirmed that he intended to continue the ban 'as a protest against what he considered to be the arbitrary and unjust decrees of the Crofters Commission in the application by the tenants of the farm of Knarston'. He reiterated the now familiar argument that the Commission had deprived him of his property and the rightful fruits of his investment. He considered that it was unreasonable to expect him to continue to treat them 'as if they were his own tenants'. Anyone who had dealings with the Commission had forfeited the right to be called a tenant. He informed the Commission that he intended to 'avail himself of all legal means to regain possession of the property of which he had been unjustly deprived'.[28]

The Commission issued its decision from Portree on 8th December

1897. It described Burroughs' conduct as 'unwarranted and oppressive' and condemned him for turning his dislike of an Act of Parliament into a 'hostile and unprecedented action against the crofting tenants of an island which was largely his own property'. Yet however much it might disapprove, the Commission could not change Burroughs' policy, and even the rent reductions which it awarded were modest. Skethaway's rent was reduced from £17:16s to £16 because of the extra expense he had to meet in obtaining building stone, and the other six applicants received similar reductions.

The ultimate condemnation of Burroughs' ban on quarrying was its futility. The original aim had been to expel crofters for allowing their buildings to become dilapidated, but not one crofter was ever forced out for this reason. Although it was expensive and time-consuming to get stones from other sources, the crofters always managed to obtain the materials they needed, not only to undertake the work of essential repairs, but also to put up new buildings. Cargoes of stones were shipped in from Westray and Egilsay and sometimes crofters might claim to have imported stone when it actually came from nearer to hand. A good deal of stone-smuggling took place. Stories are still remembered of how carts with muffled wheels would remove stones from the shore under cover of darkness and, in an island as rocky as Rousay, it was usually possible to obtain small quantities from crofters' own land when neither the laird nor his factor were in the vicinity. The ban had originated in a fit of temper brought on by a display of independence by the crofters. Thereafter Burroughs may, for a time, have genuinely believed that he could use it to force crofters out, but the prohibition was continued from sheer vindictiveness long after it had obviously failed.

15

Rousay Divided

'. . . the masses having been set against the classes, the Crofters, instead of being better off, are worse off, and it is not uncommon in this country to hear that the Crofters Act has been a curse and not a blessing to it.'   F. W. Traill-Burroughs[1]

BURROUGHS always argued that the effect of the Crofters Act had been to stir up trouble where previously there had been good relations between the different classes in the community. It was an argument which he developed on frequent occasions and the following quotation from a long article he wrote for the *National Review* is typical of his views:

> Previous to Mr Gladstone's revolution in land legislation in Ireland, prosperity and goodwill between landlord and tenant prevailed in the Orkneys. Since the passing of the Crofters Act the whole agricultural community has been set by the ears. The lairds have been traduced and plundered and the kindly feelings between them and their crofters is at an end. The large farmers now hate the crofters and the younger sons of small farmers and labourers, who looked forward to marrying and settling on crofts and now see themselves debarred from doing so by the perpetuity of tenure granted to the crofters, simply detest them.[2]

Much of this was true. One may contrast the prosperity and progress of the 1870s when there was outwardly a good relationship between landlord and tenant, with the bitterness and litigation which characterised the 1880s and 1890s when the relationship had quite obviously broken down. Landlord and crofter had perhaps never coexisted as amicably as Burroughs imagined, but their relationship had certainly deteriorated and by now could hardly have been worse. But what of the other classes — the farmers and the farm labourers?

Until the separation of croft holdings from the big farms, cottars and agricultural labourers were not distinct classes. Both were expected to supply *on ca'* labour when required in exchange for land. Insofar as there was any distinction between the crofter-cottar and the *bu-man* or full-time farm worker, the latter was to be envied since he had regular employment and substantial payments in meal as well as the use of his land. Even as late as the middle of the nineteenth century, the regular farm workers at

Westness felt themselves superior to the horde of cottar-crofters who were dependent on casual labour. A series of changes culminating in the Crofters Act had, however, reversed the status of crofter and farm servant. The cottar became a crofter and, instead of cultivating the scraps of the big farm, he had a holding of his own. He was no longer the sub-tenant of the farmer, but held his land directly from the laird. Although his land might be poor and his croft small and despite the fact that he was probably largely dependent on an income from subsidiary employment, the enterprising crofter was on the bottom rung of a farming ladder by which he might hope to rise. By piecemeal reclamation, his croft might become a farm or by careful saving he might be able to take the tenancy of a bigger place. The Crofters Act completed the process. Not only did it give him an even greater degree of security than that enjoyed by the bigger farmers with leases, but it also swept away the remaining vestiges of compulsory services.

While the crofters had improved their position, the *bu-men* had declined in status. Modern farming had converted them into farm servants paid in money and meal, but no longer cultivating their own land. Although probably better off financially than most crofters, their way up was no longer easy since, to climb the farming ladder, the farm worker had first to become a crofter. The very security the crofters enjoyed and particularly their new right to assign their tenancy to a member of their immediate family meant that it was difficult for the landless labourer to reach even the bottom rung of advancement. When they saw crofters' rents reduced to a figure which they would have been tempted to better, they resented the fact that they were excluded even from offering. But had they been free to offer and had they been successful in obtaining the tenancy, it could only have been at the expense of pushing up the rent and leaving someone else landless. The root of the trouble was land hunger — there were not as many crofts and farms as there were potential tenants.

To quite a considerable extent land hunger had hitherto been assuaged by the creation of new holdings made possible by the great expansion of the arable throughout the nineteenth century. Orkney's arable land had increased from perhaps 54,000 acres at the beginning of the century[3] to 89,500 acres in 1885, and as a result of this massive expansion it had been possible to accommodate many, but by no means all, of the landless. Between 1870 and 1885 there was an addition of 230 new holdings in the county, but by 1885 the period of expansion was over. To a large extent this was due to the fact that most of the land suitable for new holdings had already been reclaimed. But worsening economic conditions also inhibited further expansion on marginal land and the Crofters Act itself made most proprietors wary about creating new holdings. As in the rest of Orkney, new crofts had been reclaimed from the hill in Rousay, particularly on the Earl of Zetland's Sourin property, but in the period 1870-1885 when considerable numbers of new crofts were appearing on most estates, the number of holdings in Rousay declined from 123 to 117. Although the decline was not a large one, it was sufficient to cause frequent rumours of evictions and amalgamations, and any decrease in the number of holdings made the plight of the landless more hopeless.

This land hunger, which *The Orcadian* considered to be quite as severe as in the Highlands,[4] was the subject of yet another Royal Commission. Despite its title, the Deer Forest Commission concerned itself with Orkney, a land where there were neither deer nor forests. The Commission's title was a misleading one since its remit was to investigate not only deer forests and grouse moors but also grazings attached to sheep farms and to report whether these lands could be cultivated or otherwise advantageously used by the crofting population. This was the opportunity, if the government was brave enough, to restore land to crofting use and to right old wrongs. The Commission visited Orkney in late July and early August 1894 aboard the steamer *Marmion*. It visited most of the North Isles including Rousay where neither its mission, nor the fact that its chairman was Sheriff Brand of the Crofters Commission, made its members welcome guests. The Commissioners spent an afternoon and evening walking over Westness and Quandale[5] but it was hardly surprising that, although the *Marmion* lay all night under the laird's windows, they were not invited ashore to visit Trumland House. The Commission concluded its Orkney visit by taking evidence in Kirkwall[6] and, as they had done ten years earlier when Lord Napier visited Orkney, the Rousay crofters held preliminary meetings and elected delegates. Peter Yorston, the crofter who had been prevented from taking building stone from a quarry twenty yards from the door of his croft, appeared as their leader, but interest was at a low ebb. This was partly because little was expected of the Commission (quite correctly) and partly because, for reasons which will appear later, the crofters' movement in Rousay was by this time somewhat discredited.

The Deer Forest Commission eventually scheduled large parts of Rousay as suitable for crofting use. In Quandale it considered that 258 acres of old arable and 716 acres of pasture might be used to create new holdings. Three areas were also scheduled as additional hill grazings for crofters — 1,333 acres of Trumland Farm, 268 acres of Langskaill and 53 acres of the Holm of Scockness.[7]

Despite the hope that something might be done to relieve land hunger, the report of the Deer Forest Commission was left to gather dust. Buying back land formerly used by crofters was likely to be an expensive business and the Commission's many opponents seized on the mass of discrepancies in the report as a means of discrediting it. The eight-man Commission had been given the impossible task of surveying immense areas of the Highlands, and in some cases it had scheduled land which it had not even seen. Like the Crofters' Commission, it had been given a task, but not the manpower to do it properly and, after Gladstone's departure, the government also lacked the political will to carry out the Commission's recommendations.

Alarmed by the prospect of further crofting legislation which might go far beyond the 1886 Act and dismantle their estates either by a land purchase scheme or by scheduling large areas for crofting use, the Orkney lairds made one final attempt to act together. In 1893 they formed themselves into the Orkney Landowners' Association, the main object of which was to have Orkney withdrawn altogether from the scope of crofting law. The intent was to reverse the 1886 decision and the lairds proposed to achieve this by means of an appeal to Parliament.

Inevitably Burroughs was one of those landowners active in promoting the campaign. He sent to Colonel Balfour the draft of a memorial which he hoped would be adopted at the forthcoming meeting of the Landowners' Association. As usual, Burroughs proposed to meet trouble head on. His memorial was an intemperate attack on the Crofters' Commission and what he demanded was nothing less than the total abolition of the Crofters Act:—

> ... your petitioners respectfully call in question the right of any Christian government to set aside the law of God which says 'thou shalt not steal'.
> The reputations of the landowners, their lands and their incomes have been delivered over to the mercy of a Parliamentary Commission armed with the despotic power of a Czar of Russia and the infallibility of the Pope . . . This Commission stalks through the country, confiscating land without compensation and handing it over in perpetuity to those who have no just right to its ownership; it reduces rents which have been freely offered and accepted, it forgives arrears of rent which tenants are quite able to pay, it arbitrarily sists proceedings of landowners for the recovery of rent due to them and they, by their incomes unjustly arrested for years, are driven to great and unmerited hardship and even ruin.[8]

None of this appeared in the memorial which the landowners eventually presented. The wiser counsels of Colonel Balfour prevailed, the petition avoided abusive language, it was deliberately moderate in tone and deceptively constructive in its suggestions. It began by emphasising the differences between Orkney and the problem areas for which crofting legislation had been devised. Orkney had no Gaelic population, it had not been affected by the break-up of the clan system, nor did it have deer forests or grouse moors. Having greater fertility and a less hostile climate, it had not experienced the destitution which brought other areas to crisis point. Links with the sea had made Orcadians readier to emigrate and so congestion and over-population had been avoided, nor had there been that desperate competition for land which, in other areas, had forced rents to unreasonably high levels. Far from being on a downward path, the economy had been expanding right up to the time of the passing of the Crofters Act.

The lairds then enumerated the ways in which crofting legislation was, in their opinion, damaging Orkney. Improvement by the landowner had ceased, not just on crofts, but on large farms which it was feared might be broken up. This had caused a crisis in confidence and a fall in land prices. The landowners also criticised the Commission for the long delays in many of its decisions — some Orkney cases had been outstanding for six years — and for the careless and haphazard way in which land was valued. Valuing was done by strangers unfamiliar with local conditions and it was invariably done hurriedly. The landlord was not present when the valuation was made, he had no right of appeal, and income from poultry was not taken into consideration in determining rents.

In place of this system, the landowners suggested an alternative. They conceded the principle of judicially determined rents but proposed that, instead of the Commission, there should be a court for Orkney alone, sitting once a year and conducted by the Sheriff-substitute. Each party should appoint a valuer and, if they could not agree, an 'oversman' should be appointed by the Sheriff. Valuation should be done thoroughly and the rent should consist of the real letting value less improvements done by the tenant at 3½% per annum. The procedure they advocated was modelled on the traditional process for dividing run-rig lands, a method which had proved both effective and cheap. Rents fixed in this way were to run for seven years, like those fixed by the Commission. No large farms would be divided and Orkney would be exempt from any further crofting legislation.[9]

The memorial was a clever piece of writing, combining genuine criticisms of the Commission and constructive suggestions with half-truths and statements doubtfully connected as cause and effect. The reader who has followed the previous chapters will have little difficulty in identifying a number of examples. The sting was, however, in the tail of the memorial. Its sole purpose was to have Orkney withdrawn from any future crofting legislation which might affect the estates of the petitioners. On these grounds, it was condemned not only by *The Orcadian* and *The Orkney Herald* but also by the national press. From the opposite point of view the memorial was roundly condemned by Burroughs, who was unwilling to concede any restriction of his absolute freedom to determine the level of his rents. The crofters alerted Leonard Lyell to see that the petition received no misguided support from either government or opposition. There was never any real likelihood that it would succeed. Copies were sent by the Landowners' Association to every Member of Parliament but nothing further was heard of it. Soon after it was presented, *The Orkney Herald* guessed that 'it had already found its way into Lord Salisbury's and Sir George Trevelyan's pigeon holes from which it is unlikely to be exhumed'.[10] A further petition in 1896 met a similar fate.

If landless labourers resented the Crofters Act because it excluded them from competing for that scarce commodity, land, farmers had a different reason for being envious of the crofters' privileged position. In Rousay, the £30 rent limit for crofters created an arbitrary division between large crofts and small farms. They were of the same economic status, yet crofts had advantages denied farms — rent reductions, cancellation of arrears and security of tenure beyond the time limit of any lease. A letter from an anonymous Rousay farmer to *The People's Journal* in February 1892 highlighted the problems faced by farmers.[11] Not even Burroughs, the writer argued, could maintain the myth of increasing prosperity now that prices had fallen to a third of what they had been a few years previously. In such circumstances farmers were in a difficult position since they were bound by their leases and could not leave. Unlike tenants in most other areas, they had received no abatement to their rent but had to struggle on until their lease expired, when they might be excluded from offering and their farm given to someone else at a reduced rent. The writer contended that the benefits of the Crofters Act should be extended to all farmers.

The early 1890s were indeed a very difficult period for farmers in Orkney. Until then they had survived the onset of agricultural depression reasonably well since grain prices were most affected and the price of cattle held up better. The effect of the depression had merely been to reinforce the already existing trend to export less grain and to concentrate on beef. However, in the early 1890s the price of store cattle plummeted and often the money they fetched in the Aberdeen market did not even cover the cost of production and transport. Dreadful weather added to the farmers' problems. A wet summer and stormy autumn in 1891 resulted in a late harvest and the loss of much of the hay crop.[12] This was followed in 1892 by one of the worst seasons in living memory, with wintry weather in July and early August resulting in a harvest which was only beginning to ripen in October. Those who managed to harvest by mid-October managed to salvage something, but many farmers still had corn uncut in November when the crop was devastated by a severe gale, and they were still struggling with the last of the harvest as Christmas approached.[13] In 1893 the crop was little better, suffering from a summer drought and a late and stormy harvest.[14] Traditionally, poor harvests at least had the compensating advantage of good prices but now that grain, beef, mutton and even store cattle were imported from the New World, Orkney farmers had simultaneously to cope with both poor harvests and falling prices for their produce.

	Total Acres	Arable Acres	June 1893	July 1893	June 1894	June 1895	May 1896	July 1898
ROUSAY								
Banks	106	65	×					
Evradale	75	43	×					
Hurteso	81	63	×					
Faraclett	408	74	×					
Brendale	71	36		o			o	
Browland	54	32			×		o	
Classiquoy	14	2			×			
Innister	209	62	×					
Quoys	59	38		o	×			
Westness	2904	281			×			
Bigland	115	40				×		
Swandale	146	44				×		
Corse	58	16				×		
Trumland	1180	162						×
Springfield	15½	12						×
WYRE								
Helziegitha	93	40	×		×	×		
Onziebuot	95	31	×					
The Bu	94	51		o	×			
Castlehall	96	53		o	×			
Hallbreck	62	31				×		
Cavit	75	55						×

Table 9. *Turnover of Tenants on Farms and Crofts, 1893-1898* [15]
The table shows dates when farms and crofts were advertised for let during the period when farmers suffered most from depressed prices and adverse weather. Entries marked × indicate that the advertisement states that "the present tenant will not be offering". The turnover rate was very high. Few crofts appear on the table since, after the passing of the Crofters Act, they were seldom at the landlord's disposal.

The Case of John Mainland of Banks in Sourin was typical. In February 1893 he wrote asking to be relieved of the tenancy. He had only seven cattle to dispose of and, at the current price of about £8 a head, his income was bound to fall short of the £79 he needed for rent and rates. His cattle were his only income since, following the bad harvest, he had no surplus grain to sell. He had never previously been in arrears and was anxious to be quit of the farm before it ran him into debt.[16]

During these bad years the turnover of tenants on Burroughs' farms was almost complete. Each year lists of farms were advertised with the information that 'the present tenant will not be offering'. Rousay had 19 farms bigger than croft size and there were a further six on the island of Wyre. Table 9 shows the high casualty rate. In Wyre, for example, all six farms changed hands at this time.

Yet despite these difficulties there was a brisk demand for medium-sized farms and perhaps an even greater degree of competition than there was for crofts. It was this competition which kept rents above what farmers should realistically have offered in these bad years. One such casualty was Edwin Muir's father who took the tenancy of the Bu of Wyre, and it was Burroughs' high rent which started him on the downward spiral which ended in the Glasgow tenements.

The period 1883-1895 was a time of stress brought about by the conflicting interests of the landlord, farmers, crofters and farm servants. The Crofters Act, whatever its benefits — and it is difficult to see how the smaller tenants could have survived the years 1890-93 without its protection — had exacerbated the situation and contributed to the discontent. An island estate in Orkney was far from being a classless society as was sometimes fondly imagined. The classes within the community not only felt an identity of interest with others in their own group but showed signs of organising themselves along class lines; the laird was a member of the Orkney Landowners' Association; some farmers belonged to the Orkney Farmers' Association founded in 1894 'for the defence and protection of the rights of tenant farmers';[17] crofters had their meetings at local level, elected delegates to act on their behalf, and at national level involved themselves in the affairs of the Highland Land Law Reform Association; there were even proposals in 1896 for the formation of an Orkney Ploughmen's Union on the grounds that the Crofters Act had disadvantaged farm servants.[18]

Yet island communities are not entirely amenable to analysis along class lines. Older people who remember those days would deny this picture of class conflict or at least maintain that it distorts what life in Rousay was really like. For much of the time the basic tensions within the community were obscured by ties of kinship and neighbourliness which united members of different groups. Conversely the complicated personal enmities which a small island generates often divided those of similar economic status.

16

Rousay Churches

'And I suppose after all a minister preaches none the worse because he has been fighting with the heritors over gun-metal stop cocks and zinc sash chains.' *Peterhead Sentinel*[1] commenting on the Rousay manse case.

BURROUGHS' war against his tenants — the attempt to evict them, to bankrupt them, to pursue them at law, to forbid them the use of building stone, to insist on the full payment of rent no matter the difficulties they faced — shows the laird at his most despotic and his tenants at their most vulnerable. Yet Burroughs' ascendancy was never total. Even in the 1870s when his dominance of the economic and social life of the community was at its greatest, there were certain areas over which he had little control. The most obvious example was the church and another, should voters care to exercise their rights, was the democratically elected School Board. Consequently, within the community there were organisations which the crofters could control and which they could attempt to use in opposition to the laird. The crofters were not powerless, yet their opposition had to be expressed in indirect and even devious ways. This chapter and the following one describe how crofters used both Church and School Board to fight back.

The ministers of the eighteenth century church in Orkney had been firmly and comfortably fixed in the 'moderate' tradition. Their strengths and their weaknesses shine through the pages of the *Statistical Account*, those splendidly detailed parochial descriptions which the parish ministers were so well qualified to write. Often spending a lifetime in a single parish, they were familiar with every detail of the local economy and were figures of enormous influence. Their glebes were well cultivated, sometimes the only example in the whole parish of such innovations as sown grass, turnip cultivation and enclosures. Wealthy by the standards of their parishioners, they mixed socially with the lairds and shared many of their attitudes and prejudices. Theirs was a comfortable religion, little troubled by evangelical enthusiasm. Worship was sometimes irregular particularly where, as in

Rousay, Egilsay and Wyre, several islands had to be served by a single minister and stormy ferry crossings and rudimentary roads provided an excuse for a lax routine. Heritors were unwilling to do more than the bare minimum of repairs to churches which were often uncomfortable and damp.

Rousay suffered more than most parishes since its minister, the Rev James Leslie, was 'stricken with palsy' and was unable to fulfil his duties for seven years before his death in 1797. In his final illness he was acutely aware of his isolation in Rousay and particularly felt the absence of books and newspapers. He was able to potter about in his garden worrying about 'a species of mice as large as rats' which threatened to destroy the fine flowers of which he was so proud,[2] but he made no provision for his parish. For seven years his congregation were without a regular minister but met each Sunday in the church and listened to a sermon read to them by one of the proprietors.

The beginning of dissent in Rousay dates from the visit of the great evangelist, Haldane, as part of his crusade through Orkney and the North of Scotland in 1797.[3] Despite his preaching, which was always hostile to the Established Church, he was hospitably accommodated in the Rousay manse although Leslie was on his deathbed and indeed died the very night of Haldane's visit. The following morning Haldane preached to a congregation of three hundred who were visibly moved and deeply affected when he spoke of their long period without a minister. With an insensitiveness of which only an evangelist could have been capable, he assured them that, considering the usual standard of preaching in the Established Church, this was no great loss and might have been a positive advantage if it had encouraged them to read the scriptures for themselves.

From the time of Haldane's visit, a number of Rousay families were members of the Secession congregation in Kirkwall although, because of the intervening ten miles of sea, regular attendance was impossible. In 1829 Rousay became a preaching station and in 1834 a church was built and a congregation formed, United Secession initially and thereafter, as a result of union at national level, United Presbyterian. It was only in 1837 that the new congregation were able to secure a minister of their own. He was the Rev John McLellan. Rousay was his first charge and he remained there until he retired in 1874. McLellan was a powerful preacher and, with revivalist influence strong throughout Orkney, he quickly built up membership to 170 with an average Sunday attendance of about 250.[4] Thus, on the eve of the Disruption, about one third of those who belonged to the Established Church had already defected.

The minister of the Established Church at the time of the Disruption was the Rev George Ritchie. Born in Glasgow in 1798, he served three years in Westray before coming to Rousay in 1837. He was to remain in the island until his death in 1858.[5] At the Disruption, when 'moderates' and 'evangelicals' in the Church of Scotland parted company, he was one of six Orkney ministers who 'came out', bringing the greater part of his congregation into the new Free Church. In July 1843 communion was celebrated in the open air on the site of the new glebe in Sourin obtained from James Baikie of Tankerness.[6] Thus, until 1837 there had been only one minister in Rousay, but six years later there were three and the congregation in the Established Church was by far the smallest. In Orkney generally, the Established Church and the United Presbyterians were of about equal strength and both were bigger than the Free Church. In Rousay, due to Ritchie's personal following, the Free Church was unusually large and the Established Church unusually weak.[7] Ritchie's opposition to George William Traill's clearance policy gave the Free Church a reputation for radical politics and anti-landlordism. A generation later, the relative strengths of the churches were an important factor in Burroughs' struggle with the crofters.

When Ritchie 'came out' at the Disruption, he was replaced in church and manse by the Rev James Gardner. Gardner had been a schoolmaster and served for short spells as assistant minister in Stromness and Stronsay before being inducted as minister of the rump congregation in Rousay where he remained until his death forty-one years later in 1885. He was a minister of the old 'moderate' tradition — 'characterised by strong good sense, independence of judgment, kindliness of nature and an honest straightforwardness of manner. In the pulpit his style was quaint, but earnest, and in his visitations he was kindly and sympathetic to the last degree.'[8] He was also a considerable farmer since, in addition to his 15-acre glebe, he worked an adjacent 45 acres and was also tenant of the 145-acre Bu of Wyre.[9] His human flock was, however, a small one, being less than a third of the size of either the Free Church or the United Presbyterians.

The radicalism of the Free Church was fostered by the Rev Neil Rose, George Ritchie's successor. In the 1868 election campaign (when Burroughs was still in India) he was involved in an acrimonious dispute with Robert Scarth. Scarth, a leading Tory, had taken advantage of his position as factor to attempt to influence the newly enfranchised electorate to cast their votes in accordance with what he claimed were the laird's wishes. Since Burroughs was absent and indeed was strictly non-political as long as he remained in the army, a rather ridiculous controversy arose about which political party the laird supported — the implication being that it would be quite proper for the factor to influence voters provided he did so in the laird's interests. James Traill, Burroughs' shooting tenant at Westness, took issue with Scarth. He had handbills printed and distributed throughout the island pointing out that both Sir Edward Colebrooke and George William Traill had been Liberals and that it was very probable that Burroughs shared their views. Scarth countered this by sending George Learmonth to visit all voters and assure them of the laird's Tory sympathies. In private Scarth recognised that the days when a landlord could control the votes of his tenants were coming to an end, but Learmonth, less politically sensitive, attempted to exert pressure in the old-fashioned way. Riled by a uniformly hostile reception, he threatened recalcitrant voters. 'Very well! Mind your leases,' he is reported to have said, 'Mind if you go against your laird and factor.'[10]

The Rev Neil Rose furiously entered the contest. He had a blazing public row with Learmonth, accusing him of being 'just a shepherd's dog and doing what he was bidden',[11] and he exposed the whole business in the press. The visit to Rousay of Riddell, the Tory candidate, accompanied by several leading landowners, provoked a near riot. Rose's fierce onslaught disrupted the meeting, leaving the Tory chairman, Heddle of Melsetter, with a face 'blanched like a cabbage stalk'.[12] Voting (in days before the ballot) was in Kirkwall, and Rose was active at the poll, 'pulling, hauling and gesticulating'. Scarth reported to Burroughs that the minister had been very scornful of the mortgaged state of Orkney landed properties and had told the assembled voters that he might see the day when he could buy them all up! Discovering that some Rousay voters were absent, he had personally returned to the island, a round trip of twenty miles, to fetch them to the poll. Thanks to his efforts, only two tenants voted Tory. In bringing this to Burroughs' attention, Scarth also passed on the totally irrelevant but possibly useful information that the minister's father had been a Thurso blacksmith called Rosie, not Rose, and that his mother was a Caithness tinker![13]

Perhaps Burroughs' view of the affair was coloured by the fact that Scarth was his main source of information, but there is no doubt that the factor was right in attributing Tory sympathies to the laird. Having read the whole correspondence regarding the election, Burroughs dismissed the Free Church minister's contribution as 'a very silly, illiterate and vulgar effusion'.[14] After his return Burroughs remained outwardly on good terms with Rose but years later, when he received a letter suggesting that Rose might be a good candidate for the then vacant Established Church, Burroughs annotated it with three large exclamation marks and replied with a frigid acknowledgement. The irrepressible Mr Rose was no favourite of the laird.[15]

It is difficult to over-estimate the influence of those ministers who spent the greater part of their working lives in the island — Gardner (41 years), McLellan (37 years), Ritchie (21 years) and Rose (23 years). In true

Presbyterian tradition, respect for the minister was not automatic, but once it had been earned the congregation looked to the minister for a lead in temporal as well as in spiritual matters. The influence of these ministers and the revivalist atmosphere of mid-nineteenth century Orkney created a society conforming to Presbyterian standards. Church attendance was good and in both of the larger churches the Sunday congregation was measured in hundreds. The Sabbath was strictly observed, church discipline was enforced and the Temperance Movement was strong. As time passed, it appeared that the three churches were drawing closer together and that there was less and less to distinguish one from the others. The evangelicalism which had led to the formation of the United Presbyterians was now shared in almost equal measure by the other two churches. Even the episcopal laird was evangelical in his sympathies. The anti-landlordism of the Free Church was quiescent as long as agricultural prosperity lasted. Rose's radicalism was largely confined to national politics. At a time when most tenants were prospering there were fewer local issues than there had been in Ritchie's time or were to be when Rose was succeeded by MacCallum. Thus throughout the 1870s the denominations seemed to differ little. The three ministers were on amicable terms with each other and with the laird, regularly appearing together at such functions as tenants' dinners and harvest homes.

Burroughs when a young man had undergone some kind of religious experience, but his was the uncomplicated, straightforward religion of a soldier. He read daily prayers to his household and lived a model private life. He disliked bad language or any kind of profanity and, although not a total abstainer, he was of temperate habits. He was an Episcopalian and regularly took communion at St Olaf's when he was in Kirkwall but, apart from his anti-Catholicism, he was impatient of the differences between denominations. When in Rousay he first worshipped in the Established Church where his wife played the harmonium but later, having quarrelled with the minister, he transferred his allegiance to the United Presbyterians. Insofar as he had any views on inter-denominational squabbles, he felt that three churches and three stipends were more than Rousay could reasonably afford.

Between 1883 and 1886, however, events combined to force each of the churches to reassert its original character, the anti-landlordism of the Free Church, the 'voluntary principle' of the United Presbyterians, and the old 'moderate' image of the Established Church. It was the visit of the Napier Commission which revived the Free Church's antagonism to landowners, with MacCallum championing the crofters' cause and the others who gave evidence being members of his congregation. The other denominations played little part in the struggle. Gardner, whose farming activities probably made him unsympathetic, was eighty-one and his health was failing. The United Presbyterian church was without a minister at that time, so the only lead came from MacCallum and the Free Church.

Two years later Burroughs inadvertently roused the United Presbyterians to reassert their basic tenets. Gardner died in 1885 and Burroughs was appointed Convener of the Vacancy Committee entrusted with the task of searching for a successor. Following Sunday service, he astonished the congregation by standing up and proposing that they fill the vacancy by calling Mr Pirie, the new minister of the United Presbyterians and, by this means, bring about a union between the two congregations. It later transpired that Burroughs thought he had heard of a similar union somewhere else and had discussed the idea with the Session Clerk but not with other members of the Vacancy Committee or with Mr Pirie.

Pirie was acutely embarrassed, for it was naturally assumed that he must have been aware of the proposal. Previous to going to Rousay, he had been a minister of the Congregational Church, but a further move to the Established Church was an entirely different matter. He explained to Burroughs, to his congregation and to *The Orkney Herald* that his adherence to the 'voluntary principle' made it impossible for him to join a church which was dependent on the support of the state. The origins of the United Presbyterians in Rousay owed more to evangelicalism than to any great concern for the 'voluntary principle', but Burroughs had inadvertently hit on the original point of difference between the churches, and thereafter disestablishment was a particularly lively issue in Rousay.

All agreed that Burroughs had acted from the best of motives but had displayed a total lack of awareness of the complexities of inter-church politics. As *The Orkney Herald* commented, the incident had 'made manifest some weak points in his mental calibre which, had he been pleased to live contentedly in the halo of glory with which his former deeds as a soldier had surrounded him, would never have been suspected to exist.'[16]

Three months later the vacancy was filled when four candidates preached in the vacant charge and the Rev Alexander Spark was elected by a single vote.[17] If that decisive vote were Burroughs', it was a choice he quickly regretted since Spark proved to be a most expensive minister. Within six months minister and laird were engaged in a complicated legal battle about repairs to the manse — a good example of the heavy expenses which landowners had to meet at a time when the Crofters Act had made landowning less profitable. The manse case is also an illustration of the gulf between the Established Church and the crofters. At a time when the Free Church minister was fighting on behalf of the crofters, the minister of the

Established Church was preoccupied with the size of his steading, with whether or not he was entitled to marble fireplaces and with the relative merits of chain or cord for sash windows. The manse case reinforced the Established Church's moderate image and this materialistic pursuit of a standard of living associated with the landowning classes goes far to explain its small membership in Rousay.

During the long period of Gardner's incumbency, the heritors had neglected the manse. Shortly after he came to Rousay in 1844 he had been given £125 to erect a new porch on condition that he was responsible for all repairs for the next fifteen years. At the end of that time Gardner had let matters drift and it was now over forty years since any work had been done. Spark called a meeting of heritors in March 1886 and Burroughs, as virtually sole landowner, was responsible for nearly the entire cost of any repairs. The heritors, although reluctant to spend money, could not dispute that the manse was very damp and was in urgent need of repair. It was the scale of Spark's demands with which they took issue. He had produced a long list of items and had employed a local builder who estimated that the work could be done for £392. The heritors would have accepted even this if they could have been quit of the manse and Spark had agreed to be responsible for further repairs. The minister was, however, unwilling to do so and *The Orcadian* described his meeting with the heritors as 'anything but harmonious'.[18] It ended with Spark refusing to have any further dealings with Burroughs and putting the case in the hands of the North Isles Presbytery while the heritors, for their part, indicated that they would be taking legal advice. The dispute progressed from the Presbytery via the Sheriff Court to the Court of Session. No fewer than four rival architects were involved acting on behalf of the minister, the heritors, the presbytery and the sheriff and, as the case progressed, the extent and cost of repairs increased rather than diminished. Rival lawyers became involved in the most minute details of house and steading, all of which was reported in the local papers[19] and no doubt was avidly read in Rousay by parishioners who could never hope to aspire to such a standard of living. Nor was interest confined to Orkney, for the most caustic comments came from Spark's former parish near Peterhead:—

The Reverend Alexander Spark, erstwhile minister of Boddam, has been little heard of since he immured himself in the lonely solitude of Rousay; but it may interest his many friends and acquaintances in this quarter to hear that he is conducting a lively and interesting litigation with his heritors in regard to the condition of the manse. It was at one time in the Court of Session; but latterly it has been under the cognizance of the Sheriff-Substitute of Orkney, who has just issued a most elaborate and lengthy decision. His lordship sustains the claim of Mr Spark that his water main should have a gun-metal stop cock, but he refuses a whole lot of other claims by Mr Spark, who apparently has been demanding bedroom accommodation for two more people and byre accommodation for two more cattle, and sundry other luxuries. Still, Mr Spark, I gather from the Interlocutur, has made good his title to 'zinc sash chains' for his windows (the heritors wanted to put him off with ropes) and white marble chimney pieces in his dining and drawing room; and he has triumphantly vindicated the claim of a parish minister to be provided with a boiler in his scullery at the expense of the heritors. Altogether Mr Spark is to have his manse repaired and altered to the extent involving a cost of £600, which is nearly a sixth of the gross rental of the parish. And I suppose after all a minister preaches none the worse because he has been fighting with the heritors over gun-metal stop cocks and zinc sash chains.[20]

While the dispute dragged on, Spark claimed that his doctor had warned him that he was 'living in the manse at the peril of the health of his wife, his family and himself'[21] and so, in 1887, he left Rousay and took up residence in Kirkwall. Throughout 1888 he paid little attention to his parish and, for example, for over a year there was no communion service. In the winter of 1888-9, three years after his appointment and still with no start made on repairs, he announced that he would preach in Rousay only once a month. George Murrison, the factor (but acting in his capacity as Established Church elder) made an official complaint about this neglect. The North Isles Presbytery censured Spark for deserting his parish but at the same time expressed the hope that the cause of the trouble might soon be put right.[22]

Even after the repairs to the manse had been completed, Spark remained dissatisfied. He claimed that the work was defective and that on one occasion he had to remove twelve barrowloads of snow from the attic; nevertheless the terms of the decision precluded him from bringing any fresh claims against the heritors for a period of fifteen years. In 1904, when that period had expired, he reconvened the heritors and demanded that a new and bigger manse should be built, a claim which drew from Burroughs the rejoinder that it was high time the Church of Scotland was abolished. He and his fellow heritors took Spark to court with counter claims that the minister had failed to maintain the manse properly.[23] The claim for more accommodation was discounted by Burroughs' lawyer who paid a surprise visit to the manse and alleged that he had found the minister's study being used to store potatoes.[24] This charge was vigorously denied by Spark, who nevertheless maintained that he had a perfect right to use his study as a potato store if he chose to do so.

The immediate effect of the manse case was that Burroughs ceased to attend the Established Church and from that time worshipped instead with Mr Pirie's United Presbyterian congregation. It was not just that he found Spark's constant demands annoying, but they were also very expensive. As virtually the sole proprietor of Rousay, Burroughs had to meet almost all of the £600 spent on the manse, and that at a time when his crofters were staging a rent strike, when his estate was £1,000 in arrears, when his income was reduced by the Crofters Commission, when Trumland Farm was operating at a loss, and when he was paying interest charges on his heavy borrowing. His quarrel with Spark also deprived him of a natural ally. The Established Church minister with his pretentious manse and his farming interests might have been expected to be one of the leading 'Respectables', but he took no part in the struggle between laird and crofters and had deserted his parish at the time of the rent strike and the Commission's visit. The result was that from 1883 to 1889 the field was left clear for MacCallum of the Free Church to exercise the only real leadership which came from any of the Rousay ministers.

In 1889, however, MacCallum's time in Rousay came to a sudden and mysterious end. In the same month as Spark was censured by the Established Church presbytery, MacCallum appeared before the rival Free Kirk presbytery on graver charges relating to drunken behaviour, and two weeks later he had departed.

At an earlier date powerful preachers long resident in the island had exerted an enormous influence, but the more recent activities of the avaricious Spark and the alcoholic MacCallum had diminished the natural respect which the islanders felt towards their ministers. Even before his final downfall, MacCallum's following had been a faction, a group which in the eyes of many people was hardly 'respectable'. Many folk felt that a minister should not be mixed up in such matters.

There is a story told of a Kirkwall man who, when in Rousay, usually lodged with an old woman living in a croft high on the hillside. One day, when in the island, he thought he would pay her a surprise visit but he began by calling on houses lower down the hill and it was dark when he finally arrived. To his surprise, he found the old woman expecting him with everything prepared, and he asked her how she knew he was coming.

'Oh, hids easy kent whin thoo comes, for every ben lum wis reekin',' she replied. 'But,' said the visitor, 'It might have been the minister.' 'Weel,' said the old wife, 'There wis a time when hid might hiv been, but noo, for thoo sees atween Free and U.P. and Auld Kirk, unless they were aa' comin wan day, never a more reek is raised for ane o' them than wad be for mesel.'[25]

17

The School Board Affair

'... schools where lice are more abundant than lessons.' *The Orcadian*[1]

THE Free Church played an important part in the attack on Burroughs' dominance of the economic and social life of the community by providing leadership, making contact with influential supporters outside Orkney and, above all, by giving opposition a certain measure of respectability. Nevertheless church affairs provided no real battleground on which the war between the laird and his crofters might be fought. MacCallum might attack Burroughs from the pulpit but his heady sermons lost some of their effect since the laird was not in the congregation and could afford to ignore the minister's pronouncements. The School Board, on the other hand, provided a more satisfactory arena in which to act out the conflict. It was first constituted in 1873 following the Education Act and, at a time when the parliamentary franchise was restricted, it was uniquely democratic. Since heads of households who owned or occupied property worth £4 per annum were entitled to vote, many (but not all) crofters could take part in elections. Voting was by ballot and hence free from the more blatant pressures from laird, factor and minister. Elections could be used as a popularity contest and as a means of expressing public opinion on matters quite unconnected with education. In the early years there was no cause to use this weapon. Like other aspects of parish life, the Board was under Burroughs' personal control but in 1885-6 it was taken over by MacCallum and the crofters in a splendid example of ruthless power politics at parish level.

In 1873 the Board came into existence without creating any great stir. As in other parts of Orkney,[2] a public meeting was held for the purpose of selecting candidates by agreement and thus avoiding the trouble and expense of holding an election. There was little argument and it was decided that the Board should consist of the three ministers, Gardner, McLellan and Rose, along with James Sinclair of Newhouse and, of course, the laird. It had been proposed that Robert Scarth, the factor, should serve on the Board in addition to Burroughs, but the Free Church minister was of the opinion that the proposal gave too much power to the laird. The Wasbister schoolmaster had likewise objected to the election of all three ministers, a disproportionate clerical influence, he felt. This, however, was overruled since it was clear that an election could only be avoided if all three denominations were equally represented.[3] The discussion was free from acrimony. No one seemed to notice that, in an island where tenant farmers and crofters predominated, the new Board consisted of three ministers and two landowners. Despite the excuse of avoiding the expense of an election, the real purpose one feels was to avoid the dangerous novelty of the ballot box and ensure that the Board consisted of those people who usually managed such affairs. It was firmly in the control of the type of person whom Burroughs was later to call the 'Respectables'. The laird was chairman, a position which he expected to fill as of right, but the driving force came from the Rev Neil Rose who acted as secretary. Sinclair of Newhouse was officially treasurer but in practice Rose also tended to look after this side of the Board's business. The other members, being content to leave matters in his capable hands, were often rather in the dark about what was being done.

Even before the passing of the Education Act and the introduction of compulsory schooling, the standard of education in Rousay was already good. In 1841 there had been only 21 people over the age of fifteen who were unable to read and write out of a total population of 1,262 in the islands of Rousay, Egilsay and Wyre.[4] This represents a much higher degree of literacy than was common in Scotland at the time, but it was characteristic of Orkney generally. At that time the Parochial School stood on the shoulder of high ground separating the two communities of Westness and Quandale, a site abandoned when the districts were cleared. Immediately prior to the Education Act there were five schools in Rousay and, without compulsion, 78% of the age group were enrolled. The situation varied somewhat from district to district. In Wyre twenty were eligible, twenty were enrolled and twenty in attendance. On the other hand, in Frotoft, where the schoolmaster was unpopular and the school dilapidated, attendance was much less regular.[5]

As accommodation in all schools was poor, the immediate task of the new Board was to tackle an urgent building programme. The first school to be completed was at Sourin where pupils had hitherto been taught in the Free Church. The new premises consisted of a main schoolroom with a 'classroom' attached. The building cost £700 of which £542 was provided by government grant and the balance raised from the school rates.

Burroughs performed the opening ceremony in January 1876 and Rose delivered a lengthy speech reviewing the progress that had been made in the first three years of compulsory education.[6] It was a cause of satisfaction to him that, although it had to meet the cost of the new school, the Board had husbanded its finances so that each year there was a small surplus of income over expenditure even with the high salaries it had to pay — no less than £113 per annum for the teaching staff of Sourin alone. He informed his audience that attendance was good,[7] although it had dropped a little from an average of 227 in the Board's first year to 202 in 1875. The Board had been able to convince the Scotch Education Department of the need for schools on smaller islands (Egilsay opened later in the same year and Wyre one year later). Rose considered that the Board, whose term was now drawing to a close, could congratulate itself on its achievements, particularly since everything had been accomplished 'with perfect harmony'.

There was indeed general satisfaction with the work of the Board and little interest was taken in the next election. Once again it was possible to avoid the expense of a poll and the only change in membership was the advent of Mr Allardyce who came as United Presbyterian minister following the death of McLellan. Allardyce proved to be a somewhat awkward member, 'questioning whether every punctilio of the Code and Timetable had been followed by the Sourin teacher'. He took exception to the fact that Mr Rose had allowed the teacher to keep the government grant of £1 in respect of drawing when, since the class was held within normal school hours, it properly ought to have been regarded as income to the Board.[8]

By this time there were increasing complaints about the delay in obtaining a new school for Wasbister. Since the passing of the Education Act, the Board had used the former Free Church school rent-free. It was old and quite inadequate, but some members, conscious that they had built and paid for three schools, felt that they ought to avoid the expense of another one. Even after the decision was taken to build, there was further delay. Burroughs was keen to maintain his monopoly of land and, on legal advice, he refused to grant a site to the Board until he had completed the purchase of the existing Free Church site. In February 1877 Rose convened a public meeting at which these grievances were aired. The meeting ended with a unanimous call for action from the Wasbister community and from the Free Church congregation.[9]

As a result of this Free Church initiative, Rose found himself under attack. The Board split along denominational lines with Allardyce (U.P.), Sinclair (U.P.) and Gardner (E.C.) combining to oppose Rose (F.C.).

Burroughs pursued the honourable course of endeavouring to keep the peace, but he was absent from Rousay when the Board next met. Rose found himself accused of improperly taking over the financial affairs of the Board so that Sinclair, officially its treasurer, was 'in perfect ignorance' about what had been done. Rose was also censured for allowing the Sourin teacher to keep the £1 drawing grant, but he angrily refused to minute this decision until he was ordered to do so. The Board then took exception to the fact that Rose had accepted payment for six weeks' teaching when the Wasbister school had been without a schoolmaster, arguing that it was improper for him as a member of the Board also to be an employee. The Board finally decided to dismiss him from his post as secretary and appoint a clerk to conduct correspondence.[10]

From London Burroughs wrote in support of Rose and tried to patch over the quarrel. He had visited the Scotch Education Department where he found the work of the Rousay Board was held in high regard. 'I was informed,' he wrote, 'that the Rousay School Board enjoyed a pre-eminence of being of those who had quarrelled least and done most. I hope it is not about to forfeit this enviable distinction.'[11] He was back in Rousay when the Board next met. When the minutes of the previous meeting were read, it was discovered that Rose had not minuted his own dismissal and he denied that there had been any such decision — 'just some talk'. Allardyce and Gardner thereupon formally moved that Rose be dismissed and, despite Burroughs' plea that he be allowed to remain, their motion was carried. The Board then proceeded to appoint Mr M'Crie, the Inspector of Poor, as its 'neutral clerk'.[12]

Thus, several years before the dispute with the crofters, the Board split into those groupings which became 'Respectables' and 'Crofters'. The appointment of M'Crie further exacerbated the situation since, as Inspector of Poor, he was associated with the laird's policy of minimal relief and identified with the indignities which accepting charity involved. For these reasons he was not likely to be acceptable to the Free Church crofting community, and the fact that he had ousted their own minister made him even less popular. Rose's departure from Rousay did not end the dissension. He was replaced by the Rev Archibald MacCallum, who was to prove a much more formidable opponent of the 'Respectables' on the Board.

Meanwhile the long awaited Wasbister school was eventually completed and was officially opened by Burroughs. It had been designed and built by Alexander Gibson, a Wasbister man, and the Board was pleased with it, there being 'nothing to match it in Orkney or any rural area'. The opening ceremony gave Burroughs an opportunity to enlarge on his views about education. Cleanliness, always one of his obsessions, was, he said, next to Godliness and he urged the teachers and pupils to be tidy, methodical and punctual. Once the boys had finished their schooling, he strongly advised them to serve for a few years in the Volunteers to be 'straightened up and smartened up' and to learn obedience to commands. Schooling, he felt, ought to be much more practical and should prepare boys for their future occupations, for farming, fishing or a trade. The Germans followed these principles, he understood, and that was why there were so many German waiters.[13] Although one may criticise his ideas as an attempt to teach the lower classes to know their place in society, there is something refreshing and modern about his advocacy of practical subjects to augment the over-formal nineteenth century curriculum. The Wasbister folk, however, can have known little of the prevalence of German waiters, nor was such a career necessarily the limit of their ambition.

Elections were avoided in 1879 and again in 1882 but, as the time for the renewing of the Board approached in 1885, it became obvious that membership could no longer be quietly arranged. By this time Rousay was divided by the events following on the visit of the Napier Commission. MacCallum complained that, ever since he had given evidence to the Commission, the other members had automatically opposed anything he suggested, and for a time he considered giving up his seat.[14] As on previous occasions, a public meeting was held for the purpose of selecting candidates but it quickly became apparent that the first real election was inevitable. The Board had now passed through two stages, the initial period 1873-6 when there had been good relations between members, and the years 1876-85, when, although membership could still be arranged, there had been a 4 to 1 split, with the Free Church minister, first Rose and then MacCallum, in opposition to the other 'Respectable' members and forming a one-man nascent 'Crofters' party. Now there was to be a real election and the real battles would begin.

It was the nomination of James Leonard, the evicted crofter, which set the election alight. He was by this time a paid lecturer of the Scottish Temperance League in addition to being an official of the Highland Land Law Reform Association. He was due to visit Rousay shortly to deliver a series of temperance lectures. Other candidates included three retiring members, Burroughs, MacCallum and Sinclair, and four new candidates, George Murrison, the factor, John Craigie of Hullion, the postmaster, Samuel Gibson of Bigland, and James Johnston of the Hall of Tankerness who represented the Baikie estate interest in Egilsay. The results were sensational:—

James Leonard (Crofters Party)	82
Rev Archibald MacCallum (Crofters Party)	70
General F. W. Traill-Burroughs (Respectable)	60
John Craigie (Independent Respectable)	54
James Johnston (Respectable)	33
James Sinclair (Respectable)	24
Samuel Gibson (Respectable)	16
George Murrison (Respectable)	15

(These 'party affiliations', although real enough, were not used in the election. Local papers, however, often printed the candidates' religious denominations as a party ticket.)

The results were a personal triumph for James Leonard and the Rev Archibald MacCallum, finally disposing of Burroughs' claim that their evidence to the Napier Commission reflected the views of a disaffected minority of troublemakers. Burroughs was important enough to do quite well personally, but his factor was bottom of the poll with a mere 15 votes. Yet, when the euphoria cleared, it became obvious that the Crofters had not achieved actual power; the Board was in fact very evenly balanced. It was also obvious that a five-man committee which included Leonard, MacCallum and Burroughs was an explosive mixture and that the Board could hardly be expected to function properly with such a composition.

Trouble began even before the first meeting. Leonard arrived in Rousay to deliver his temperance lectures and applied for the use of school premises. His request was considered by the old Board which somehow contrived to meet after the election. Leonard's application was turned down and he was unable to hold his proposed series of meetings.[15] A subsequent request was rejected in even more peremptory terms when it was discovered that Leonard had used the Egilsay School to address the islanders on 'The Land Question' without obtaining permission from the School Board.[16]

At the first meeting Johnston moved that Burroughs be appointed chairman. It was a position he had held since the inception of the Board, a position which he felt was his by right. Craigie, however, moved that Leonard be chairman since he had topped the poll. Eventually an uneasy and rather ridiculous compromise was reached whereby Leonard took the chair while the meeting was opened with a prayer, after which Burroughs was allowed to take his accustomed place. The Board then turned its attention to financial matters and examined an apparent discrepancy in M'Crie's accounts. In vain the clerk tried to explain that this discrepancy had arisen in Mr Rose's time and that, in any case, it did not represent a real loss. It was sweet revenge to pursue M'Crie for the very same discrepancies which had led to Rose's dismissal and M'Crie's appointment. Eventually Craigie moved that M'Crie be dismissed. Burroughs opposed this and threatened to resign if the motion was carried. It was a dangerous threat to make but for the moment it worked and the motion was withdrawn.[17]

The next meeting was even more stormy. Burroughs as chairman proposed to open the meeting with a prayer as he always had done, but MacCallum objected to the form of the prayer and, after a lengthy wrangle, Burroughs temporarily left the meeting while MacCallum conducted prayers.[18] He then returned to the chair for the remainder of the meeting which lasted a further six hours. Arrears of school fees were discussed. For some reason M'Crie had been in the habit of charging an extra sixpence on the fees of Sourin pupils and it was alleged that this showed a bias against the Free Church and the crofting community. Leonard and MacCallum again proposed his dismissal and, with Craigie's vote, this was carried. Burroughs now found himself trapped by his earlier threat to resign if M'Crie were dismissed. He gave notice of his resignation and angrily left the meeting.[19] The Board finally adjourned with much of its business uncompleted and, after such fireworks, it was not surprising that there was a good attendance of the public when it re-convened.

One month later the question of filling the vacancy caused by Burroughs' resignation arose. It was suggested that the first unsuccessful candidate in the recent election be co-opted. But since this was James Sinclair of Newhouse, a former member of the 'Respectable' Board and known to be unsympathetic to the crofters, MacCallum and Leonard proposed that the place be filled by James Grieve, the other evicted crofter. MacCallum was now chairman and, with his casting vote, the proposal was carried. This victory was an important one since the addition of Grieve gave them a 3:2 majority, even without Craigie's now wavering support.[20]

With their new power, the crofters began to attack the conduct of the old Board under Burroughs' chairmanship. They criticised the re-opening of the Sourin school after it had been closed during a recent whooping cough epidemic. It was claimed that the school had been opened too soon and before proper clearance had been obtained from the Medical Officer, with the result that there had been several relapses and one fatality. Such a charge was highly emotive. The Board also began proceedings for the dismissal of three of its five teachers, Miss Calder in Wyre, Mr Moyes in Sourin and Mr Cooper in Wasbister. In Wyre there may have been grounds for dissatisfaction with the standard of education. It was a school which suffered from a rapid succession of teachers, none of whom stayed long. The inspector who visited schools annually for the purpose of awarding the grant from the Education Department reported that it was 'not satisfactory', and he particularly criticised the pupils' copy books.[21] In contrast, the inspector's reports on Sourin and Wasbister were on the whole favourable. In 1885, when the dismissals were first threatened, he commented on the 'creditable appearance' of the Sourin school after its recent closure during the epidemic. Analysis and composition were somewhat weak in senior classes and the grant for History and Geography was given only with hesitation because of the pupils' meagre knowledge of History. Writing, on the other hand, was neat and both sewing and singing were of a reasonable standard. Wasbister also received quite a favourable report but, because of the standard of drill, the grant in respect of discipline was withheld.[22] The inspection of Sourin the following year showed that Mr Moyes had been endeavouring to correct some of the weaknesses revealed in the previous inspection:—

> The school on the whole made a fairly good appearance. The discipline is of an excellent character, the children being quite remarkable for orderliness, attention to work and thorough honesty while under examination . . . The class grant for History and Geography was this year most creditably earned.[23]

The impression from these reports is of schools of a quite normal standard, if anything rather better than commonly found in remote rural areas. It is clear that the motive for getting rid of the teachers had little to do with the standard of education. In part it was merely the continuation of a feud which had originated long before the Education Act when the Sourin school was run by the Education Committee of the Established Church's Assembly. Set in a district with a predominantly Free Church allegiance, the school had frequently been the centre of disputes. Soon after the Disruption, Free Church intrigue had secured a decision to remove a previous teacher, although on that occasion Robert Scarth had been able to bring pressure to bear on the church to have the dismissal reversed.[24] In Mr Moyes' time ill-feeling between the school and the community continued. Some parents neglected to send their children, others refused to supply the peats the pupils were required to bring with them, and there were constant rows about fees.[25] When asked to explain its decision to dismiss Moyes, the School Board stated that it was not bound to give explanations, but the culminating reason was obvious enough. As *The Scotsman* commented in an article condemning the frequency of School Board disputes in rural areas where religious denominations complicated matters:—

> Two boys in Mr Moyes' school were suspected of having concocted (the anonymous letter to Burroughs) and the Procurator Fiscal, having obtained a warrant, went to the school house and seized the copy books of the two boys in order to use them for the purpose of evidence. Now Mr Moyes' offence is that he did not resist the Procurator Fiscal and defy the warrant of the Sheriff. On that ground, and on that ground alone, the crofters and their friends rose up against the schoolmaster to boycott him.[26]

Moyes was having an increasingly difficult time as quarrels between 'Crofters' and 'Respectables' spilled over into the school. There was trouble between the son of John Mainland of Banks and the children of Mr Gray, the Sourin miller. Gray was present at the November meeting of the Board, complaining that his children were annoyed by other pupils and 'had no life to live'. He had complained to Mr Moyes, who had warned a number of pupils about their behaviour. Mainland, however, had encouraged his boy to further mischief and told him to come straight home if he was punished for it. When inevitably this happened — three strokes of the tawse — Moyes had a visit from the angry Mainland parents who subsequently complained to the Board that their son had been 'unjustly and unmercifully punished'. The Board informed Mr Gray (Respectable) that it could do nothing to protect his children since the incidents happened out of school (actually in the playground). On the other hand, it advised Mr Mainland (Crofter) that he ought to take legal action against Mr Moyes since the matter was too serious for it to deal with.[27]

Pressure for Moyes' dismissal also came from the general public. A petition was circulated in Sourin and eventually gathered 43 signatures. Moyes was never allowed to see it but one jaundiced 'Respectable', an ex-member of the Board, reported that half those signing were female; fourteen of the signatures were in coloured pencil and in the same handwriting.[28]

Mr Cooper of Wasbister School was pursued on even vaguer grounds. He had been censured for leaving his school at New Year under the care of 'a person who might have been a carter' and for carelessness in stating arrears of school fees. The real reason for the attack was that he was the son-in-law of John Gibson of Langskaill, the tenant of one of the island's biggest farms and a leading 'Respectable'. Similar family connections probably account for the Board's action against Miss Calder in Wyre. She was related to the factor of the Balfour estate, the man whom Burroughs had employed to allocate common grazing to individual farms (see p. 108).

The Board met again in November 1885 to consider the dismissals. MacCallum and Leonard, the two original 'Crofters', were due to be joined by Grieve as newly co-opted member. They were opposed by Johnston and Craigie — the latter, although hitherto often voting with the 'Crofters', now disapproved of the way they were proposing to exercise their power. Johnston and Craigie deliberately stayed away from the November meeting, having put it about that the Board could not receive a new member unless there was already a quorum before he joined. Since the quorum was three, they argued that any action of the Board in their absence would be illegal. The Board rejected this argument but felt it wiser not to proceed with anything so controversial as the removal of the teachers from office when there was a doubt about the legality of its meeting. It had, however, much pleasure in refusing an application from M'Crie, its late clerk, who asked permission to hold a Parochial Board meeting in school premises.[29]

The deadlock was broken by the resignation of James Johnston, who had experienced quite enough of the Rousay School Board and its squabbling. He had represented the Egilsay interests and, at the suggestion of Egilsay people, he was replaced by Hugh Marwick of Guidall,[30] the father of Dr Hugh Marwick, the Orkney writer and scholar. Marwick senior had spent much of his early life in New Zealand. He had served an apprenticeship as a shipwright and at one point had supervised the building of a schooner in Fiji. On his return to Rousay he found employment as shopkeeper, cabinetmaker and carpenter. Although neither a crofter nor a member of the Free Church (he was United Presbyterian), he was believed to be much under the influence of MacCallum, and thus the 'Crofters' now had a 4:1 majority on the Board, with John Craigie left in the isolated position of being the only 'Respectable'.

Although the 'Crofters' now had a secure majority, the Board did not immediately proceed with the dismissals; the position was now further complicated by the Board's having lost its copy of William Cooper's terms of agreement. It had to resort to asking him to provide a copy and this he naturally refused to do. Apart from censuring him again, there was little that it could do about it.[31] The Board was also running into financial difficulties since its grant was dependent on furnishing the Scotch Education Department with a certificate as to the good character of its teachers. This it could not very well provide while at the same time trying to dismiss them.

The next four monthly meetings were held in private with a notice of motion to dismiss the teachers on the agenda on each occasion. Before the meeting in May 1886 the teachers, who had never been given the opportunity of a hearing, announced that they intended to present themselves and demand to be heard. Like recent meetings this took place in secrecy, but a highly coloured version appeared in *The Orcadian*, no doubt leaked by John Craigie:—

> On Saturday 1st May a meeting of the School Board of Rousay and Egilsay was held in the Sourin Public School. The meeting was held in private, but the following report is believed to be pretty accurate:— All the members were present. As soon as the members had entered, the Chairman (Mr MacCallum) asked the clerk if he had locked the door. He received an answer in the affirmative which, however, did not seem to satisfy him, as he went and personally examined the fastenings of the back entrance of the school room. He then opened the meeting with a prayer on the conclusion of which a loud knocking was heard at the door. One of the members (i.e. Craigie) remarked to the Chairman that the two teachers of whose dismissal notice

P

had been given for that meeting, were seeking admittance and ought to be admitted. The Chairman said he would admit them when he was ready for them. The minutes of the last meeting were then read — Mr Craigie objected to an entry censuring Mr Cooper, teacher, for having written two letters — one addressed to the editor of one of the local newspapers and the other addressed to the Chairman of the Board in answer to a private note from that gentleman, asking him to explain or withdraw the former letter. Mr Craigie said the Board had no occasion to censure Mr Cooper for these letters and asked for that part of the minute to be deleted. The request being refused, Mr Craigie tendered his resignation and asked liberty to withdraw. The Chairman said they would retain Mr Craigie for a month and refused to allow Mr Craigie to exit from the room. A minute or two later, on Mr Craigie expressing an opinion on the business under discussion, he was told by the Chairman that he had no right to speak, as he had resigned his seat. Thereupon Mr Craigie demanded to be allowed to withdraw and threatened to break open one of the windows if the door were not opened for him. The Chairman said such a manner of exit was illegal, and would render him liable to an action for damages, and Mr Craigie retorted that it was also illegal to hold him against his will. He was permitted to retire and the door was locked behind him.[32]

Behind closed doors, the motion to dismiss the teachers was now carried.[33] The Board's anxiety to detain Craigie stemmed from more than the fear that, if he was let out, the angry teachers might get in. A Board was prohibited from dismissing teachers in the first six months of its term of office and there were now so many new members on the Board that the legality of a dismissal might be questioned on these grounds. Craigie was, in fact, persuaded to come to the next meeting and then, with his attendance recorded, the Board was quite willing to let him go. After his departure it was entirely composed of 'Crofters'. In exactly a year they had moved from a minority position to one-party dominance — a victory achieved by ruthless tactics and an over-hastiness on the part of the 'Respectables' to resign.

It was a further two months before the teachers were served with notice of dismissal. At Sourin MacCallum entered the school and recorded in the log that Moyes had ceased to be the teacher.[34] He went at once, employing another teacher to act during his period of notice. Cooper, on the other hand, served out his notice and was temporarily succeeded by the Clerk to the School Board until another permanent teacher could be found.[35] Moyes' career was not damaged by his dismissal. He was soon able to obtain a school at Dornoch and within three years was earning almost double the salary he had received in Rousay.[36]

His successor in Sourin was Alexander Oswald, who took up his duties in November 1886. He was very disparaging about the general standard of the pupils' work and recorded in the school log that he found the basics of Arithmetic totally lacking and 'the manners of the children most boorish'.[37] These remarks contrast with the quite favourable report from the inspector and were no doubt coloured by the knowledge that

MacCallum frequently visited the school and examined the log. Oswald, however, did not have an easy time in Sourin. His stay was short and, at one point, he too was threatened with dismissal by the School Board.[38]

Having been expelled from the Board, the 'Respectables' attempted to rally support in the community at large. As former members they knew very well that the accounts had been in a state of confusion for many years and that there had been irregularities which no one could now explain. The same irregularities which the 'Respectables' had used to dismiss Rose in 1876 and which the 'Crofters' had used in 1885 to get rid of M'Crie, were now used by the 'Respectables' again in a general attack on the Board. Burroughs first tried to persuade the Parochial Board to demand an enquiry,[39] and when that failed he organised a formal request by five ratepayers to inspect the accounts. Three of these ratepayers were ex-members, Burroughs himself, James Sinclair and John Craigie. The other two were William Seatter of Saviskaill and John Gibson of Langskaill (father-in-law of Mr Cooper, the dismissed Wasbister teacher). George Murrison, the factor, and M'Crie, the ex-clerk, were also associated with the group's activities. The ratepayers gave notice that they would present themselves at the November meeting and requested that the accounts be laid out for their inspection. MacCallum had to admit that they had a legal right to see the accounts but set about making it as difficult as possible for them to do so.

When Burroughs entered the meeting and made his request, MacCallum answered that the ratepayers were late; twelve o'clock had been the appointed time; it was now past the hour and the meeting was a private one. Burroughs became extremely angry and there were heated exchanges between the Board and the ratepayers. MacCallum as chairman protested that he 'would not be annoyed in this rude manner' and the ratepayers had to withdraw, the accounts unseen.

They then adjourned to a room at the back of Munro's shop which was near the school and, with some formality, Burroughs was appointed their chairman and M'Crie clerk. They drew up a minute of their encounter with the Board and sent off a protest to the Scotch Education Department. This document was, in due course, passed back to the School Board for its comments. The Board pointed out that its opponents did not represent a genuine body of ratepayers but largely consisted of former Board members 'cast out by the electors for their fatuous maladministration'. This was hardly a fair comment since two of the ratepayers (Burroughs and Craigie) had been successful in the elections but had subsequently resigned. By this time the Board itself was in a similar position, with only two members who had been elected (MacCallum and Leonard), the others having been co-opted to fill vacancies. In its comments the Board made much of the interrelationships of the ratepayers' group, representing it as a family clique. Gibson was the father-in-law of the dismissed Wasbister teacher, Craigie was a brother-in-law of Burroughs' footman, Gibson was married to a daughter of Burroughs' yachtmaster, Sinclair was an uncle of the footman's wife, and his niece was married to Seatter's nephew who in turn was a brother-in-law of Craigie! No doubt it might have been possible to find similar relationships in almost any group of people in a small island, but the Scotch Education Department found it all very confusing. The Department wrote to Burroughs informing him that the Chairman of the Board had been entirely justified in putting him out of the meeting, having been 'provoked by the irregular and grossly rude conduct of the ratepayers'.[40] MacCallum continued to concede their right to inspect the accounts but continued to prevent them ever actually doing so. Eventually the ratepayers gave up.

These battles had little to do with education and there is a good deal of evidence to suggest that the children were the ones who suffered. With an overbearing and interfering School Board liable to censure and dismiss its teachers, the turnover of staff was high. During the five years of 'Crofter' control no fewer than 17 head-teachers were employed in the four schools on the Burroughs estate:—[41]

	Permanent Appointments	Temporary Appointments
Wasbister	3	1
Sourin	3	1
Frotoft	3	2
Wyre	4	0

As *The Orcadian* commented, Rousay teachers were on the lookout for a new appointment within a month of arriving and once clear of the island, they could not have been tempted back for double the salary.[42]

Nor did the 'Crofters' make use of their control to push for improvements and advance the standard of education. The old 'Respectable' Board had built new schools in Sourin (1876), Egilsay (1876), Wyre (1877) and Wasbister (1881) and had stoutly resisted suggestions from the Scotch Education Department that proper schools were not needed on the smaller islands. Thereafter very little was achieved. The Frotoft school was in need of attention, with ill-venting chimneys, bad ventilation, poor equipment and an undrained playground. Other schools complained of a penny-pinching attitude and small requests being denied them. The collection of fees had never been easy in a crofting community and the main aim of the 'Crofters' was not to improve education but to keep it cheap. Ironically this policy reduced the contribution which Burroughs made as largest ratepayer. His assessment had amounted to £35 immediately before the passing of the Education Act when, under his own management, it jumped to £53, thereafter gradually rising to £56 in 1881. Under 'Crofter' control his rate dropped to £48 in 1889.[43]

For the bright pupil, progress through the Rousay schools was not easy. One may contrast the seemingly effortless accomplishments of Burroughs' nephew at Harrow, who won prizes for Latin hexameters, Latin Alcaics, Greek epigrams and knowledge of the scriptures and of whom his headmaster said, 'Go weep like Alexander, for truly there are no more kingdoms for you to conquer',[44] with the young Hugh Marwick who had only his inherent ability to aid him as he climbed his way through the Sourin school. As a very young child he began his education under Mr Moyes at a time when his father was a Board member intent on securing the teacher's dismissal. Eventually reaching the status of pupil-teacher, he won second prize from the Orkney and Zetland Association for an essay highly critical of landlordism.[45] At that time it was virtually unknown for Rousay pupils to pursue their education at Kirkwall. Hugh Marwick went direct from the Sourin school to the Free Church Training Centre in Aberdeen where he was able to secure a place only as the result of a last-minute withdrawal. It was only after three years of Primary teaching and intensive private study that he was able to enter Edinburgh University.[46]

The behaviour of their elders also had its effect on the standard of conduct of the pupils. A series of articles in *The Orcadian*[47] on 'The Inefficiency of School Boards' was based almost entirely on what had happened in Rousay. By no means an unbiased account, it was part of the war of words between 'Crofters' and 'Respectables', possibly the work of M'Crie. It criticised the conduct of the 'Crofter' Board, its relationship with its teachers, its inefficient accounting, the insanitary conditions of its schools ('where lice are more abundant than lessons') and ended with a diatribe against the behaviour of pupils:—

> . . . morality has fallen to a low level in the schools. Under the old regime neither evil word or evil deed or evil thought was laid to a scholar's charge. Now what? The language of the Schools outwith School hours — both on the playground and on the road would make the hair stand on end and the flesh creep. Am I mis-stating facts? Go listen for yourselves. No parent, however fallen, could endure to hear his children pouring out from their lips molten words of iniquity! Boys torment girls — do unbecoming deeds — swear, use filthy words, and girls are no less guilty. The teacher disowns control outside his school. The minister has no control outside his Kirk. The parents have no control outside their homes. The School Board has no control outside its sederunt. So the children are like wild beasts without government. Parental and ministerial advice but mock at the evil, and while some Christian attempts are being made to further morality, the weeds of wickedness are allowed to grow and develop. The Mahommedan priests would make short work of such a moral plague. They would sharpen their knives and cut out the filthy tongues and thus put a

period to the spread of moral evil . . . If the three schools of Rousay are bad, surely Sourin carries the palm. The children insult passers-by — calling names, using horrible insinuations, men of respectability, women of respectability, ministers or elders, all the same, the foul fiends with poisoned lips pour out dirty lava like volcanoes.

While every generation fears that the standard of its youth is declining, it seems highly probable that persons of 'Respectability' and that some of the ministers and elders were indeed likely to meet with a torrent of abuse when they passed the Sourin school playground.

Despite these criticisms, the 'Crofter' administration was vindicated when the Board came up for re-election in 1888. Burroughs did not stand, no doubt wishing to avoid the indignity of being defeated, or if elected, finding himself once again in a minority position. James Leonard was also missing, since by this time he had left Orkney. There was a heavy poll and a victory for the 'Crofters' who occupied the first four places. James Sinclair of Newhouse was the only 'Respectable' ex-member to stand and he finished bottom of the poll — a condemnation of the part which he had played in the ratepayers' attack on the retiring Board.[48] MacCallum was re-elected chairman, but eight months later he left Rousay and was replaced by the Rev A. I. Pirie of the United Presbyterians.[49] With the advent of Pirie, the Board began to follow more moderate policies and the rule of the 'Crofters' was over.

What is one to make of the activities of the Rousay School Board between 1885 and 1889? In many ways they were petty and parochial in the extreme, damaging the reputations of all those who were connected with the Board's affairs. No one emerged from these squabbles with credit. Under 'Crofter' control the Board was dictatorial, secretive, its accounts muddled and its records probably deliberately destroyed. Its battles were not about education and it was not fighting the cause of reform. It was as parsimonious as any Board dominated by the landowner could have been. Relations with teachers were bad and the standard of education slipped back rather than advanced.

By the nature of the battle, it was one without a final goal, but it was more than just an expression of purely personal animosities. It was a demonstration, a public exhibition of the power of the crofters to humiliate the landowner and those who supported him. The Board was an arena in which laird and crofter could meet as equals with one vote each. It was also the means of establishing the authority of those who claimed to act on behalf of the crofting community and who were delegates to meetings of the Highland Land Law Reform Association or who appeared before the Napier or Crofters' Commission. A vote for these people did more than entrust them with the management of the schools; indeed that sometimes seemed almost incidental. It was a mandate for them to speak on behalf of the Rousay crofters.

Even more fundamentally, it was a battle about the landlord's unquestioning assumption that he had a right to dominate the social life of the community in the same way as he dominated its economic life. A laird might see this as a duty rather than a right but, however well-meaning, his influence was paternalistic and authoritarian. In Rousay this was particularly so since Burroughs was the only landowner of consequence; he had controlled not only the statutory bodies such as the School Board and the Parochial Board, but also most of the recreational and voluntary organisations. The extension of the franchise, backed by the Rev Neil Rose's vigorous electioneering, had broken the political power of the laird. The Crofters Act, for small tenants at least, had secured a large measure of economic independence. In the same way the School Board affair destroyed Burroughs' dominance of the social life of his estate. It left him disillusioned with life in Rousay. He was convinced that the people for whom he had done so much had proved ungrateful. Their rejection of him was a bitter blow to his pride.

18

Finale

'That the inhabitants of Rousay and Viera are totally exempt from all the ills that flesh is heir to, I do not pretend to say.' F. W. Traill-Burroughs[1]

WHEN the crofters were at the height of their power, with their management of the School Board vindicated at the poll and their rents recently reduced by the Crofters' Commission, the crofters' movement received a blow from which it never properly recovered — the scandal of MacCallum's departure. Unmarried and living alone in the damp and cheerless Sourin manse, his drinking bouts were becoming increasingly frequent. His lapses were at first a closely guarded secret in the Free Church congregation but the point was eventually reached when the problem could be concealed no longer. Moyes, the schoolmaster, when he was about to be dismissed, had threatened to reveal the secret and was only silenced by the prospect of a libel action. In fact nothing became public until in December 1888 *The Orcadian* revealed that the Free Church Presbytery had been holding a series of meetings to consider the alleged drunkenness of one of their ministers.[2] Even then no name was mentioned and MacCallum's departure from Rousay was arranged without his being publicly identified as the minister in question. Two weeks after the presbytery meeting he submitted his resignation 'as his health did not agree with the climate conditions in Orkney'.[3]

Such events caused a grave scandal in Rousay where the Temperance Movement was strong and supported by all sections of the community. Temperance meetings were well attended and a visiting lecturer had once noted with approval that Rousay was a most sober community, although he deplored 'the filthy rot-gut ale' which was still brewed by some of the small farmers.[4] The Temperance Movement was particularly associated with James Leonard, who was a paid lecturer of the Scottish Temperance League and had conducted meetings in Rousay on many occasions. It will be remembered that he had been prevented from holding a series of such lectures in 1885 when Burroughs had denied him the use of school premises. This had been entirely due to Burroughs' belief that he would

206

use the occasion to speak on crofting matters and not from any opposition to temperance. The laird was an enemy of any kind of drunkenness and it was his influence which kept the island free of licensed premises. Such was Rousay's reputation for sobriety that, being an island and licence-free, it 'was much resorted to as an asylum for inebriates'.[5] In these circumstances MacCallum's conduct was highly damaging to the crofters' cause.

He received more understanding than perhaps one might have expected. Initially the Free Church congregation rallied to the support of their minister with a unanimous call to stay. They listed his services to the church and School Board and stated that it was particularly important that they should keep a minister who could help them gain full advantage from the new crofting legislation. It appears that they were willing to forgive his drinking bouts. Not so the North Isles Free Church Presbytery who, although individual members expressed sympathy at his departure in 'such circumstances', did nothing to persuade him to stay.[6] The discovery of further scandal averted a clash between congregation and presbytery. Within the closely guarded confines of the Kirk Session it was revealed that Hannah, James Leonard's daughter, was pregnant and that the father was the minister himself. It says much for MacCallum's domination of his congregation that, even in these impossible circumstances, he still had his followers on the Session. However, a motion asking him to reconsider his decision to leave was defeated and the last of his supporters resigned from the eldership.[7]

There was a measure of understanding from General Burroughs too. For several years he had been aware of the minister's failings. As early as 1885 he had asked the Rev J. B. Craven, rector of the Episcopal church in Kirkwall, to make confidential enquiries into MacCallum's background. Craven reported that the Free Church minister, when filling a temporary vacancy in Rothesay, had 'gone on the spree and become quite maddened by drink', breaking a window and throwing a mirror into the roadway. On a further occasion at Newhills, he was rumoured to have taken to his bed for three weeks as a result of his drunken excesses.[8] It says much for the General's sense of honour that, although there must have been a considerable temptation to use MacCallum's behaviour to discredit the crofters, he never made mention of it even after it became common knowledge. His only comment was an entirely private one. When pasting the relevant newspaper cuttings into his scrapbook, he marked them prominently with three large exclamation marks — !!! Yet throughout the controversy surrounding the Crofters Act and the affair of the School Board, Burroughs possessed information which he could have used to destroy MacCallum. Had their situations been reversed, it is unlikely that the minister would have been so scrupulous.

Thereafter MacCallum's story is one of rapid decline into alcoholism. He spent the next three years living at Arisaig but without a church,[9] then switched to the Established Church and was settled in the parish of Knock in Lewis. For a minister with a drink problem, a move to Lewis was the worst step imaginable. Soon after his arrival he was reprimanded by the Lewis Presbytery, having been seen making his way out of Stornoway, stumbling through a crowded countryside and very much the worse of drink. Further incidents followed and in 1895 the presbytery decided that steps should be taken to remove him.

His trial before the presbytery was of 'sensational magnitude'. In Lewis, of all places, such charges were a matter of scandal and that the scandal affected a minister of the Established Church, a renegade from their own Free Church, made it all the better. The trial lasted for four days and was conducted before the entire presbytery with over a hundred witnesses for the prosecution. Both sides were legally represented and both had their medical experts. Despite its size, the trial was supposedly conducted in private, but on each of the four days large crowds congregated outside the hall to pick up any scraps of information. In the end MacCallum was found guilty on all charges. Typically he fought back, announcing his intention of appealing to the synod and initiating slander actions against some of the principal witnesses.[10] The following week the presbytery met again to consider other offences which had subsequently come to light. They had discovered that, on a recent visit to Glasgow, MacCallum had been found drunk and incapable and had spent the night in the police cells.[11]

MacCallum's final appearance was in April 1895 when his appeal was heard by a meeting of synod at Strome Ferry. It was an evening meeting and the ministers' departure for their parishes could not be delayed beyond the following morning. MacCallum, in the best tradition of his Rousay days, decided that, if he could not persuade his fellow ministers by argument, he would simply wear them down. He began by insisting that the transcript of the original trial be read. Relays of weary ministers took it in turn hour after hour to go through the mass of evidence. This was followed by a three-hour speech from MacCallum in which he denied all charges and embarked on lengthy explanations. For example, when he told the barmaid in a Stornoway hotel that all Free Church ministers could go to hell, he had done so for a spiritual end and to indicate a real possibility so that the girl might see the error of her ways and leave the Free Church. The synod, however, were not convinced and at 4.30 a.m. the meeting ended with the rejection of his appeal.[12]

MacCallum then appealed from the synod to the General Assembly which was due to meet the following month but, before his case could be heard, he suddenly resigned both from the parish of Knock and from all ministerial status.[13] Little was heard of him thereafter. A year later there were reports that he had been arrested at Marash in the Turkish Empire while distributing relief. The Turkish authorities suspected that money intended for charitable purposes was being used to assist revolutionary movements. Knowing MacCallum's character, it seems quite possible. It required the intervention of the British ambassador in Constantinople to secure his release.[14] Soon after this incident he was believed to have emigrated to America.[15]

The subsequent history of James Leonard was equally improbable. Whatever the minister's intentions may have been towards the pregnant Hannah, her father had no intention of permitting a match. Leonard's break with MacCallum was complete and final. For his daughter's sake he uprooted his entire family from Orkney and moved to the Oban area where he was able to find employment as Sheriff's officer. It was an unlikely role for the crofters' champion, since Oban too was in crofting country and disputes between landlord and tenant often landed in the courts as they had done in Rousay. In his new job Leonard was poacher turned gamekeeper.

In October 1889 the inevitable happened. Donald MacDermid, a crofter in Glendryan, Ardnamurchan, was being pursued by his landlord for arrears of rent and Leonard was entrusted with the task of seizing and auctioning his cattle. On his arrival at Glendryan he was met by an angry crowd, mainly consisting of women and led by the crofter's sister, a redoubtable lady of seventy-six. She protested that, since MacDermid had applied to the Commission, no one could touch his property. Fearing a serious disturbance and surely feeling some sympathy for the crofters, Leonard declared himself to be 'deforced' (prevented from carrying out his legal duties) and returned defeated to Oban.[16]

For her part in the disturbance, the old lady was eventually sentenced to ten days in gaol. On her release she discovered that she had become a popular heroine. A large crowd met her at the door of the prison and, with pipes playing, she was escorted along the street to where a breakfast had been prepared. An Oban baillie made a speech and presented her with a purse containing £9. Her supporters, some of them from as far away as Taynuilt, then led her in triumph to the steamer which was to take her back to Ardnamurchan.[17] James Leonard must have reflected that he had never enjoyed such a reception in Rousay. He soon gave up his post as Sheriff's officer and found employment as a coalman.[18] A regular wage provided more than he would ever have won from the stony soil of Digro, yet he found little happiness in his new life in Oban. Of those involved in Rousay's troubled years, no one emerges with more credit than the stern, unbending James Leonard and no one was called on to make greater sacrifices. He never returned to Orkney.

The third protagonist, Burroughs himself, would also have left Rousay in 1889 if he had been able to do so, but for a proprietor who was unfortunate enough to be encumbered with a crofting estate, it was not so easy to move as it was for a poor crofter or an unattached minister. Because of depressed agricultural conditions, it was difficult to get a good price for an estate, particularly so if the land was held on crofting tenure. Burroughs' own actions — the publicity there had been about bad landlord-tenant relations — made the sale of Rousay doubly difficult. The best prospect of a good price was to sell it as a sporting estate for, although the market for agricultural land was slack, there was a brisk demand for places with good shooting and fishing.

Burroughs set about the task of disposing of his estate in a systematic way. First he wrote a long article which appeared in *Rod and Gun* as one of a series on the sporting estates of Scotland.[19] All possible attractions were mentioned. He described the house, its outbuildings, policies and pleasure gardens, expanded on the scenic beauty of Rousay and emphasised its sporting potential. Grouse shooting was good and because of the climate and the favourable nature of the ground, disease was unknown among the birds. About 300 brace could be expected and, although this figure had been exceeded, he had lately limited the number to 150 for Trumland and 150 for Westness. In addition the sportsman could expect 200 snipe, 20 to 30 woodcock, 25 to 30 golden plover, 25 to 30 wood pigeons, 20 wild duck, 50 brown hares and 200 rabbits. Burroughs also mentioned the possibility of swans, seals, otters and whales. Almost the only thing omitted was that he had once shot an osprey![20] Trout fishing was excellent and there were possibilities of introducing salmon and culturing oysters. In addition, Rousay was a delightful holiday home with opportunities for yachting, sailing, rowing, bathing, riding, driving, picnicking and playing lawn games. Optimistic to the last, Burroughs described the estate as very low-rented and considered that 'as soon as the agricultural outlook improves, it would admit of a considerable increase'.

He followed his article with a series of advertisements in *Rod and Gun* but, although they appeared intermittently over the next few years, he failed to find a buyer. His price was £100,000[21] but, as Orkney agriculture became increasingly depressed in the 1890s, he was less and less likely to find anyone willing to offer as much as that. Eventually he resigned himself to remaining on the island.

After the discomfiture of the 'Crofters', Burroughs even regained a little of his authority in his last years. Such was the traditional grip of landlordism that, despite his recent treatment of his tenants, in 1889 he was returned unopposed as Rousay's first County Councillor and re-elected on a low poll in 1892.[22] Habits of obedience to the laird had not been destroyed by six years of revolt. Perhaps an even more remarkable comeback was his reappearance on the School Board in 1897 when he came third out of ten candidates and had the satisfaction of seeing the Rev John MacLeman, MacCallum's successor, and the Rev Alexander Spark both defeated.[23] Spark, indeed, finished bottom of the poll with a mere 12 votes but this was the least of his troubles. Like the laird, the minister was deep in debt and for a number of years the stipend was paid to a committee of his creditors. However, he had the consolation of receiving a marble clock to mark his silver wedding anniversary and no doubt it went very nicely with the marble fireplaces in the manse.[24]

For Burroughs there were honours in old age. He was appointed honorary colonel both of the Warwickshire Regiment and of his own regiment, now amalgamated to form the Argyll and Sutherland Highlanders, and he was a popular figure at their regimental dinners. In 1904, a year before his death, he received a knighthood and he saw this as a recompense for his failure to win the Victoria Cross at Lucknow. His homecoming after his investiture was the last occasion on which the full ceremonial of an estate welcome was performed, and *The Orkney Herald* reported it in the same detail as it had recorded his arrival in Rousay thirty-four years earlier.[25] There was an eerie similarity, as if the Crofters Act and the troubles in Rousay had never been. The tenantry of Rousay and Viera were gathered in 'full muster' when Sir Frederick and Lady Burroughs arrived at Trumland pier aboard the *Fawn*. They stepped ashore to the accompaniment of three hearty cheers and were led through a triumphal arch of evergreens on which was written the word 'Welcome' in large red letters. The Rev A. I. Pirie then stepped forward to read a prepared speech, after which Burroughs replied briefly and invited the tenants into a flag-bedecked Trumland House where refreshments had been prepared for them. It was to be the last occasion of its kind. In November Burroughs was taken ill just before he was due to act as chairman at a regimental dinner to mark the fiftieth anniversary of Balaclava, and his illness developed into a sharp attack of jaundice.[26] By the end of the year he was well enough to move to London but he suffered a relapse and died there on 9th April 1905.

Even after thirty-five years' residence in Rousay, Burroughs remained a curiously alien figure. He might own Rousay but he never belonged to it. Ownership was important to him, but he had originally wanted more than that. Part of his ideal had been to settle into the community and become part of it. Money could buy ownership, but belonging — that close identification with a place and its people — was a more difficult matter. It was ownership and the gulf it created between laird and tenant which made belonging impossible.

In the Bu of Wyre directly across the sound from Trumland, the young Edwin Muir, with one of those clear flashes of perception which sometimes occur in childhood, was aware of this alien quality in Burroughs and later recaptured it in his *Autobiography*:—

> He came over to Wyre to shoot the wild birds. I remember one soft spring day when the light seemed to be opening up the world after the dark winter; I must have been five at the time, for it was before I went to school. I was standing at the end of the house; I think I had just recovered from some illness, and everything looked clean and new. The General was walking through the fields below our house in his little brown jacket with the brown leather tabs on the shoulders, his neat little knickerbockers and elegant little brown boots; a feather curled on his hat, and his little pointed beard seemed to curl too. Now and then he raised his silver gun, the white smoke curled upwards, birds fell, suddenly heavy after seeming so light; our cattle, who were grazing in the field, rushed away in alarm at the noise, then stopped and looked round in wonder at the strange little man. It was a mere picture; I did not feel angry with the General or sorry for the birds; I was entranced with the bright gun, the white smoke, and particularly with the soft brown tabs of leather on the shoulders of his jacket. My mother was standing at the end of the house with me; the General came over and spoke to her, then, calling me to him, gave me a sixpence. My father appeared from somewhere, but replied very distantly to the General's affable words. He was a bad landlord, and in a few years drove my father out of the farm by his exactions.[27]

Notes

Abbreviations:

Estate Accounts   Mss Estate of Rousay and Viera, Factory Accounts (1840 to 1889), 2 vols, Orkney County Library, D19/1 and D19/2 and vouchers, D19/3-7.

N.S.A.   *New Statistical Account of Scotland, Orkney Islands*, Edinburgh, 1842.

O.A.D.S.   Orkney Agricultural Discussion Society.

O.C.L.   Orkney County Library.

Orkney Crofters   W. R. Mackintosh, *The Orkney Crofters*, Kirkwall, 1889 (The evidence taken on the first visit of the Crofters Commission, 1888).

O.S.A.   *Old (First) Statistical Account.*

Napier Commission   *Evidence taken by Her Majesty's Commissioners of Inquiry into the Condition of the Crofters and Cottars in the Highlands and Islands of Scotland*, Edinburgh, 1884 (Orkney evidence is in Vol 2).

P.O.A.S.   *Proceedings of the Orkney Antiquarian Society.*

S.R.O.   Scottish Record Office.

Chapter 1   Homecoming, 1870

1   *The Orkney Herald*, 2nd August 1870.
2   The description of Burroughs' arrival in Rousay is from *The Orkney Herald*, 2nd August 1870.
3   The description of the dinner at Westness is from *The Orkney Herald*, 17th August 1870.

Chapter 2   The Family in India

The records of the National Army Museum relating to the careers of George William Traill, Frederick William Burroughs (senior), Frederick William Traill-Burroughs and Charles Adolphe Maria de Peyron are used throughout this chapter.

1   *The Napier Commission*, p.1571.
2   *Mémoires de Mme du Barry*, Paris, 1830, and *Lettres de Marquis de Mirabeau*, Paris, 1832.
3   *The Napier Commission*, p.1569.
4   T. E. Colebrooke (ed), *Miscellaneous Essays*. Vol 1 contains a life of his father, Henry Thomas Colebrooke.
5   Mss letter, Frederick William Burroughs (senior) to F. W. Traill-Burroughs, 5th October 1864, O.C.L. D19/8/8.

6   Mss letter, F. W. Burroughs (senior) to Mr Bethune, n.d. (1867) O.C.L. D19/8/10.

7   Mss diary of F. W. Traill-Burroughs, National Library of Scotland, MS 2234.

8   The account of G. W. Traill's career in Kumaon is largely based on Sir William Wilson Hunter's *The Life of Brian Houghton Hodgson*, London, 1896.

9   A. L. Munn, *Five Months in the Himalaya*, London, 1909.

10   George William Traill, *Report on Kumaon for 1822-23*, reprinted in *Official Reports on Kumaon*, Agra, 1851.

11   Kenneth Mason, *Abode of Snow*, London, 1955, p.69.

12   Sir William Wilson Hunter, *The Life of Brian Houghton Hodgson*.

13   *The Times*, 22nd November 1847 and *Allen's Indian Mail*, 23rd November 1847.

14   Mss letter, David Balfour to F. W. Traill-Burroughs, 16th June 1866, in possession of Mr A. J. Skinner, St Albans.

Chapter 3   Early Development of the Estate

1   David Balfour, *Odal Rights and Feudal Wrongs: A Memorial for Orkney*, Edinburgh, 1860, p.3.

2   This rental is printed in Alexander Peterkin's *Rentals of the Ancient Earldom and Bishoprick of Orkney*, Edinburgh, 1820.

3   The tack is summarised in Hugh Marwick's *The Place Names of Rousay*, Kirkwall, 1947, pp.36-7.

4   Printed in Peterkin's *Rentals*.

5   Hugh Marwick, *The Place Names of Rousay*, p.18.

6   Map, O.C.L. E29.

7   Map, O.C.L. E29 (accompanying text).

8   For a description of the run-rig system in Orkney, see J. Storer Clouston's *History of Orkney*, Kirkwall, 1932, pp.346-55.

9   Strictly speaking the coogild was related to the number of marks of land which in turn was related (not uniformly) to the pennyland value.

10   Map, O.C.L. E29.

11   Rev Dr Barry, *History of the Orkney Islands*, London, 1808.

12   Joseph Anderson (ed), *The Orkneyinga Saga*, Edinburgh, 1973, pp.105-9.

13   Rev J. B. Craven, *History of the Church in Orkney, 1662-1688*, Kirkwall, 1893, pp.76-7.

14   Alexander Peterkin, *Rentals*, p.78.

15   Alexander Peterkin, *Rentals*, p.74.

16   J. Storer Clouston, *Records of the Earldom of Orkney*, Edinburgh, 1914, p.34.

17   The record of the assize and sale is printed in J. Storer Clouston's *Records of the Earldom of Orkney*, pp.160-5.

18   Robert S. Barclay, *Orkney and Shetland Court Books 1614-15*, Edinburgh, 1967, p.21.

19   A complaint, partly written by John Traill, regarding the burning of Westness, is printed in B. H. Hossack's *Kirkwall in the Orkneys*, Kirkwall, 1900, pp.217-20.

20   Mss Account of a House built in Westness in Rousay by John Firth in the Summer of 1792, O.C.L. Balfour Papers, D2/8/29.

21   The account of the Traills of Frotoft is based on a voluminous mss correspondence with William Watt, O.C.L. Watt of Breckness Papers, D3/47, D3/408, D3/412, D3/396 and D3/38.

22   W. S. Hewison, 'Smuggling in Eighteenth Century Orkney', in *Orkney Miscellany*, Vol 3, Kirkwall, 1956.

23   Mss unsigned letter, O.C.L. D3/104.

24   W. R. Mackintosh, 'Running an Illicit Cargo in Rousay', in *Around Orkney Peat-Fires*, Kirkwall, 1905.

25   J. Storer Clouston, *The Orkney Parishes*, Kirkwall, 1927, p.239.
26   This is the number of landowners involved in the division of commonty, O.C.L. D13/5/12.

Chapter 4   The Age of Improvement

1   John R. Tudor, *The Orkneys and Shetland*, London, 1883, pp.107-8.
2   The outline of the growth of Orkney's trade between 1800 and 1883 is based on statistics contained in a number of sources. The position at the beginning of the century is described in John Shirreff's *General View of the Agriculture of the Orkney Islands*, Edinburgh, 1814, supplemented in certain respects from the *O.S.A.* Comparable information for 1833 is contained in the *N.S.A.*, p.215. The *N.S.A.* figures were periodically updated, for 1848 in *Anderson's Guide*, for 1861 by the Rev Charles Clouston's *Guide to the Orkney Islands*, for 1866 in a new introductory chapter to the 3rd edition of Barry's *History of the Orkney Islands*, for 1871 in R. O. Pringle's *On the Agriculture of the Islands of Orkney*, Trans. Highland and Agric. Soc. 4th series, Vol 6, 1874, for 1882 in the *Orkney Herald*, 3rd May 1882, and for 1883 in *The Scotsman*, 11th May 1883.
3   W. S. Tait, 'Farming in a Bygone Day', *Journal O.A.D.S.*, Vol 11, p.13.
4   This estimate is based on a comparison with the arable acreages given for most parishes in the *N.S.A.* with the agricultural returns first made in 1866.
5   John R. Tudor, *The Orkneys and Shetland*, pp.107-8.
6   Rev Dr Barry, *History of the Orkney Islands*, footnote in 2nd edition, London, 1808, p.372.
7   *O.S.A.*, Shapinsay.
8   *O.S.A.*, South Ronaldsay and Burray.
9   A number of generalisations about seed/yield ratios are to be found in the *O.S.A.* Actual figures for individual farms in the eighteenth century in published records include Hugh Marwick's *Merchant Lairds of Long Ago*, Kirkwall, 1939, Vol 2, p.36 and, by the same author, 'An Orkney Jacobite Farmer', *Journal O.A.D.S.*, Vol 5, p.64.
10   *O.S.A.*, Shapinsay.
11   James Wallace, *A Description of Orkney* (1693), reprinted Edinburgh, 1883, p.15
12   Hugh Marwick, 'Two Orkney Inventories', *P.O.A.S.*, Vol 12, pp. 47-54.
13   John Shirreff, *General View of the Agriculture of the Orkney Islands*, pp.95-105.
14   William P. L. Thomson, *Kelp Making in Orkney* (forthcoming).
15   Act 10 Geo. IV Cap. 152.
16   A letter, Robert Scarth to John Watson, and quoted in the latter's *Tenancy and Ownership* (Cobden Club Prize Essay c.1891).
17   R. O. Pringle, *On the Agriculture of the Islands of Orkney*.
18   Hugh Marwick, 'An Orkney Jacobite Farmer', p.64.
19   W. S. Tait, 'Farming in a Bygone Day'.
20   *Napier Commission*, p.1481.
21   *N.S.A.*, Cross and Burness. (This account was written by Robert Scarth, not the parish minister).
22   Eileen Power, *Medieval People*, London, 1937, pp.11-33.
23   *Orkney Crofters*, p.16.

Chapter 5   The Quandale and Westness Clearances

1   The Estate Accounts are the main source used throughout this chapter, both for the clearances and for the management of Westness Farm. Some crofts which disappeared before 1840 have been identified from Hugh Marwick's *Place Names of Rousay*, Kirkwall, 1947.

2 *Napier Commission,* p.1571.

3 Mss letter, George Traill M.P. to Captain William Balfour, 10th November 1827, O.C.L. Balfour Papers 8/24.

4 Mss letter, Captain William Balfour to John Balfour, 17th November 1837, O.C.L. Balfour Papers, D2/24/2.

5 J. Storer Clouston, 'Old Orkney Houses' *III, P.O.A.S.,* Vol 2, 1923-4.

6 Quoted in Clouston, 'Old Orkney Houses'.

7 *The Orkney Herald,* 1st August 1894.

8 Mss Notes Written by Mr Marwick, Corse (locus of original not known). These notes were written soon after the clearance since Alexander Marwick died in 1858.

9 Notes Written by Mr Marwick, Corse.

10 *N.S.A.,* Cross and Burness, p.109.

11 *John o'Groat Journal,* 13th, 20th and 27th February 1846.

12 *Napier Commission,* pp.1548-54.

13 Information from Mrs J. Leslie, Kirkwall, a great-granddaughter of George Leonard.

14 Mss letters (Bills of Removing), O.C.L. D19/2/3.

15 *Napier Commission,* p.1535.

16 R. O. Pringle, 'On the Agriculture of the Orkney Islands', *Trans. Highland and Agric. Soc.,* 4th series, Vol 6, 1874.

17 J. M. H. Robertson, 'Can the Six Year Rotation in Orkney be Improved upon?' *Journal O.A.D.S.,* Vol 3, p.19, 1928.

18 Mss Memo on the Cost of Letting Trumland, O.C.L. D19/2/3.

19 T. E. Buckley and J. A. Harvie-Brown, *A Vertebrate Fauna of the Orkney Islands,* Edinburgh, 1891. T. E. Buckley, 'A Few Notes on the Mammals and Birds of Rousay', *Trans. Nat. Hist. Soc. Glasgow,* Vol 1, new series 1884, p.44.

20 *The Scotsman,* 1st January 1889.

Chapter 6   Lucknow

1 Mss 'Sutherland Highlanders: Historical Records, 1800-91', Stirling Castle, R26.

2 Quoted by Burroughs in a letter to *The Guardian,* 23rd January 1899.

3 Mss letters from George William Traill *et al.* to Burroughs when he was a schoolboy at Blackheath and Hofwyl, O.C.L. D19/8/6.

4 *Aberdeen Free Press,* 25th March 1870.

5 Richard Collier, *The Indian Mutiny,* London, 1966, p.276.

6 *The Thin Red Line Almanac,* Edinburgh, 1908.

7 Mss letter, George William Traill to F. W. (Traill)-Burroughs, n.d. (1847), O.C.L. D19/8/6.

8 William Forbes-Mitchell, *Reminiscences of the Great Mutiny,* London, 1893, pp.235-41. Forbes-Mitchell states that Burroughs attended the Ecole Polytechnique but there is no record of his having been a student nor, indeed, any unaccounted-for time in his career when he could have been. Forbes-Mitchell is inaccurate in several other respects.

9 The description of Burroughs' duties on Deeside is based on the memoirs of his superior officer on the Balmoral guard, Lt General John Alexander Ewart, *The Story of a Soldier's Life,* 2 vols, London, 1881.

10 Forbes-Mitchell, *Reminiscences of the Great Mutiny.*

11 John A. Ewart, *The Story of a Soldier's Life.*

12 Mrs Courtney Downman (Burroughs' sister Charlotte), *The Gentlewoman,* 5th March 1892. (First prize for a true account of a strange personal experience).

13 Lt Colonel W. Gordon Alexander, *Recollections of a Highland Subaltern,* London, 1898.

14   This incident and the following account of the picket in the Dilkusha Park are based on Alexander's *Recollections*.

15   *The Standard*, 22nd and 28th January 1897.

16   John A. Ewart, *The Story of a Soldier's Life*.

17   W. G. Alexander, *Recollections of a Highland Subaltern*.

18   Surgeon General William Munro, (1) *Reminiscences of Military Service with the 93rd Highlanders*, London, 1883. (2) *Records of Service and Campaigning in Many Lands*, 2 vols, London, 1887.

19   William Forbes-Mitchell, *Reminiscences of the Great Mutiny*.

20   Mss letter, R. Burgoyne to F. W. Traill-Burroughs, National Library of Scotland, MS 2235.

21   Sir Colin Campbell (Lord Clyde), dispatch from Lucknow dated 18th November 1857.

22   *Ayr Advertiser*, 28th January 1858, private letter from Burroughs to his sister, published without his consent. He expressed his annoyance in his diary.

23   Mss 'Sutherland Highlanders; Historical Records'.

24   Mss Diary/account book, National Library of Scotland, MS 2234.

25   Mss Diary/account book.

26   *The Guardian*, 23rd January 1899, letter from F. W. Traill-Burroughs.

27   Surgeon General Munro, 1883, and *The Broad Arrow, the Naval and Military Gazette*, a letter from 'Lieutenant General' (Burroughs).

28   Mss 'Sutherland Highlanders; Historical Records'.

29   Surgeon General Munro, 1883, and *The Broad Arrow* letter.

30   Official report on the 93rd Highlanders quoted in Burroughs' obituary, *The Orkney Herald*, 12th April 1905.

31   *The Lucknow Times*, 22nd April 1868.

32   *The Aberdeen Journal*, 30th March 1870.

33   Quoted in *The Orkney Herald*, 12th April 1905.

34   *The Broad Arrow* letter.

35   Mss 'Sutherland Highlanders; Historical Records'.

36   William Forbes-Mitchell, *Reminiscences of the Great Mutiny*.

37   *The Belfast News Letter*, 29th March 1898.

Chapter 7   Rousay Society in the Years of Prosperity, 1870-1883

1   *The Orkney and Zetland Telegraph*, 25th March 1880, a letter from 'A Scribbling Pedestrian in Rousay'.

2   Information from Mrs Alexina Craigie who, in her hundredth year, recalled her days as a servant in the Burroughs household.

3   Mss Notes Written by Mr Marwick, Corse, c.1850.

4   Undated newspaper cutting in Burroughs' scrapbook, 'Records of Rousay', O.C.L.

5   *The Orkney Herald*, 25th February 1874 and *The Orcadian*, 19th August 1874.

6   *The Orcadian*, 27th June 1874.

7   *The Orcadian*, 27th October 1874.

8   *The Orcadian*, 11th September 1875.

9   *The Orcadian*, 9th December 1878.

10   *The Orkney Herald*, 12th August 1874.

11   *The Orkney Herald*, 19th June 1889.

12   Printed advertisement bound in with the Estate Accounts.

13   *The Orkney Herald*, 9th November 1887.

14   *Napier Commission*, p.1569.

15   The description of the construction of the roads and the levying of the road assessment is based on Estate Accounts and mss accounts of the Road Committee of the District of Rousay (1859-77), O.C.L. D19/8/4.

16   *Napier Commission*, p.1569.
17   The background to Orkney road legislation may be found in the evidence of John MacRae to the Select Committee on the Orkney Roads Bill of 1886 (conveniently summarised in *The Orkney Herald*, 9th June 1886).
18   *The Orkney Herald*, 20th and 27th January 1886.
19   *The Court Journal*, 12th February 1887.
20   *The Times*, 12th February 1887.
21   *The Scotsman*, 25th May 1887.
22   *The Orcadian*, 25th March 1893.
23   *The Orkney Herald*, 6th December 1876.
24   *The Orkney Herald*, 23rd April 1877.
25   *The Orcadian*, 21st December 1877.
26   *The Orkney Herald*, 29th November 1878.
27   *The Orcadian*, 12th April 1879.
28   A. and A. Cormack, *Days of Orkney Steam*, Kirkwall, 1971, pp.116-9.
29   A. and A. Cormack, *Days of Orkney Steam*.
30   *The Orcadian*, 23rd August 1879.
31   *The Orkney Herald*, 31st August 1880.
32   A. and A. Cormack, *Days of Orkney Steam*.
33   *The Orkney Herald*, 30th January 1884 and *The Orcadian*, 14th February and 31st March 1884.
34   *The Scotsman*, February 1884.
35   *The Orkney Herald*, 24th October 1883, a letter from James Grieve, a recently evicted crofter.
36   *The Orkney Herald*, 24th August 1887.
37   A. and A. Cormack, *Days of Orkney Steam*.
38   *The Orcadian*, 17th August 1889.
39   *The Orcadian*, 9th April 1892 and 30th April 1892.
40   *The Orcadian*, 14th October 1893 and *The Orkney Herald*, 18th October 1893.
41   *The Orkney Herald*, 31st May 1876.
42   *The Orkney Herald*, 25th May 1880.
43   *The Orkney Herald*, 13th September 1883.
44   *The Orcadian*, 29th November 1891 and *The Orkney Herald*, 3rd October 1892.

Chapter 8   Rack-Renting

1   This chapter is based on the Estate Accounts. Bound in with the accounts are four sets of printed *Conditions and Regulations* dated 1852, 1874, 1876 and 1880.
2   *The Orkney Herald*, 17th August 1870.
3   Plan of the Township of Wasbister, Rousay, 1842, Sheriff Court Records, Kirkwall, SC.11.58.
4   Mss letters, Sir Edward Colebrooke to F. W. Traill-Burroughs, O.C.L. D19/8/6; Judicial Factor's accounts, O.C.L. D19/2/8.
5   B. H. Hossack, *Kirkwall in the Orkneys*, Kirkwall, 1900, p.329.
6   Robert Scarth's obituary in *The Orcadian*, 5th July 1879.
7   *The Orkney Herald*, 17th August 1870.
8   The considerable arrears of rent in 1847 (see Fig. 9) do not represent a real deficit. The year's accounts were closed earlier than usual due to the death of G. W. Traill, and at that time many tenants had not yet settled their rent.
9   *The Orkney Herald*, 14th May 1884 and *Napier Commission* (Report).
10   Arable acreages from the *N.S.A.* have been ignored as being grossly inaccurate. Note that figures quoted from Agricultural Returns include Egilsay which was not Burroughs' property.
11   Plan of Township of Wasbister; Plan of the Lands of Frotoft, Rousay, 1844, Sheriff Court Records, Kirkwall, SC.11.58.

12 Sheriff Court Records, Kirkwall, SC.11.58.

13 Information from Mr R. W. Marwick, Penicuik, whose forebears farmed Scockness.

14 Mss papers relating to the voluntary agreement to divide the Rousay commonty, O.C.L. D13/5/12.

15 The final date of the division is noted in Burroughs' handwriting in Estate Accounts.

16 Mss Memo regarding Rent of Grazings, O.C.L. D19/2/2.

17 Mss Established Church North Isles Presbytery Minutes, St Magnus Cathedral, Kirkwall.

18 Mss Report on Contemplated Improvements by Mr Marcus Calder and Mr Robert Walker, 1875, O.C.L. D19/2/6.

19 *Orkney Crofters*, pp.230-57.

Chapter 9   Money Problems and the Financing of Improvement

1 'Statement prepared by General Burroughs for Crofters Commission', printed in *Orkney Crofters*, p.257.

2 Thomas W. Traill, *Genealogical Sketches*, privately printed, 1902, p.62. The other main legatee was an illegitimate daughter, Mary Traill.

3 The extent of Burroughs' borrowing, the financing of improvement and the study of public burdens on the estate are based on Estate Accounts.

4 Mss letter, Sir Edward Colebrooke to F. W. Traill-Burroughs, 25th June 1853, O.C.L. D19/8/7.

5 Mss letter, Caroline Burroughs to F. W. Burroughs (senior), 24th September (1857) O.C.L. D19/8/6.

6 Mss letter, F. W. Burroughs (senior) to Mr Bethune (1867) O.C.L. D19/8/10.

7 Mss letter, Sir Edward Colebrooke to F. W. Traill-Burroughs, 30th December 1853, O.C.L. D19/8/7.

8 Mss letter, A. Lillie to F. W. Traill-Burroughs, 16th April 1856, O.C.L. D19/8/7.

9 Mss letters, James C. Traill to F. W. Traill-Burroughs, 14th January 1857, O.C.L. D19/8/7 and Sir Edward Colebrooke to F. W. Traill-Burroughs, n.d., O.C.L. D19/8/15.

10 Mss letter, Caroline Burroughs to F. W. Traill-Burroughs, 2nd July 1862, O.C.L. D19/8/7.

11 Mss letter, A. Lillie to F. W. Traill-Burroughs, 19th December 1856, O.C.L. D19/8/7.

12 Mss letter, F. W. Burroughs (senior) to F. W. Traill-Burroughs, 15th October 1864, O.C.L. D19/8/8.

13 Mss letter, F. W. Burroughs (senior) to F. W. Traill-Burroughs, 16th September 1872, O.C.L. D19/8/11.

14 Mss Memo Touching Selling Out, or Purchasing an Unattached Majority, 4th August 1862, National Library of Scotland, MS 2235.

15 Mss letters, Robert Scarth to F. W. Traill-Burroughs, 24th July 1860 and 14th November 1864, O.C.L. D19/8/8.

16 Mss letter (draft), F. W. Traill-Burroughs to Robert Scarth, 31st December 1870, O.C.L. D19/8/11.

17 *The Orkney Herald*, 19th June 1889.

18 *Napier Commission*, p.1572.

19 F. W. Traill-Burroughs, 'Land Legislation: A Plain Tale and a Warning', *National Review*, October 1891.

20 F. W. Traill-Burroughs, *National Review*.

21 Mss papers relating to the Scottish Drainage and Improvement Company Loan, O.C.L. D19/7/11.

22   The regular losses on Trumland Farm appear to be genuine. They are not, for example, the result of passing personal or estate expenditure through the farm account.
23   *N.S.A.*, Rousay, p.84.
24   *O.S.A.*, Rousay.
25   *Napier Commission*, p.1582.
26   *Napier Commission*, p.1556.

Chapter 10   *The Napier Commission*

1   This chapter is based on *Napier Commission*, pp.1533-62 and pp.1569-83.
2   *Napier Commission*, p.1558.
3   Rev Dr Barry, *History of the Orkney Islands*, London, 1808, p.343.
4   Mss draft of letter to newspaper by F. W. Traill-Burroughs (not sent), O.C.L. D19/7/8.

Chapter 11   *Trouble in Rousay*

1   Quoted in *Napier Commission* (Report).
2   *The Orkney Herald*, 2nd August 1870.
3   *The Orkney Herald* , 17th October 1883. This account does not mention Gibson by name. A copy of a letter from Burroughs to Gibson thanking him for circulating the counter-memorial appears in Burroughs' scrapbook, 'The Crofters Question', O.C.L.
4   Mss postcard, postmarked Edinburgh, 27th July 1883 and annotated by Burroughs 'Anonymous No.I', in possession of Mr A. J. Skinner, St Albans.
5   *Napier Commission* (Report).
6   *Napier Commission*, p.1564.
7   *The Orcadian*, 1st September 1883.
8   *The Orkney Herald*, 12th December 1883.
9   Mss Sourin School Log, entry for 17th August 1883, O.C.L.
10   *The Orkney Herald*, 14th May 1884.
11   *Napier Commission* (Report).
12   *The Daily Review*, 22nd January 1884.
13   *The Orkney Herald*, 12th December 1883.
14   Mss postcard, postmarked Edinburgh, 26th January 1884, in possession of Mr A. J. Skinner, St Albans.
15   *The Orkney Herald*, 14th May 1884.
16   Mss draft of letter, F. W. Traill-Burroughs to J. Leonard, n.d., O.C.L. D19/7/7.
17   Mss Memo of Meeting between James Leonard and F. W. Traill-Burroughs, O.C.L. D19/7/7.
18   Mss letters, J. Leonard to F. W. Traill-Burroughs, 1st and 4th October 1883, O.C.L. D19/7/7.
19   *The Scotsman*, 13th October 1883 and *The Daily Review*, 22nd January 1884.
20   *The Orkney Herald*, 21st November 1883.
21   *The Orkney Herald*, 17th October 1883.
22   *The Orkney Herald*, 31st October 1883.
23   *The Scotsman*, 17th October 1883.
24   *The Daily Evening Traveller* (Boston, U.S.A.), 18th August 1883.
25   *The Scotsman*, 1st February 1884.
26   Mss letter, George M'Crie to F. W. Traill-Burroughs, 1st December 1883, O.C.L. D19/7/7.
27   *The Orkney Herald*, 14th May 1884.

Chapter 12   Support for the Crofters

1   A quotation from the Rev A. MacCallum's speech to the Highland Land Law Reform Association at Dingwall, *The Orkney Herald*, 24th September 1884.
2   *The Orkney Herald*, 21st November 1883.
3   *The Orkney Herald*, 28th November 1883 and *The Scotsman*, 29th November 1883.
4   *The Orkney Herald*, 28th November 1883.
5   James Hunter, *The Making of the Crofting Community*, Edinburgh, 1976, p.155. Hunter minimises the role of Free Church leadership in the crofters' movement in the Highlands. At least in Orkney, its involvement was crucial.
6   *The Times*, 27th May 1885.
7   *The Oban Times*, 8th May 1886.
8   James Hunter, *The Making of the Crofting Community*, p.169.
9   *The Orkney Herald*, 27th May 1885.
10 *The Orkney Herald*, 19th December 1883.
11 *The Scotsman*, 1st February 1884.
12 *The Orkney Herald*, 6th February 1884.
13 *The Pall Mall Gazette*, 6th February 1884.
14 *The Orkney Herald*, 13th February 1884.
15 *The Scotsman*, 15th February 1884 and *The Orkney Herald*, 26th March 1884.
16 *The Scotsman*, 23rd January, 1885.
17 *The Orkney Herald*, 24th September 1884.
18 F. W. Traill-Burroughs, 'The Crofter Question', *Liberty Review*, 1893.
19 Flett expounded his ideas on land purchase to the point of boredom in a stream of letters to local newspapers. The most comprehensive statement of his views is contained in an address delivered to the Glasgow Orkney and Shetland Literary and Scientific Society, reported in *The Orkney Herald*, 20th January 1892.
20 The aims of the League were set out in a lecture by A. W. Johnston reported in *The Orcadian*, 23rd October 1886. Proposed fiscal arrangements are to be found in *The Orcadian*, 7th September 1886.
21 Correspondence between A. W. Johnston and Colonel D. Balfour, made public in *The Orcadian*, 7th September 1886.

Chapter 13   The Crofters Act

1   The Rev A. MacCallum used this text, Matthew Chapter 5, verse 10, when preaching on the occasion of receiving the news that the Crofters Act was to apply to Orkney, *The Orcadian*, 11th December 1886.
2   David Turnock, 'Small Farms in North Scotland: An Exploration in Historical Geography', *Scot.Geog.Mag.*, Vol 91, No 3, 1975.
3   *Orkney Crofters*, pp.v-vi.
4   *The Orkney Herald*, 30th November 1886.
5   *The Orcadian*, 11th December 1886.
6   *The Orcadian*, 11th December 1886.
7   *The Orcadian*, 11th December 1886.
8   F. W. Traill-Burroughs, 'The Crofter Question', *Liberty Review*, 1893.
9   *The Orcadian*, 13th January 1894.
10 *Orkney Crofters*, 'Statement prepared by General Burroughs', p.260.
11 P. J. Perry, *British Farming in the Great Depression, 1870-1914*, Newton Abbot, 1974, p.74.
12 The account of the first visit to Orkney of the Crofters Commission is based on *Orkney Crofters*.
13 *The Orkney Herald*, 3rd May 1882.

14   Mss draft of letter in Burroughs' handwriting dated 14th May 1887 to be sent to certain tenants, O.C.L. D19/2/1. The Estate Accounts, however, indicate that a reduction was not made until the following year.

Chapter 14   The War Against the Crofters

1   *The Orcadian,* 17th July 1897.
2   Letter from F. W. Traill-Burroughs to Mr Cromb, Dundee, author of the then recently published *Highland Brigade,* the letter contained in an undated newspaper cutting in Burroughs' scrapbook, 'Records of Rousay', O.C.L.
3   *The Orcadian,* 12th February 1887.
4   *The Orcadian,* 19th February 1887.
5   *The Orcadian,* 7th May 1887.
6   *Orkney Crofters,* p.290 and *The Orcadian,* 7th May 1887.
7   Mss Records of the Kirk Session of the F.C. of Rousay and Egilsay, St Magnus Cathedral, Kirkwall.
8   *The Scotsman,* 7th March 1889, and F. W. Traill-Burroughs, 'The Crofter Question', in *Liberty Review,* 1893.
9   Undated newspaper cutting (c.1890) in 'Records of Rousay'.
10   *The Orcadian,* 10th November 1888.
11   *The Orkney Herald,* 16th January 1889.
12   *The Orkney Herald,* 23rd January 1889.
13   *The Orcadian,* 29th December 1888.
14   *The Orcadian,* 21st January 1889.
15   Archibald Geikie, *The Scenery of Scotland,* London, 1865; Burroughs' correspondence with Geikie and papers relating to mining enterprises, O.C.L. D19/1/1 and D19/7/9.
16   *The Orkney Herald,* 12th November 1890.
17   *The Orkney Herald,* 8th October 1890.
18   *The Orcadian,* 4th October 1890.
19   *The Orcadian,* 4th October 1890.
20   *Exodus,* Chapter 5, verses 10-11.
21   *The Orcadian,* 18th October 1890.
22   *The Orcadian,* 12th December 1890.
23   *The Orcadian,* 12th December 1890.
24   *The Orcadian,* 20th June 1891.
25   *The Orkney Herald,* 12th November 1890.
26   *The Orkney Herald,* 22nd October 1890.
27   *The Orcadian,* 17th July 1897.
28   *The Orkney Herald,* 15th December 1897.

Chapter 15   Rousay Divided

1   F. W. Traill-Burroughs, 'The Crofter Question', in *Liberty Review,* 1893.
2   F. W. Traill-Burroughs, 'Land Legislation: A Plain Tale and a Warning', in *National Review,* 1892.
3   The estimate of Orkney's arable acreage at the beginning of the nineteenth century is based on slightly differing figures in two contemporary sources — John Shirreff's *General View of the Agriculture of the Orkney Islands,* Edinburgh, 1814, p.99 and the Rev Dr Barry's *History of the Orkney Islands,* London, 1808, p.352.
4   *The Orcadian,* 4th August 1894.

5   *The Orkney Herald,* 1st August 1894 and *The Scotsman,* 30th July 1894.
6   *The Orkney Herald,* 8th August 1894 and *The Orcadian,* 4th August 1894.
7   This figure for the 'old arable' in Quandale is much greater than the acreage which actually existed c.1845 according to the Estate Accounts (Chapter 5, Table 3).
8   Mss draft memorial drawn up by F. W. Traill-Burroughs, O.C.L. Balfour Papers 17/13.
9   *Memorial of the Landowners of Orkney on the Crofters Holdings (Scotland) Act of 1886* (printed), 1893. A copy with Burroughs' hostile annotations is in O.C.L. D19/7/10.
10   *The Orkney Herald,* 3rd March 1893.
11   *The People's Journal,* 18th February 1892.
12   W. J. Moar, 'Climate and Weather of Orkney', *Journal O.A.D.S.,* Vol 6, 1931, p.8.
13   *The Orkney Herald,* 31st December 1892.
14   *The Orkney Herald,* 25th December 1893.
15   Advertisements for letting farms appearing in *The Orkney Herald,* 7th June 1893, 12th July 1893, 16th June 1894, 17th June 1895, 16th May 1896, 20th July 1898.
16   Mss letter, J. Mainland to D. J. Robertson (Burroughs' lawyer), February 1893, O.C.L. D19/7/8.
17   *The Orkney Herald* advertised the formation of the Orkney Farmers' Association in September 1894.
18   *The Orcadian,* 3rd October 1896.

Chapter 16   Rousay Churches

1   *The Peterhead Sentinel and Buchan Journal,* 17th August 1888.
2   Mss letter, Rev James Leslie to William Watt, O.C.L. D3/196.
3   J. Haldane, *Journal of a Tour through the Northern Counties of Scotland and the Orkney Isles,* Edinburgh, 1798, p.62.
4   William MacKelvie, *Annals and Statistics of the United Presbyterian Church,* Edinburgh, 1873; Robert Small, *History of the Congregation of the United Presbyterian Church, 1733-1900,* Edinburgh, 1904, pp.507-8; *N.S.A.,* p.84.
5   William Ewing, *Annals of the Free Church of Scotland,* Edinburgh 1914, Vol 1, p.216.
6   Mss Records of the Kirk Session of the F.C. of Rousay and Egilsay, St Magnus Cathedral, Kirkwall.
7   The relative strengths of the Rousay churches in 1890 were as follows (*The Orkney Herald,* 13th June 1892):

		Established Church	Free Church	United Presbyterians
ROUSAY	Communicants	59	195	200
	Stipend	£180	£151	£175
	Income/Christian liberality	£7	£67	£130
ORKNEY	Communicants	4,279	3,743	4,301

8   From Gardner's obituary, *The Orcadian,* 4th April 1885.
9   Estate Accounts.
10   Mss letter, Rev N. P. Rose to G. Learmonth, 10th December 1868, O.C.L. D19/8/10.
11   Mss letter, Rev N. P. Rose to G. Learmonth.
12   *The Edinburgh Courant,* 16th December 1868.
13   Mss letters from Scarth, Learmonth and Rose regarding the 1868 election, O.C.L. D19/8/10.
14   F. W. Traill-Burroughs' annotation on letter from Rev N. P. Rose to G. Learmonth.

15   Mss letter, Francis J. Grant to F. W. Traill-Burroughs, 30th March 1885, O.C.L. D19/8/12.
16   *The Orkney Herald,* 20th May 1885; *The Orcadian,* 16th May 1885.
17   *The Orcadian,* 8th August 1885.
18   *The Orcadian,* 17th April 1886.
19   *The Orkney Herald,* 19th February 1887; *The Orcadian,* 30th April 1887.
20   *The Peterhead Sentinel and Buchan Journal,* 17th August 1888.
21   *The Orkney Herald,* 23rd March 1887.
22   Mss Minutes of the E.C. North Isles Presbytery, St Magnus Cathedral, Kirkwall.
23   *The Orkney Herald,* 7th December 1904.
24   *The Orcadian,* 21st November 1905.
25   Mss letter, R. Marwick to A. W. Johnston, in possession of Mrs J. Leslie, Kirkwall.

Chapter 17   The School Board Affair

1   *The Orcadian,* 22nd November, 1890.
2   David A. Eunson, The Influence of the Education (Scotland) Act 1872 on Education in Orkney, unpublished M. Ed. dissertation, University of Stirling, 1979.
3   *The Orcadian,* 17th March 1873.
4   *N.S.A.,* p.84.
5   Rousay and Egilsay School Board Minutes, O.C.L. Unfortunately the minutes are missing for the later crucial period of 'Crofter' control, reputedly deliberately suppressed.
6   *The Orkney Herald,* 19th January 1876.
7   The average attendance at the Board's schools was as follows (*The Orkney Herald,* 16th August 1875, 27th September 1876)—

	1874-5	*1875-6*
Sourin	61	64
Wasbister	60	50
Frotoft	45	42
Egilsay	21	18
Wyre	15	14

8   *The Orkney Herald,* 31st May 1876.
9   *The Orkney Herald,* 9th February 1877.
10   *The Orkney Herald,* 9th February 1877.
11   *The Orcadian,* 17th March 1877.
12   *The Orkney Herald,* 25th April 1877.
13   *The Orcadian,* 12th November 1881.
14   *The Orkney Herald,* 1st April 1885.
15   *The Orkney Herald,* 13th May 1885.
16   Mss letter, G. M'Crie to F. W. Traill-Burroughs, 1st November 1884, O.C.L. D19/8/2.
17   *The Orcadian,* 4th May 1885.
18   The written version of the prayer which Burroughs used at Board meetings is preserved in O.C.L. D19/8/2. It seems quite innocuous, the objection probably being the very fact that it was written.
19   *The Orkney Herald,* 17th June 1885.
20   *The Orkney Herald,* 22nd July 1885.
21   *The Orkney Herald,* 23rd September 1885.
22   *The Orkney Herald,* 23rd September 1885.
23   Mss Sourin School Log, O.C.L.
24   Mss letter, D. Horne to Robert Scarth, 9th December 1851, O.C.L. D19/8/2.

25 Mss letter, Alex Taylor (Scotch Education Department) to F. W. Traill-Burroughs, 19th February 1883, O.C.L. D19/8/2.
26 *The Scotsman*, 19th July 1886.
27 *The Orcadian*, 5th and 12th December 1885.
28 *The Scotsman*, 25th July 1886.
29 *The Orcadian* 14th November 1885.
30 *The Orcadian*, 17th April 1886.
31 *The Orcadian*, 14th November 1885.
32 *The Orcadian*, 8th May 1886.
33 *The Orkney Herald*, 5th May 1886.
34 Mss Sourin School Log, O.C.L. Entry for 16th August 1886.
35 Mss Wasbister School Log, O.C.L. Entry for 1st September 1886.
36 *The Orcadian*, 8th November 1890.
37 Mss Sourin School Log. Entry for 8th November 1886.
38 *The Orcadian*, 8th November 1890.
39 *The Orkney Herald*, 5th May 1886.
40 The Board's dispute with the ratepayers is described at length in *The Scotsman*, 1st December 1886 and *The Orcadian*, 2nd April 1887.
41 Mss Sourin, Wasbister and Frotoft school logs, O.C.L.
42 *The Orcadian*, 8th November 1890.
43 Estate Accounts.
44 *Society*, 9th July 1898.
45 *The Orcadian*, 12th December 1899.
46 Bruce Dickens, 'An Orkney Scholar: Hugh Marwick', in *The Saga Book*, Vol 17 Part 1, Viking Society for Northern Research.
47 *The Orcadian*, 8th, 15th and 22nd November 1890.
48 *The Orkney Herald*, 2nd May 1888.
49 *The Orkney Herald*, 17th April 1889.

Chapter 18   Finale

1 F. W. Traill-Burroughs, 'Statement prepared by General Burroughs', in *Orkney Crofters*, p.202.
2 *The Orcadian*, 29th December 1888.
3 *The Orkney Herald*, 16th January 1889.
4 *Organ of the Scottish Temperance League*, 24th October 1892.
5 *Organ of the Scottish Temperance League*.
6 *The Orcadian*, 9th February 1889.
7 Mss Records of the Kirk Session of the F.C. of Rousay and Egilsay, 2nd February 1889, St Magnus Cathedral, Kirkwall.
8 Mss letter, Rev J. B. Craven to F. W. Traill-Burroughs, 1st September 1885, O.C.L. D19/7/7.
9 *The Orcadian*, 30th March 1895.
10 *The Scotsman*, 25th March 1895 and *The Orcadian*, 30th March 1895.
11 *The Scotsman*, 30th March 1895.
12 *The Orkney Herald*, 4th April 1895.
13 *The Orkney Herald*, 29th May 1895.
14 Foreign Office Telegrams, Public Record Office, FO-78-4727-X/K-6363.
15 William Ewing, *Annals of the Free Church of Scotland*, Edinburgh, 1914, Vol 1, p.216.
16 *The Orkney Herald*, 14th October 1889.
17 *The Orkney Herald*, 18th December 1889.

18   Information from Mrs Christine McKinlay, Glasgow, great-granddaughter of James Leonard.

19   *The Orkney Herald,* 19th June 1889, an article reprinted from *Rod and Gun.*

20   Undated newspaper cutting (c.1879) preserved by Burroughs.

21   Advertisements in *Rod and Gun,* 30th May and 20th June 1889 and 24th September 1892.

22   Burroughs received 8 votes and John Gibson 3 votes. Contrast this apathy to the voting figures in School Board elections.

23   *The Orcadian,* 1st May 1897.

24   *The Orkney Herald,* 9th January 1904.

25   *The Orkney Herald,* 13th July 1904.

26   *The Glasgow Evening News,* 21st November 1904.

27   Edwin Muir, *Autobiography,* London, p.15.

Index